ISLAMIC INSTITUTIONS

ENCYCLOPAEDIC SURVEY OF ISLAMIC CULTURE SERIES

ISLAMIC INSTITUTIONS

Edited by
MOHAMED TAHER

ANMOL PUBLICATIONS PVT. LTD.
NEW DELHI-110 002 (INDIA)

ANMOL PUBLICATIONS PVT. LTD.
4374/4B, Ansari Road, Daryaganj
New Delhi-110 002

Islamic Institutions

First Edition 1998
ISBN 81-7488-942-6

PRINTED IN INDIA

Published by J.L. Kumar for Anmol Publications Pvt. Ltd., New Delhi-110 002 and Printed at Mehra Offset Press, Delhi.

Contents

Preface

The *Encyclopaedic Survey of Islamic Culture* is a unique reference source. This series seeks to anthologise the most important primary and secondary materials on a wide variety of topics and writers of Islamic culture and civilisation. The scholar, the student and the layman will find in various volumes not only a generous selection of reprinted articles, but original essays, bibliographies, and other materials brought for the first time in a comprehensive and exhaustive fashion.

The need for this collation grew out of our awareness that there is no comprehensive source of information for the study and research of the field. Other published works are too specialised in the topics discussed or neglect the institutional as well the individual role which the Islamic system plays. Few encyclopaedic works do exist, and few anthologies also have appeared. Fewer books, again, have systematically covered such topics as Islam in Africa, Islamic sociology, Islamic polity, Islamic thought, etc. Although these topics have been addressed separately, no attempt has been made to discuss them as part of a united treatment of the literature of the field.

Islam brought a total change in all spheres of life. It revolutionised many societies, both in the east and the west. But this is not always accepted and acknowledged. To quote Major Arthur Leonard from his work: Islam; her moral and spiritual value:

"Never to this day has Europe acknowledged in an honest and whole hearted manner the great and everlasting debt she owes to Islamic culture and civilisation. Only in a lukewarm and perfunctory way has she recognised that when, during the dark ages, her people were sunk in feudalism and ignorance, Muslim civilisation under the Arabs reached a high standard of social and scientific splendour that kept the flickering members of European society from utter decadence.

"Do not we, who now consider ourselves on the top most pinnacle ever reached by culture and civilisation, recognise that, had it not been for the high culture, the civilisation and intellectual, as well as the social splendours of the Arabs and soundness of their school system, Europe would to this day have remained sunk in the darkness of ignorance. Have we forgotten that the Muslim maxim was that, the real learning of a man is of more public importance than any particular religious opinions he may entertain, that Muslim liberality was in striking contrast with the then intolerant state of Europe? Does the magnificent valour of the Arabs, inspired as it was by a theism as lofty as it was pure, not appeal to us? Does not the moderation and comparative toleration shown by them to the conquered, notwithstanding the fierce and burning ardour to regenerate mankind that impelled them onward to conquest, also appeal to us? Does it not all the more appeal to us when we contrast this with the bitterness of the attitude of the Christian sects towards one another? Especially when we consider that in Christendom, as it was then constituted, extortion, tyranny and imperial centralisation, combining with ecclesiastical despotism and persecution, had practically extinguished patriotism, by substitution in its place schismatic and degenerate Church?"

Further the same writer continues to say:

> "Is it possible that Europe is unmindful of, and has the ingratitude to ignore the splendid services of the scientists and philosophers of Arabic? Are the names of Assamh, Abu Othman, Alberuni, Albeithar, Abu Ali Ibn Sina (Avicenna) the great physician and philosopher, Ibn Rushd (Anempace) besides a host of others but dead letters? Is the great work that they have done and the fame they have left behind them in their books to be consigned to the limbo of oblivion, by an ungrateful but antipathetic Europe?

"It cannot be that already we have lost sight of the amazing intellectual activity of the Muslim world during the earlier part of the `Abbaside' period more especially. It cannot be that we have quite forgotten the irrecoverable loss that was inflicted on Arabian literature, and on the world at large, by the wanton destruction of thousands of books that was promoted by Christian bigotry and fanaticism? It cannot be surely said of Christian Europe that for centuries now she has done her best to hide obligations to the Arabs; yet most assuredly, obligations such as these, are far too sacred to lie much linger hidden."

This is one side of the story. The other side is that the West has definitely absorbed much of the Islamic contributions and is "unaware." To quote Marcus Marby and William Underhill "Bold new visions from ancient landscapes" (*Newsweek*, May 29, 1995): Christian and Islamic civilizations have been in conflict for most of their history. But as often as they have clashed, they have enriched each other. In this ninth century, Moors brought advanced architecture, astronomy and medicine to occupied Spain. While Europe lingered in the Dark Ages, courtly poetry from Persia inspired the troubadours, whose verse evolved into the literature of the early French Renaissance. Even whiling away hours over coffee and conversation—the basis for the cafe—came from Arab culture… France's most popular dish today is not escargots but couscous. French slang is peppered with Arab words like kif-kif (50-50) and Insha Allah (God willing). The hottest new music is Arab-inspired rai" (p. 28). The list of Arabic borrowed words in English and Western usages are many more, not mere algebra, alchemy, azimuth, albatross, timbal, zenith, etc.

There is, in short, a lot of misinformation and incorrect representation about Islam. And more so there is a need today to describe and interpret the issues and express in clear terms what this thought actually deals with. Due to social and cultural changes, the salient aspects of the field require examination. The post cold war era has left the world with a unipolar political system. Islam is a system which promises the world that if applied in toto it would solve the multi-dimensional problems of the modern era. But is there any one who wishes to test this module and try it in a space and time to see the truth of the statement?

The primary purpose of this encyclopaedic survey is to serve as a basic handbook on significant topics of Islamic culture. To facilitate an understanding of the field, the series presents a survey and an analysis of the various socio-cultural forces that shape both the structure and functions of the field as well as by the way this society has changed. We also analyse the larger forces outside the community, such as assimilation and acculturation, and forces inside the community, like, role of the leadership, role of the social and cultural groups and the so much alleged 'imbalance' in the theory and practice of the faith.

We are confident that this work will make a permanent and significant contribution to the study of Islam. Its style is simple, and it is presented in a style accessible to a wide audience. Its target audience is faculty, students, and all concerned with the understanding of the faith of the second largest following in the world. While it has scholarly materials, it is nevertheless also of use to those who have no knowledge of the field, as well as to those who are working in related and allied fields. Most important, we hope that this series will be useful in teaching and learning as an educational resource in the academic world.

The series is planned to be both, multi-volume and multi-faceted set, which will run into hundreds of numbers. The compilation of such a huge set is a gigantic task and requires the support and encouragement of all concerned. It requires feed-back and also support from the literary market place and literary circles all over.

A collection of articles, or an anthology, has many benefits, like, it renews our acquaintance with literature which we have neglected, it reveals to us material of which we were ignorant, and it exposes relationships where we did not suppose them to exist. This is the ultimate purpose of our efforts and we wish and pray that this is fulfilled.

A word of acknowledgement is due to the inspiration of the idea of a comprehensive, commulative and compact set of literary works on the Islamic culture. These inspirers are from all walks of life and their efforts must be acknowledged which includes contributors, authors and editors, as well as the publishers who have graciously contributed to this project and we duly acknowledge their cooperation. The well wishers are many more and listing all the concerned by names is impossible here. Each must be duly rewarded for this gesture, and this is our sincere prayer.

—Editor

1

Islam and Knowledge

ABDEL HALIM MAHMOUD

(Abstract: In Islam Knowledge (or al-Ilm) is part of the purpose for which the Divine message was revealed; Islam allied itself from the first to last with knowledge--and stood against ignorance; Islam encouraged seeking of knowledge all through; and the knwoledge propounded by Islam is knowledge of everything beneficial both for physical and metaphysical world).

The Object of the Islamic Message:

In the name of Allah, Most Merciful, Most Gracious
All praise is due to Him
The Cherisher and Sustainer of all the worlds.
Blessings and Salutations of Allah
Be upon the most noble prophet,
Our belobved, Muhammad, his children and his companions
And Those who follow his guidance
Till the Day of Judgement.

In various verses of the Glorious Quran the object of the Islamic Call is Defined and specified. In one of the verses we read:

"It is He who has sent
Amongst the unlettered
An Apostle from among themselves,
To rehearse to them His signs.
To sanctify them and to instruct them

In Scripture and wisdom,
Although they had been, before,
In manifest error."

The Almighty refers to His Bounty upon the believers in that He chose his Messenger from amongst them and specified the wisdom and purpose underlying this choice :

"Allah did confer a great bounty
Upon the believers
When He sent among them an Apostle
From among themselves,
Rehearsing unto them the Signs of Allah
Sanctifying them,
And instructing them

In Scripture and Wisdom
Although before this
They were in manifest error.

They praise the Glory of Allah, the Sovereign, the Holy One, the exalted in Might, the Wise.

The above verse and those of their kind do not require great reflection to grasp their import. To understand their meanings there is no need for exertion and hard thinking. They are as clear as crystal. They point out of wisdom in sending the Prophet (P.B.U.H.) which are basically :

1. Knowledge and Science.
2. Sanctification and Purification.

According to the above verses, knowledge is the twinhalf of the entire Islamic Message while the other twinhalf which is actually based upon the former is sanctifying and purity. It is not conceivable that purification and sanctification could be fruitful with ignorance.

Islam Emerged as an Ally to Knowledge

A cursory glance upon the early years of Islam, when it emerged with its glory, will show the great importance Islam has conferred upon knowledge and science. Imam Ismail el-Bukhari, may Allah rest his soul in peace, narrates the most widely quoted tradition reported by Aesha, "mother of the believers" and which is found in most authentic books. It is the tradition relating to the "Commencement of Revelation." The tradition is lengthy and it relates the gripping scene that took place in the cave of Mount Hira, while the prophet was meditating. There according to the tradition, an Anglel appeared unto him saying ;

Read ! (O Muhammad !)
The Prophet replied, "I do not know how to read
Then the Prophet described how the angel embraced
him and enveloped him tightly. On releasing him the
Angel repeated, "Read ! (O Muhammad !)
The Prophet said, "I do not know how to read."
The Prophet went on to say, "He held me
for the second time with all his might
then released me saying, "Read ! (O Muhammad)
I said, "I do not know how to read."
He continued describing, "He then embraced
me for the third time. After releasing me he said,
Read !
In the name of thy Lord and Cherisher
Who created.
He created man
Out of a (mere) clot
Of congealed blood.
Read ! And thy Lord
Is most bountiful ;
He Who taught
(The use of) the Pen

Taught man that
Which he knew not.

Commenting on the above verse, Sheikh Muhammad Abduh makes the following remark ;

"There isn't a more eloquent statement nor a more decisive evidence of the superiority of reading, writing and knowledge in all its aspects for the introduction of God's Book and the commencement of Revelation."

God commenced the Revelation of the Islamic Religion with these eternal verses which eulogize reading, writing and knowledge and more than once they touch on the subject of knowledge. After these verses come the following verse :

"Nun. By the Pen
And by (Record)
Which (men) write.

This time the Almighty commenced His Revelation with an alphabet and addressed man with an oath of the Pen, and that which it writes. It was the first oath mentioned in Quran. As for the name of the Book that was revealed, theologians say,

"This Book is named The Quran because it has the essence of all the books revealed.
In fact it has collected the essence of all the sciences. The Quran points to this fact in the following words ;
"Fuller explanation of everything," and
Statement on everything." This goes to prove that the Quran:

1. By its very name
2. By the very first verse that was revealed.
3. By the first oath it mentions draws the attention of man directly and by way of revelation to pursue knowledge

by all means whether by writing, reading or acquiring knowledge.

Position of Knowledge in Islam by Way of Stories

The Holy Quran from its inception emerged as an ally to knowledge. It shed its light with the glad tidings of knowledge. Thereafter the Quran encouraged the pursuit of knowledge in various methods. For instance it explains to us that when Allah created Adam He taught him all the names :

"And He taught Adam
The names of all things."

By virtue of this knowledge Adam's rank was elevated. He was much higher in station than the angels :

"Then (He) placed
Them before the angels and said,
Tell me the nature of these
If ye are right."

The Angels were unaware of these names and in modesty said:

"Glory to Thee ;
Of knowledge we have none,
Save what Thou
Hast taught us.
In truth it is Thou
Who art perfect
In knowledge and wisdom.

In the following verse God, indirectly, portrays the rank and exalted position of Adam :

"O Adam
Tell them the names

Of things."

Then Adam rattled out the names of things. The unique result of this is eloquently portrayed in the following words :

"Did I not tell you
That I know the secrets
Of Heaven and Earth.
And I know what ye reveal
And what ye conceal."

A very significant aspect of this, which is often not studied seriously lies in the following verse :

"And remember,
We said to the angels ;
Bow down to Adam ;
And they bowed down
Not so Iblis.
He refused and was haughty
He was of those who reject Faith."

In the above verse God commands the angels to bow down to Adam after making it clear that Adam's knowledge was superior to theirs. The angels responded and prostrated accordingly. The context of the above verse reveals that man by virtue of his knowledge is elevated to such a supreme position that even the angels prostrate to him.

In the Quran, there is another story of invaluable significance. It is charged with wisdom, meaningfulness and import. The Messengers of God (P.B.U.THEM.) are the most exemplary members of the human society. By Virtue of their being God's Messengers their rank and station, knowledge and wisdom are supreme. Their positions remain the lofties. Despite this we have the illuminating story of the Prophet Moses (PBUH.) Moses and his companion, once, were in search of a learned man whom God had informed them. After strenuous efforts and great patience they found the man. God describes this beautifully :

> "So they found one
> Of Our servants
> On whom We had bestowed
> Mercy from Ourselves
> And whom We had taught
> Knowledge from Our own presence
>
> Moses said to him :
> "May I follow thee,
> On the footing that
> Thou teach me something
> Of the (higher) Truth
> Which thou has been taught
> (The other) said. "Verily
> Thou will not be able
> To have patience with me !
>
> "And how canst thou
> Have patience about things
> About which they understanding
> Is not complete ?"
>
> Moses said : "Thou wilt
> Find me, if God so will,
> (Truly) patient : nor shall I
> Disobey thee in aught.
>
> The (man) said, "If then
> Thou wouldst follow me,
> Ask me no questions
> About anything until I
> Myself speak to thee concerning it.

The Prophet Moses accompanies this humble man. They continue travelling together and Moses, the Messenger of God acquires knowledge from this ordinary man. He learns of the things he had no knowledge of.

Imam el-Baidawie commenting on the significance of this story has the following to say:

1. Man should always pursue knowledge.
2. Mans should show humble obedience to those who import knowledge to him.
3. Man should observe courtesy and etiquette when discussing.

Imam el-Sayootie make the following remarks :

1. "Travel in pursuit of knowledge is extremely desirable.
2. A learned man must further his knowledge.
3. A student should make means for his travels which is not contrary to placing trust in the providence of God.
4. Attributing undesirable things and foregtfulness to the devil is metaphoric. Such expressions are adopted as a mark of respect to God.
5. A student must show humbleness to his tutor even the latter be below him in rank and station in life.
6. The one offers knowledge has the right to excuse himself in doing so if he feels that his student is unable to absorb and benefit from the knowledge.
7. A person should express his doubts in advance in mutual matters.
8. A person has the right to place conditions upon the person who wishes to follow him or benefit from him.
9. Once a condition is made it is obligatory to fulfil it.
10. Man is not reprimanded for forgetfulness and faults arising from lack of memory.

We may now round up our Quranic stories pertaining to knowledge by making to a third story. Thereafter we may project our attention to the direct inferences made in the Quran regarding knowledge followed by the traditions of the Prophet (PBUH).

Here is the Prophet Solomon. He sits majestically with his most intimate companions discussing the paganistic tendencies of the Queen of Sheba who worshipped the sun. He discusses the presents he flung back at her which she had sent to pacify him and conciliate him. At this point he said,

"Will you give me abundance in wealth ?
But that which Allah has given me
Is better than that which
He has given you !
Nay it is ye
Who rejoice in your gift
Go back to them
And be sure We shall come to them
With such hosts as they
Will never be able to meet
We shall expel them
From there in disgrace
And they will feel humbled (indeed).

Solomon then addresses the people around him saying:

"Ye chiefs! which of you
Can bring me her throne
Before they come to me
In submission ?"

One of the large, powerful jinn, reputed to be wicked and crafty replied,

"I will bring it to thee
Before thou rise from thy council
Verily I have full strength

For the purpose and am trustworthy."

Another jinn replied : The Quran portrays his answer in the following words:

"One who had knowledge of the Book
said, "I will bring it to thee
Within the twinkling of an eye !"

The latter who was versed with the knowledge of the Book implemented his word and within split seconds presented the throne to Solomon. When Solomon observed the throne firmly placed before him he said,

"This is by the grace of my Lord !
To test me whether
I am grateful or ungrateful
And if any is grateful,
Verily his gratitude is for his own soul
But if any is ungrateful,
Truly my Lord is free
Of all Needs
Supreme in Honours !"

By illustrating this story, the Quran emphasizes the wonders of knowledge. It shows us that knowledge can do more than what a jinn can do. It also shows that the power of a learned man surpasses that of the most crafty jinn. With knowledge he travels across the globe, removes distances and accomplishes miracles.

The Status of Knowledge in the Quran

We may now draw our attention to the view of the Quran pertaining to knowledge in a direct manner. We would discuss the verses that dwell upon knowledge exhorting it and glorifying it. God mentions:

"Verily only those possess knowledge
Among His servants
Truly fear Allah."

A man's fear of God lies in his deep knowledge gained by sincere pursuance and true zeal. The greater the depth the greater the fear. This is so because he sees the precision in God's creating and in the Laws of the Universe. He observe wisdom in the wonderful plannings of God which forces him to fall in prostration to his Creator and his Maker.

These are the people who by attaining a sound knowledge of anatomy or by specialization in it see the co-ordination and minutest precision in the various organs of the human body and in their minutest parts. This forces them to prostrate to the Creator of such co-ordination, order and creation.

Anatomy is not the only science that bewildered the well versed scientist; in fact astronomy dazzles the astronomer and biology the biologist and so forth. It is in this way that the human mind is bewildered in the sciences of every field pertaining to the universe its earth, heavens and that which is between.

"Blesed is He
In whose hands is dominion
And He has power
Over all things.
"He who created death
And life, that He
May try which of you
Is best in deed
And He is the Exalted
In Might, oft Forgiving.

He who created

The seven heavens
One above another
No want of proportion

Will thou see
In the Creation of the Most Cracious
So turn thy vision again ;
Seest thou any flaw ?

"Again turn thy vision
A second time : (thy) vision
Will come to thee
Dull and discomfitted
In a state worn out."

The Almighty Lord is True in His Proclamation :

"Verily, only those who possess knowledge
Among His servants
Truly fear Allah."

The fear of the Lord which is the fruit of knowledge is one of the most important basics of Islam. It is from here that Islam sees knowledge as a necessity and not as a luxury. This in itself is an Islamic principle and an essentialiy in an Islamic personality. A Muslim personality must be versed with knowledge; knowledge of the universe, of man and of the mind. In fact in every field that this word may entail.

Where does the fear of the Lord lead ?

Where do the sincere believing scholars end up ? What is the import of the following verse? :

"There is no god but He :
That is the witness of Allah
His Angels, and those endued

With knowledge, standing firm
On justice. There is no god but He,
The Exalted in Power, The Wise.

By way of knowledge which produces fear of God, man reaches the realms of monotheism. According to el-Bayruni, monotheism is the hall-mark of Islam and it is also the characteristic of true religion. The concept of monotheism is witnessed by God and His pure angels. In co-relating and corresponding the Ulemas with the Angels the Almighty has elevated the position of knowledge to the noblest rank.

The tenet of monotheism is the fundamental principle in Islam. It is :

"I bear witness that there
Is no god but Allah
And Muhammad is His Messenger."

This is witnessd in full by the learned only. In the same way monotheism which is the height of spiritualism is also witnessed by the learned in faith. God has presented monotheism to mankind in various ways. The presentation is unique, precise and often very deep. It is only comprehended by the learned and those who are versed with knowledge :

"Say ; Praise be to Allah
And peace on His servants
Whom He has chosen
(For His Message) (Who)
Is better ?
Allah or the false gods they associate
(With Him) ?

Or, Who has created
The heavens and the earth
And Who sends you down

Rain from the sky ?
Yea, with it We cause
To grow well planted orchards
Full of beauty and delight ;
It is not in your power
To cause the growth
Of the trees in them.
(Can there be another)
god besides Allah ,
Nay they are a people
who swerve from justice.

"Or who has made the earth
Firm to live in ; made
Rivers in its midst ; set
Thereon mountains immovable ;
And made a separating bar
Between the two bodies
Of flowing water ?
(Can there be another)
god besides Allah ? Nay, most
Of them know not.

Or, who listens to the (soul)
Distressed when it calls
On Him, and who relieves
Its suffering, and makes you
Inheritors of the earth ?
(Can there be another)
god, besides Allah
Little it is that ye heed

Or, who guides you

Through the depths of darkness
On land and sea, and who
Sends the winds as heralds
Of glad-tidings, going before
His Mercy ?
(Can there be another)
god besides Allah ?
High is Allah above what
Thou associate with Him.

Or who originates Creation
Then repeats it,
And who gives you sustenance
From heaven and earth ?
(Can there be another)
god besides Allah ?
Say, "Bring forth your argument
If ye are telling the truth.

Following the above verses, God makes a further remark. According to the Lord, no man's knowledge, however encyclopeadic, can ever comprehend the unknown. The unknown is far greater and none save Allah comprehends everything. This apparently means that knowledge has no end and as long as the earth and heavens exist knowing the unknown will never come to finality :

"Say, None in the heavens
Or on the earth, except Allah
knows what is hidden :
Nor can they perceive
When they shall be raised
Up (for judgement.)

Islam has laid great stress on knowledge. It has encouraged mankind to acquire it and made it one of the basis of religion. This it has done for man to reach the stage of monotheism in faith and to reach the highest point where mankind can reach. In stressing on knowledge Islam has reached an unchallengeable point; point where none compete with.

For the purpose of monotheism in faith or for the specific purpose for man to reach the highest point possible, Islam has encouraged the pursuit of knowledge. In fact Islam has made knowledge an integral part of its system. The Quranic verses an traditions of the Prophet pertaining to knowledge are plenty and most beneficial. Since the learned people bear witness to the concept of monotheism together with God and the angels, their positions became very noble and their ranks, too, are noble.

> "Allah will raise (to suitable ranks)
> Those who believe
> And who have been granted
> Knowledge.
> And Allah is well-acquainted
> With what you do."

Because of the extremely elevated position of knowledge and the learned people, the Lord, especially asked His messenger who is an ideal example for the Muslims, to say the following :

> "O may Lord !
> Advance me in knowledge."

O Lord ! advance me in knowledge every day; in fact every second. This should be the motto of the believing Muslim. Obviously if a Muslim's knowledge increases, his fear for the Lord, too, will increase. With that Islam would be established in full and will be absolutely perfect.

A point that should never be forgotten, in fact always remembered is the first word that was revealed to the Prophet (PBUH.); the first word that gave the glad-tidings of a new era full of new light. It was the word "Read."

The Status of Knowledge in the "SUNNAH" of the Prophet (P.B.U.H.)

We may now allude to the teachings of the Prophet (P.B.U.H.) from where we can take a beautiful pattern of conduct in matters pertaining to life in general and knowledge in particular :

"There is indeed
In the Apostle of Allah
A beautiful pattern of conduct
For you ; for anyone whose hope is
In Allah and the Final Day
And who engages much
In the praise of Allah."

Abu Hurairah reports the following :

"Whosever relieves a believer from an affliction in this world Allah relieves him from an affliction on the Day of Judgement, and whosoever conceals a believer's shortcoming Allah protects him both in this world and the Hereafter. Allah assists every person who is preoccupid in helping his brother.

"Whosever travels in search of knowledge Allah makes his way easy to heaven. Indeed, whenever a people gather in the house of Allah reciting and studying the Book of Allah, the angels welcome them, peace is showered upon them and Allah's mercy envelops them. Allah mentions them among those who are close to Him.

"A person whose noble deeds and actions are nil can never be rescued by his noble genealogy." (In Islam deeds and not lineage counts for eternal bliss.)

Anas bin Malik reports the following :—

The learned on the earth are like the stars in the sky. Guidance is available by them during dark nights on land and sea. Once the stars disappear the guides are on the verge of falling astray.

Kusair bin Qabas narrates the following : He said,

> "I was sitting with Abu Darda in amosque in Damascus. A man came forward and said, O Abu Darda ! I have come from the city of the Prophet (P.B.U.H.) I have not come for anything except that I heard the Prophet (P.B.U.H.) say : "Any person who travels for the acquisition of knowledge Allah puts him on one of the paths to Heaven. The angels stretch their wings welcoming a student in search of knowledge. All the things that exist between the heavens and the earth including the fish in the sea ask the Almighty to accept the repentance of the learned.
>
> A learned man, in comparison to an isolated worshipper is superior. He is like the full moon in comparison to the stars. The learned are the heirs of the Prophets. The Prophets of Allah have not bequested money or wealth. The inheritance left by them is knowledge. Who inherits that, inherits something considerably great."

Abu Omama el-Bahily reports :

> "Two persons were discussed by the Prophet (P.B.U.H.); one a worshipper and another a learned man. The Prophet said,
> "The status of a learned man compared to a worshipper, is lik my status, compared to the most inferior ones amongst you." The Prophet then added, "Verily Allah, His Angels and all His creation in the heavens and the earth, including the ants in their moles and the fish, pray for the learned who imparts the good things to people."

Aesha reports the following :

> "I heard the Prophet saying,
> "Allah has revealed it to me
> That He paves the way to Heaven
> For those who travel in search of knowledge.

He confirms Heaven for those
Who have lost their two daughters.
The bounty of knowledge is superior to
The merits of worship and the
most noble aspect of religion
is God-consciousness."

Anas reports :

"The Messenger of Allah said,
Whoever travels in search of knowledge
is in the path of Allah until
he returns."

Abdullah bin Masood reports :

The Messenger of Allah said,
"Only two people may be envied :
One who is endowed with abundant
Wealth and is engaged in spending it
in the way of Truth and another
Whom God has given wisdom
and he imparts it to the others
and judges with it."

Awn bin Malik reports :

Abdullah bin Masood said,
Who can never quench their gluttony;
One, the learned man and the other,
The worldly man. These two can never be equal.
As far as the learned man is concerned
He increases the pleasure of God
While the worldly man continues
In his transgression. Abdullah

Then read the following verse of the Quran:
"Nay, but man doth
Transgress all bounds,
In that he looketh
Upon himself as self-sufficient."
And then he read,
"Verily only those who possess knowledge
Among His servants
Truly fear Allah."

Abu Hurairah reported:

"After a mandies his relations
Are severed from everything
Save three: charity that continues
In his name, knowledge with
Which people benefit and
His progeny that pray for him."

Abu Hurairah reported:

"After the death of a believer the rewards of the following deeds are bestowed upon him:

(1) Knowledge he learnt and imparted to others
(2) Noble progeny he leaves behind.
(3) A Quran he leaves in his legacy.
(4) A mosque he built for the public.
(5) A way-house he built for the wayfarer.
(6) A river or a canal he introduced for general welfare.
(7) Wealth he offered in charity while alive and sound in health.

Safwan bin Ussal al-Muradie reports:

"I approached the Messenger of Allah

While he was sitting and resting on a red sheet.
I told him, 'I have come in search of knowledge'.
He said, 'Welcome to a seeker of knowledge.
He is welcomed by the Angels who spread.
Their wings for him in groups soar up
in heaven conveying
This news in great delight.'

Abu Hurairah reports that the Prophet (P.B.U.H.) said,

"The finest charity for a

Muslim is to study
Knowledge and then impart it to
his Muslim brother."

Abu Hurairah reports that the Prophet (P.B.U.H.) said,

"Knowledge that benefits none
is like treasure not spent in the way of Allah."

The Type of Knowledge Advocated by the Quarn and the Hadith of the Prophet (P.B.U.H.)

Some people, basing their ideas on suppositions, feel that the knowledge towards which the Quran appears so desirous in nothing but theology. By this they mean knowledge about God, His Angels, His Books, His Messengers, the Hereafter and knowledge about religious obligations such as Prayers, Fasting, Poor-Tax, Haj and knowledge about Islamic Legislation and Islamic Divinity.

It is a fact that Religious knowledge implies faith, morals and legislations encouraged by Islam. In fact, they rank in the first division. Faith is the most essential fundamental of any religion. Man's knowledge about God and relations with Him through His Prophets is the noblest knowledge for the individual. It is also the most worthy knowledge for the security of the society and the safety of its honour, life and blood.

However, despite the fact the knowledge of Allah through His Messengers rank the highest in Islam and in the domain of religion, the Quran itself tells us that whole universe is a Book of knowledge regarding God. The universe is a vast complex of natural phenomena with their complexities, precisions and natural laws. The advancement of knowledge in these fields lead to greater comprehension about God which in turn leads one to fear God all the more.

Let's ponder together on the following verse :

"Seest thou not that
Allah sends down rain
From the sky ? With it
We then bring out produce
Of various colours.
And in the mountains
Are tracts white and red,
Of various shades of colour
And black intense in hue.
And so amongst man
And crawling creatures and cattle,
Are they of various colours
Those truly fear Allah
Among His servants
Who have knowledge
For Allah is Exalted in Might
Oft-Forgiving."

This leads us to the fact which we discussed earlier regarding the co-ordination, order and creation found in this world of matter. We were forced to admit,

"Varily only those who possess knowledge
Among His servants
Truly fear Allah."

The Quran has exhorted the Muslims to pursue knowledge in various fields regarding the universe. It exhorted them to learn about the historicity of the world which it calls "Ayyam-Allah" (The passage of time.) How those who followed the teaching of God and were steadfast in their faith prospered and how those who continued in evil and sins pershde. The passage of time portrays the successive lives of God's friends and the absolute dejection of those who remained the enemies of the Almighty.

"Says : Travel through the earth
And see how Allah did
Originate creation; so will
Allah produce a later creation.
For Allah has power over all things."

"Say : Travel through the earth
And see what was the End
Of those before (you)
Most of them worshipped
Others besides Allah."

"Do they not travel
Trough the earth, and see
What was the End
Of those before them ?
They were superior to them
In strength : They tilled
The soil and populated it
In greater numbers than these
Have done : There came to them
Their Apostles with clear (signs)
(which they rejected, to their
Own destruction) : it was not
Allah who wronged them, but

They wronged their own souls."

"See they not how many
Of those before them
We did destory ?
Generations we had established
On the earth, in strength
Such as We have not given
To you, for whom
We poured out rain
From the skies in abundance
And gave (fertile) streams
Flowing beneath their (feet)
Yet for their sins
We destroyed them,
And raised in their wake
Fresh generations
(To succeed them.)

The Quran also exhorted the Muslims to study astronomy when it adjured them by taking oaths of certain stars : By way of oaths and adjuration the position and rank of the stars are brought to light. This calls for great research, reflection and thinking. God uses the following oaths :

"By the Star when it goes down."

"Furthermore I call to witness
The setting of the Stars
And that is indeed
A mighty adjuration
If ye but knew."

God says that He is the Lord of the Mighty Star.

"That He is Lord
Of Sirius (The Mighty Star)."

God discusses the great precisional wonders in the system of the planets and heavenly bodies and their movements :

"It is not permitted
To the sun to catch up
The moon, nor can
The night outstrip the day
Each (just) swings along
In (its own) orbit
(according to Law.)"

Describing His Creation, God goes on to say :

"Blessed is He
In Whose hands is Dominion
And He hath power
Over all things."
"And He Who created Death

And Life, that He
May try which of you
Is best in deed.
And He is the Exalted
In might, Oft-Forgiving."
"He Who created
The seven heavens
One above another
No want of proportion
Wilt thou see
In the Creation
Of (God) Most Gracious

So turn thy vision again
Seest thou any flaw ?"

"Again turn thy vision
A second time : (thy) vision
Will come back to thee
Dull and discomfitted
In a state worn out."

By the oaths and adjurations of the stars and planets God has declared that He has made them subservient to man. In doing so God has bestowed great bounty upon us. The following verses illustrate this fact:

"And He hath made subject
To you the sun and the moon,
Both diligently pursuing
Their courses; and the night
And the day hath he (also)
Made subject to you."

"He has made subject to you
The Night and the Day
The sun and the moon
And the stars are in subjection
By His command :
Verily in this are signs
For men who are wise."

"Seest thou not that
Allah merges Night into Day
And He merges Day into Night
that He has subjected the sun
And the moon (to His Law)
Each running its course

For a term appointed
And that Allah is well acquainted
With all that ye do ?"

The significance that is concealed in these statements which Allah loves to bring forth and which man should be grateful of, lies in the following : Man should study the laws operating in the universe and the Kingdom of Nature. This done, man should make them subservient to him and consequently have control over them. Eventually man should own them.

When discussing space exploration and travels to the moon, it is sheer ignorance to say that Islam opposes such a proposition. It is nonsensical to utter such a fallacy. The Quranic view pertaining to the planets and heavenly bodies is one of reality and factuality. It reduced them to their proper status while others had sanctified them and even worshipped them. Regarding those who prostrated to them and worshipped them the Quran has the following to say :

"Do not prostrate to
The sun and the moon
But fall in prostration
To Allah Who
Created them."

The sun and the moon and all the plants are mere creation of God. He is their Creator and Lord. He is the Lord of the mighty planet Sirius and is also the Lord of all the planets and all the stars. He created the moon and the sun and the entire heavens which He beautified with the stars.

As the Quran exhorted the Muslims to study the historicity of creation, to think hard and deep on the question of the stars and the planets, in the same way it has, in general, induced them to think and ponder deeply about the universe. The Quranic verses assist and co-ordinate the efforts of man in trying to discover the laws operating in the Kingdom of Nature which is God's Nature Book.

> "Behold ! In the creation
> Of the heavens and the earth
> In the alternation
> Of the Night and Day
> In the sailing of the ships
> Through the ocean
> For the profit of mankind
> In the rain which God
> Sends down from the skies
> And the life which He gives therewith
> To an earth that is dead ;
> In the beasts of all kinds
> That He scatters through the earth ;
> In the change of the winds,
> And the clouds which they
> Trail like their slaves
> Between the sky and the earth ;
> (Here) indeed are Signs
> For a people that are wise."

> "Behold ! In the creation
> Of the heavens and the earth
> And the alternation
> Of Night and Day
> There are indeed Signs
> For man of understanding."

The Ra'd or Thunder commences with the following Verses:

> "A.L.M.R. These are the Signs (Verses)
> Of the Book : that which

Hath been revealed unto thee
From thy Lord is Truth ;
But most men believe not."
"Allah is He Who raised
The heavens without any pillars
That ye can see ; is firmly

Established on the Throne (of Authority)
He has subjected the sun
And the moon (to His Law !)
Each one runs (its course)
For a term appointed
He doth regulate all affairs,
Explaining the Signs in Detail
That ye may believe with certainty
In the meeting with your Lord."
"And it is He Who spread
Out the earth, and set thereon

Mountains standing firm
And (flowing) rivers; and fruit
Of every kind He made
In pairs, two and two
He draweth the Night as a veil
O'er the Day. Behold, verily
On these things there Signs
For those who think."
"And in the earth are tracts
(Diverse though) neighbouring,
And gardens of vines
And fields sown with corn
And palm trees growing
Out of single roots or otherwise :

Watered with the same water,
Yet some of them we make
More excellent than others to eat
Behold, verily in these things
There are Signs for those
who understand !"

Out of His Grace and Mercy by way of these verses, God, showers bounties upon the whole of mankind. For the intelligent and enlightened ones He illustrates examples. He does this to induce them to make researches and studies and concentrate their attention to what God says in the following verses :

"So (give) Glory to Allah
When ye reach eventide
And when ye rise
In the morning.'

"To Him is all praise due
In the heaven and on the earth ;
And in the late afternoon
And when the day
Begins to decline."

"It is He Who brings out
The living from the dead
And brings out the dead
From the living, and Who
Gives life to the earth
After is is dead ;
And thus shall ye be
Brought out (from the dead.)"

"Among His Signs is this
That He Created you

From dust ; and then
Behold, ye are man
Scattered (far and wide.)"

"And among His Signs
Is the creation of the heavens
And the earth, and the variations
In your Languages
And your colours : verily
In that are Signs
For those who know."
"And among His Signs
In the sleep that ye take
By night and by day
And the quest that ye
(make for livelihood)
Out of His bounty ; verily
In that are Signs
For those who hearken."

"And among His Signs
He shows the lightning
By way both of fear
And of hope, and He sends
Down rain from the sky
And with it gives life to
The earth after it is dead ;
Verily in that are Signs
For those who are wise."

"And among His Signs is this,
That heaven and earth
Stand by His Command
Then when He calls you

By a single call, from the earth
Behold, ye (straightway) come forth."

"To Him belongs every being
That is in the heavens
And on earth : all are
Devoutly obedient to Him."

"It is He Who begins
(The process of) creation ;
Then repearts it : and
For Him it is most easy
To Him belongs the loftiest
Similitude (we can think of)
In the heavens and the earth ;
For He is Exalted in Might
Full of Wisdom.

God has also made the sea subservient to man

"It is Allah Who hath created
The heavens and the earth
And sendeth down rain
From the skies, and with it
Bringeth out fruits wherewith
To feed you ; it is He
Who hath made the ships subject
To you, that ye may sail
Through the sea by His Command ;
And the rivers (also)
Hath He made subject to you."

"It is He Who has made
The sea subject, that ye

May eat thereof flesh
That is fresh and tender
And that ye may extract
Therefrom ornaments to wear,

And thou seest the ships
Therein that plough the waves
That ye may seek (thus)
Of the bountry of Allah
And that ye may be grateful."

"And He has set up
On the earth mountains
Standing firm Lest it should
Shake with you ; and rivers
And roads; that ye
May guide yourselves."

"Seest thou not that
The ships sail through
The ocean by the grace
Of Allah ? that He may
Show you of His Signs ?
Verily in this are Signs
For all who constantly persevere
And give thanks."

The Quran rounds up the whole subject by making it clear that God has made the whole universe subservient to men :

"Seest thou not that
Allah has subjected
To your (use) all things
In the heavens and on earth."

Do they not look
At the sky above them ?
How We have made it
And adorned it
And there are no
Flaws in it ?
"And the earth
We have spread it out
And set thereon mountains
Standing firm, and produced
Therein every kind of
Beautiful growth (in pairs)
To be observed
And commemorated
But every devotee
Turning to (Allah)
And We send down
From the sky Rain
Charged with blessing
And We produce therewith
Gardens and Grain for harvest ;
And tall (and stately)
Palm-trees, with shoots
Of fruit stalks, piled
One over another ;
As sustenance for
(God's) servants ;
And We give (new) life
Therewith to land that is
Dead; thus will be
The Resurrection."

"Do they not look
At the camels
How they are made ?"
"And at the sky
How it is raised high ?"
"And at the mountains,
How they are fixed firm ?"
And at the earth
How it is spread out ?"

We have quoted abundantly from the Quran. These verses are absolutely unambiguous in their import. They enhance and induce the Muslim nation to study the Open-Book of Nature, to make deep researches in matters pertaining to the world and its various complexities and in general, make a thorough study of the heavens and the earth and all that exist in them

"Soon will We show them
Our Signs in the (furthest)
Regions (of the earth) and
In their own souls, until
It becomes manifest to them
That this is the Truth.
Is it not enough that
Thy Lord doth witness
All things ?"

The Significance of Theology and Religious Learning

Despite the fact that we have hitherto, in general, discussed aspects of knowledge ; pertaining to the Natural phenomena and matter which is observed and felt and despite the fact that various questions and verses of the Quran have been cited to show how Islam encourages learning in general, there is no doubt that there are numerous traditions that reflect on the importance and significance of theology itself. Whatever, we have mentioned in the form of quotations, speaking generally of knowledge and especially of theology is in no way a full study of the matter. We are only mentioning some highlights of it.

It is reported by Ibn Abbas that the Prophet (P.B.U.H.) said,

> "The people who are nearest in rank
> to prophethood are
> The learned and the men of Jehad.
> The former guide mankind to the teachings
> of the prophets and the latter fight in
> the way of the Lord with their swords
> according to the dictates of the prophets."

Abu Hurairah reported that the prophet (P.B.U.H) said,

> "Whenever a people
> gathered in any place of worship
> and recited the Quran and
> studied its contents together
> it has been certain that
> peace enveloped them, mercy overwhelmed them,
> the angels welcomed them and God
> registered them among His intimate ones."

Moaweya reported that the Messenger of Allah said,

> "With whom Allah desires goodness
> He endows with understanding
> In religion. Verily Allah is the
> Giver of Knowledge and I
> am the distributor."

Ibn Masood reports that the Prophet (P.B.U.H.) said,

> "May Allah brighten and cherish the person

who hears my statement, remembers it,
understands it and fulfils its
obligations. There are many that are versed
in religious understanding and yet don't understand.
Many well versed in religious understanding convey
my message to those who understand it better.
A Muslim's heart never envies three things ;

1. Sincerity in deeds solely performed for Allah.
2. Advice to Muslims.
3. Loyalty to their congregational unity. Their prayers disrupt those who remain aloof.

Ibn Abbas reports that the Prophet (PBUH.) said,

"A single person
endowed with understanding (learned in religion)
is better than a thousand
worshippers (who do not understand.)"

Abu Sufyam reports that Omar bin Khattab once asked Ka'b, "Who are the learned people ?"

He replied, "Those who act upon the things they know ; whose actions correspond with their knowledge."

He asked further, "What has caused knowledge to disappear from the hearts of the learned ?"

He replied, "Greed and covetousness."

Abu Hurairah reports that he treasures the following tradition from the Prophet (PBUH.)

"At the commencement of each century
Allah raises are former in this
nation who is responsible for its
renaissance."

Some Etiquettes and Manners of the "Ulema"

The Prophet (PBUH) has warned the learned and has cautioned them. He outlined the necessary etiquettes and manners expected from people of learning and their attitude towards knowledge itself. These exhortations are many but it would suffice here to mention a few.

Abdullah bin Masood reports that the Prophet (PBUH) said,

> "O People !
> Whoever learns something should speak it out.
> And who has not learnt anything should say
> 'Allah known best.' It is knowledge, in the case
> of a person who does not know, to say
> 'Allah knows best."

The Almighty Lord has addressed His Prophet saying,

> "Say : No reward do I ask
> Of you for this (Quran)
> Nor am I a pretender."

Ibn Abbas reported that the Prophet (PBUH) said,

> "Some of my people will be versing themselves
> with religious knowledge. They will be reading
> the Quran saying
>
> "We will approach the rich, enjoy a share of their
> worldly possessions and preserve our religion to
> ourselves. Such is impossible. One can only pluck
> thorns from a thorny tree. In the same way from
> the wealthy people one can never share but,
> according to Mohammed bin Sabbah, "sins."

Omar bin Khattab said the following to one of the Sahabas (companions of the Prophet) :

"Do you know what destroys Islam ?"
He said, "No."
Omár added, "The slip of the learned, arguments of the hypocrites
in matters pertaining to the Quran and the rule of such leaders who mislead.

Abu Hurairah reports that the Messenger of Allah said,

"Any person who possess some knowledge
and withholds it when asked about it,
will be bridled with fire on the
Day of Judgement."

The Companions of The Prophet (P.B.U.H.) and Knowledge

The Muslims in encouraging and inducing people to pursue Knowledge followed the Quaran and the noble traditions of the Prophet (P.B.U.H.). In reference it may suffice to quote Ma'z bin Jabal as reported by Imam el-Gazzalie in his "Ihya-el-Uloom."

Ma'z Ibn Jabal reports from the Prophet (P.B.U.H.) as having said.

"Seek knowledge. Seeking it purely for Allah's sake is fearing Him ; pursuing it is worshipping Him ; discussing it is remembering Him ; searching it is Jehad ;imparting it to others is charity an spending it for the benefit of the family is affinity. All this is because knowledge is the boarderline between the prohibited and permissible ; the light to the inroads to heaven ; the friend in isolation the companion intravel, the person to discuss with in solitude ; the guide in happiness and sorrow ; bringer of peace to the enemy, and an ornament to the intimate friend. With the power of knowledge Allah raises a people and make them leaders of virtues. Their footsteps and deeds are imitated and people conclude with their opinions. The angels show anxiousness in their friendship and spread their wings for them. Every animate and inanimate being prays for their salvation ; the fish and creatures in the sea, the animals and beasts on the land, all ask for repentance for the learned. This is so because knowledge give life to the hearts from ignorance and works as a lamp for the sight during darkness. Man reaches the rank of the selected ones of God and reaches supreme heights through knowledge both in this world and the Hereafter. To ponder in matters of knowledge is equivalent to fasting and studying it is equivalent to praying throughout the nights, knowledge brings one closer to his relatives and verses him with the facts of the prohibited and permitted things. Knowledge remains the leader while actions remain the followers. It inspires the fortunate and de prives the wicked.

Fruits of Islamic Encouragement of Knowledge

The result of the Islamic encouragement was staggeringly great. Muslims rushed to seek knowledge in every field whether spiritual, theoretical or physical. Suddenly there emerged an Islamic civilization which produced men of learning like Jabir bin Habban in Chemistry, Ibn el-Hay-sam in Physics, Abu Bakr Razi and Ibn Sina in Medicine and Philosophy, Gazzali in spiritualism, Ibn Rushed in Philosophy and Rationalism, Ibn Khaldun in Sociology and Historiography, Khawarzumi in Algebra and so many others.

Distinction of Muslim Thinkers

We may now by way of example, illustrate the distinguished position attained by some Muslim thinkers in the field of knowledge.

In the Encyclopaedia of Islam, TJ. De Boer has the following to say :

> He was therefore still regarded by Cardan, a philosopher of the Renaissance, as one of the twelve subtlest minds.
>
> "Al-Kindi was celebrated in the Middle Ages as an astrologer, he was numbered among the nine judices of astrology but he dealt not only with what we call astrological fantasies but with exact astrological measurements and calculations.

Al-Kindi was well versed in music theoretically and practically. In treating his patients he combined music with medicine. An interesting story is related about him in this respect. Irrespective of whether there is any truth or not in the story, it does go to show that he knew both medicine and music and its combinated effect.

The author of "Akhbar al-Hukama" relates the following story:

> (Writers) have mentioned an interesting story about Al-Kindi which was prevalent among the people. They said that a very rich merchant was his neighbour who was operating his business on a very grand scale. He had a son who did all the buying, selling and handling of expenses and expenditures on his behalf. The said merchant was extremely prejudiced towards Al-Kindi and spared no scruples in slandering him. Not only was this merchant obsessed with animosity but was even proud of his attitude and as such aggravated the situation.
>
> It so happened one day that his son suddenly fell in a coma. He lost consciousness of everything including the debts owed by the people and his obligations towards other merchants. The father was overwhelmed with fear and made it his duty to consult every physician available in the city. He prevailed upon them to visit his son and offer treatment.

Many physicians, on knowing the critical situation and the seriousness of the failed to respond. Those who responded were unable to produce any satisfactory result. Then the merchant was told, "But you are the neighbour of the greatest philosopher of his time and the finest physician for the treatment of this sickness. If you consult him you will certainly get what you desire."

Compelled by necessity and ashamed of embarrassment, he delegated his brother to call on Al-Kindi. The response was favourable. Al-Kindi went to the merchant's house and diagnosed his son by feeling his pulser-rate. He ordered his students who were well versed in music, efficient in playing the lute, and knew all the melancholic and gey notes to call upon the patient.

Four of the students arrived and began to play music near his head. They followed the instructions of Al-Kindi and played the notes he had taught them. They continued playing the same music while Al-Kindi studied its effects. He was reading the pulse-rate which showed that it was being effected gradually. The patient began to breathe and his pulse began to stimulate. Slowly he began to move then he sat up and began to talk. The musicians were instructed not to cease playing music.

At this stage Al-Kindi beckoned the father of the patient to ask him the things he wanted to know and to write them down so as to preserve them. The dialogue began by the father asking and the son replying to each query. When the father had completed all his questions and had written everything, Al-Kindi ordered his students to stop. With the cessation of music the patient returned to his state of unconsciousness. The father immediately asked for the music and tried to persuade Al-Kindi to instruct his students to replay the music. To this Al-Kindi replied,

> "I am very very sorry !
> The little that he lived was his last.
> Neither I nor anybody in the world
> can extend the period of life that
> comes to its end.
> Once life has fulfilled the part God
> has bestowed upon it, then
> no mortal can bring it to life again."

Ibn Al-Haitham (Al-Hazen)

He used to select the appropriate places for the observation of his optic test. Later he wrote a book on his experiments which remained to be a source of inspiration for many western scholars in optics and heat.

Sartun had the following to say about Ibn Haithm "He is the greatest authority in optics for all times."

Inb Al-Nafees

The West applauds William Harvey as the discoverer of "Blood Circulation." They forget or try to forget the observations, tests and experiments made by Ibn Nafees who discovered the basis of blood circulation many centuries before Harvey. He proved that blood was never static in the veins that it circulated in every part of the body.

Ibn Yunus

Ibn Yunus devoted most of his time studying how to develop a watch. He invented the clock pendulum known as "al-Refas." Dr Abdul Halim Muntasar has the following to say about him in his book "Science among the Arabs."

"He observed the eclipse of the sun and the moon in Cairo He described the methods adopted by Arab astronomers during Caliph Mamoon's time to measure the circumference of the earth.

It was he who invented the "Pendulum" and so preceded Galilio. In spherical trigonometry he was supreme and his discoveries surpassed those of any mathematician. He was first to propound the prosthapherical formula which before the invention of Logarithms was of great value to astronomers as it transformed the complicated multiplication of trigonometrical functions expressed in sexagesimal fractions into an addition. He also showed great skill in the solution of several difficult exercises in spherical astronomy with the help of orthogonal projection of the celestial sphere on the horizon and the plan of meridian."

Al-Beiruni

A German Orientalist who published a number of his books says, "He is the greatest rationalist that history has ever seen. His books on Indian religions and Indian Society during his time is considered to be references of the first degree during our times. An actual story of the extent of his enthusiasm to study is illustrated in the following report:

In his book "Majam Al-Udoba" Yaqooth reports the following from the Muslim Theologian, Ali Bin Iesa Al-wal-walji :

> "I called upon Abu Rayhan (al-Beiruni)
> when he was at his death bed. Joyously
> he was departing from this world and was
> in a state of agony. On seeing me
> said, 'How did you explain the question of
> Inheritance for maternal grandmothers ?'
> Out of consideration and sympathy I said,
> 'You want me to repeat that while you are in
> such a critical state ?'
> He replied, 'How can this be ?
> Is it not better that I depart from
> this world knowing this question than dying
> ignorant of it ?'
> I had no alternative but to explain
> it to him and he began remembering it.
> When I left the and was on my way I
> heard a shriek." (He was dead.)

It is true that Al-Beiruni was one of the great scholars in all history. The German Orientalist goes further and mentions, benignly, that "He is the greatest rationalist history has ever seen and that he is a great astronomer. Dr. Abdul Wahab Azzam says : "He is one of the greatest scholars in the entire history of mankind."

We do not wish to relate the history of Muslim scholars but it would suffice to quote Dr. Abdul Haleem Muntasar and what he said about Ibn-Al-Haithamand Al-Beiruni in his magnificent book "Lectures on Science among the Arabs."

> "Ibn Haitham said, as long as he lives
> he will spend all his energy and money
> in writing, with three things in mind.

Firstly : People should, after his death,
discover in his writings the benefits and
the knowledge he offered during his life-time.
Secondly : He does it for pleasure and
contentment with the above views in mind.
Thirdly : By means of his writings he prepares
for the future when he is old and helpless.

One day a rich scholar approached Ibn Haitham and offered him wealth in abundance. This he did not accept saying, "It suffices me to have enough food for the day and my servant. I do not want more, for if there does remain any surplus it would entail two things. I would be preserving it which would mean that I am your storeman or I would be generously spending it. In that case that would imply that I am your agent dispensing with your charities.

In any case if I got involved in these two matters who would then fulfil my obligations and duties in the field of knowledge?"

Finally he accepted only the amount he required and some inexpensive moderate clothes.

Ibn Haitham returned the remuneration given to him by one of the amirs whom he had taught. When returning the money he said, "Take all your money back. I do not require it. You are in greater need of it especially when you return to your Lord and go back to your eternal place. And remember in the perorfmance of good deeds there is no remuneration, no gifts and no bribery." Sarturn has the following to say about Ibn Haitham, "He is the greatest Muslim physicist and the greatest optician of all times. The basis of his moral was "Sacrifice of rights and pursuit of knowledge."

"Don't we observe in this great Egyptian Arab scholar, Ibn Haitham, the morals of an exemplary scholar ? Don't we find his life an ideal imitated in his life time and followed not only by the very generation in which he lived but for a thousand years thereafter."

In the same way Al-Beiruni was distinguished for his absolutely rare intelligence and rational mind. We can place him among the most subtlest minds of modern times. It is amazing how he was distinguished to possess knowledge of varied and variegated fields.

He was, according to the best European and Arab authorities in astronomy a superb astronomer. And according to the best geologist of our time he is an authority in geology. He is a voracious historian reputed for his wide knowledge, depth in thinking and infering.

He was able to accumulate such vast knowledge because of his extraordinary ability to study and undertake research work together with this supernatural intelligence and rational mind.

It is reported that when Al-Beiruni completed his book "Al Masoodi" he was called by the Sultan who was desirous to reward him for this gigantic work. The Sultan sent him three camels laden with money and silver. Al-Beiruni replied this kind gesture saying, "Verily I serve knowledge for knowledge and not for money."

Professor Ahmed Abdur Rahim Al-Sayeh enumerates the name of some Muslim scholars and then goes on to say, "Islam, with its call to seek knowledge. is solely responsible for producing the great men of culture, learning, polities and theology like :

Ibn Al-Haitham (Ahiazen), Al-Kindi, Alfarabi, Ibn Sina (Aviccina) Al-Beiruni, Al-Faragani, Al-Tousi, Al-Baghdaudi, Al-Dainwari, Al-Razi Al-Azwani, Al-Antaki, Al-Zaharawi, Al-Khawarzami Al-Sarfie Jaber, Jahez, Ibn Al-Baitar, Ibn Nafees, Ibn Hayyam, Ibn Hamza, Al-Idrees, Al-Masoodi Ibn Batuta and Ibn Zahra.

These great minds and many of their kind were the furits of the Islamic call which in matters pertaining to the encouragement of knowledge, had reached the ultimate height.

Contradiction Between Islam and Science : A Myth

The question of religion and science and the relation between them whether of co-ordination or unity, dipute or variance, has occasionally been discussed in the newspapers, books and by scholars in their institutes and lecture rooms.

Western writers have written profusely in this respect. In fact they were the first ones to write on this subject. From the West the controversy reached the East where many Eastern writers wrote on this subject They were, however, equally disunited in their finding like their predecessors in the West.

> Amil Buthro, a French scholar of great repute gives a picture of the situation in this respect. He writes, "The relation between religion and science, when observed through the passage of time, stirs great amazement. Despite the fact that now and again religion and science appear to have come to terms and despite the efforts of the greatest thinkers who tried their best to solve the dispute in a rationally enlightened way, the struggle between religion and science continues unabated. The battle is not over. Not only are either sides trying to overpower the other but they are all out to completely destroy each other.
>
> These two institutions are still in existence. The efforts of religion to subject knowledge and keep it under its influence has been proved fatally vain. Knowledge has liberated itself from this serfdom and slavery.

Sheikh Mustapha A. Razik has the following comment :

> "Knowledge began its campaign of threat to annihilate religions. But religions remained lofty and high. The fierce struggle proved the vitality and tenacity of religion to live."

Sheikh Mustapha continues,

"We do not wish to present a historical survey of the

relationship between religion and knowledge throughout the ages and the various periods of peace and war that existed between them. Such a survey would be too tedious and lengthy and quite out of context with our present book. However, it would not be out of place to make reference to what Amil Bothor said regarding religion and knowledge during our present times."

He says,

> "Apparently, as it stands now, there is no dispute between religion and knowledge as two entities. The dispute is actually in the spirit that governs religions and scientific learnings. A learned man never intends to convince anybody that the religious fundamentals comply with scientific facts. This is no because the basis upon which religious facts are considered to differ from the basis upon which scientific facts are taken into account.
>
> Religion imposes its facts as articles of faith which must be believed in. This means subjecting the winds and feelings of man to faith. Religion presents its facts in a way showing that man is connected with certain things that are inexplicable and incomprehesible. in the natural way. This obligates the scholar even if he does not refuse the facts, to refuse the fact-finding method adopted by the religious man. On the other hand, if a religious man finds all his articles of faith, spiritual feelings and scientific facts explained and proved by knowledge he would be the farthest one in accepting peace with science. Ones these matters are explained in a thoroughtly scientific way religion loses its grandeur and characteristics."

This statement of Amil Buthro, which Sheikh Mustapha has transmitted, is in reality a reflection of the Christian European atmosphere. It portrays Europe gripped in a Christian spell, and as such quite foreign to the Islamic atmosphere. It is therefore erroneous to transfer this dispute from the European Christian scene to the Eastern Islamic scene of course, as far as it concerns the European Cristian Society. Any person who has studied the relation between religion and knowledge in Christian Europe, knows this very well.

In its history the Church, on several occasions has adopted the views of Aristotle both in physics and metaphysics. The views of Aristotle which at one time were religious in matters concerning physics, were accepted and adopted by the Church. These views were absolutely baseless.

They were neither correct nor were supported by factual evidences. They had no relation with Christianity whatsover. Those were in fact rumours and myths which found their way into the Church and became religious.

After the "Renaissance" a new era of observation, test and experiment began. Through observation centres and laboratory experiments the scientists began to gradually trace the flaws of Aristotle's views. They arived to the conclusion that the views of were not absolutely flawless. They began exposing these errors one after the other.

During this period the Church had its dominating authority well settled in Europe. The law courts were ready to execute the wishes of the Church and so execute those who went against it or betrayed its teachings. The period of persecution and torture against the learned scientists began in a way absolutely devoid of mercy and sympathy.

This did not deter the scientists from continuing their studies and research undertakings and declaring their findings openly. When the Church saw this, its fury and animosity became fierce. Everyday a scholar met his martyrdom. The number of the martyrs became so great that the masses began to think that there existed contradiction, animosity and war between the Christian faith and knowledge.

The truth is that there does exist contradiction, animosity and war between knowledge and the particular kind of faith adopted by the Church. This particular type of faith adopted by the Church cannot be called religion. If the Church held firmly to the teachings of Jesus (P.B.U.H.) and did not concoct its own doctrines there would have never been a controversy between religion and knowledge.

On the other hand, if the controversy between knowledge and religion was a product of Christian Europe for reasons given above, then it is superfluous to drag it to the East and discuss it in an Islamic atmosphere. Islam emerged as an ally to knowledge. It encouraged knowledge and lauded it in every term. In fact Islam made the pursuit of knowledge an obligatory issue, thereby giving it the highest priority possible.

After all said and done we would like to make a general remark in this respect. The question of contradiction between knowledge and religion, when seen in its reality is merely superficial.

This is because knowledge and those who truly represent it know for certain in unambiguous terms that the centre of their researches is "matter ;" the felt and seen object. And their reliance comes from observation and experiment. They generally start with the parts of matter and later by observations and experiments upon the parts and particles they formulate their opinions.

The scientific method is therefore a method to know all the things pertaining to matter. Once the search goes beyond matter and substance it gets out of the realm of knowledge. On this basis knowledge has absolutely nothing to do with matters concerning religion whether in affirmation, confirmation, negation or rejection. If any person argues that knowledge proves certain spiritual matters it would suffice us to withdraw our confidence in him as a scientist and in the same way if he argues that knowledge rejects certain spiritual matters it would suffice us to withdraw our confidence in him as a scientist also. This as mentioned earlier is because knowledge cannot confirm or negate any spiritual fact on the basis of what we have expressed earlier. This is clear.

With all this, knowledge has its advantages. Its researches offer opportunity to create a link between the universe, its co-ordination, its creation and the smooth functioning of its entire mechanism and its deep mysterious realities.

Biology for instance, offers complete knowledge of the entire body and the animate mechanism of the body. This knowledge offers the religious authorities means upon which they can base their sermons, exhortations, advices and statements issuing from the fact that the world is not a result of some blind accident or some meaningless effort. From the results obtained of things in the universe they base their conception on the fact that these are signs and witnesses that they are all created by a God who is Supreme in His Creation.

Religion does not unite with knowledge and therefore, there is no contradiction between the two. Knowledge does not discuss articles of faith as articles of faith, nor does it discuss the concept of virtue and sin at moral realities. In matters of legislation it does not concentrate on what is obligatory upon the nation and what rules it should make for itself. These are fields where only religion appears to be operating. It declares the revelation of God and directs mankind to the right way. It declares all that is obligatory and voluntary ; all that is permissible, prohibited and unlawful.

To transmit the idea of a contradiction between religion and knowledge from an isolated area with its peculiar circumstances to the whole area covered by religion and all the fields it operates in, is certainly a blind imitation of an evil. It also indicates a clear provocation and the hidden ill-motivation. It is certainly a very ignoble practice to convey an idea born in a Christian atmosphere to an Islamic atmosphere where such an idea is absolutely foreign and where its very inception begins with "Read" and leads the learned to believe and bear witness that God is One.

Scientific Methods Between Islam and Modern Civilization

There is no doubt that modern civilization has come into existence with intense rapidity by the adoption of two methods in the pursuit of knowledge. Both differ from each other and are opposite in nature. A cold war exists between these two methods. They are :

1. The Baconian Method based on experiments, tests and observations of matter and substance.
2. The Rational Method or the De Cartian Method which is explained by the rationalists as the swift movement of the mind to the object desired.
   Both these methods developed in an atmosphere of antagonism to the Aristotlian method.

Both these methods see the Aristotlian method as that of picture and form and they have no relation whatsoever to reality and implementation. That is why they called it Pictorial Rationalism meaning the logic of the picture and form and not the essence.

The Baconian Method is a scientific method and the Carte Method is a philosophical and an experimental one. Modern civilization is based on the latter method and it would therefore behove us to limit our discussion on this method. The latter method is based on investigation of particles and substances which can be subjected to experiment, failing which they can be placed under observation to allow a decision to be taken ; a decision showing the general laws that operate in them. In other words, to come to some conclusions about the general laws that operate in the Natural Phenomena.

The field of investigation is nature and its substances for investigation is done on them. The instrument that is applied in these fields is sensory because its function is to investigate and observe the perceptible. The modern European culture and all that it stands for is based on the foundation of this method of investigation and observation. In chemistry, astronomy and all fields of matter and substance, this remains their basic and fundamental method.

It is on the same method that they will continue making progress in the future both in quality and quantity. This method owes its origin, as is famously known to Francis Bacon.

Students of European history and European thinkers do not share this view. They attribute this method to Rogers Bacon more than anyone else. Scientists and Research students are of the opinion that Rogers Bacon was more penetrating and precise in explaining and implementing the investigation on any method. Against the view of many of his countrymen he eloquently and in unambiguous words explicitly acknowledges the fact that this method was pursued by the Arabs and by their culture to which he is indebted.

This reality which the Western writers have tried to obliterate and conceal is being openly brought to light by some judicious modern thinkers. In his book "The Construction of Humanity" Professor Brifolt, traces the roots of Western civilization. He writes :

> "Rogers Bacon studied the Arabic Laugage and Arabic sciences at Oxford by his tutors from Andalous.
>
> Neither Bacon nor his followers have the right to place the crown of inventing the experimental method on themselves ; Rogers was none other than a messenger among the messenger of the Islamic method who conveyed it to Christian Europe. On the other hand Rogers himself was never tired of admitting that to get to the truth it is imperative upon his contemporaries to study the Arabic Language and sciences. The discussions and counter-discussions regarding who the original founders of this method are, reflects one of the great adultrations and concoctions in the origin European Civilization."

The Arabic method of experiments flourished in Europe during the time of Bacon. It was on a very wide scale and students throughout Europe flocked to learn it. In this respect Brifolt has the following to say :

"Knowledge brought by the Arab Civilization, remains to be the most important contribution to the modern world but its fruits were in maturing. The genius created by the Arab Culture in Spain did not bloom to its full until a long time had elapsed after that civilization had disappeared in darkness."

It is not only knowledge that was responsible to bring back life to Europe. In fact there were many other influences of the Islamic Civilization that sent their batteries of illumination to European life. Brifolt has the following to say in this respect :—

"Our knowledge is not indebted to the knowledge brought by the Arabs, in their breath-taking discoveries and unique conceptions only, in fact our knowledge is indebted to Arab culture. Still more than this we are indebted to the very existence of Arab knowledge and culture. For as far as the old world is concerned we are fully aware that it had no room for knowledge at all. The astronomy and mathematics that flourished in Greece were all foreign. They had gained these knowledges from others but never in their long history did these sciences become dissolved in their Greek culture wholly.

The Greeks had organised the religions, had generally spread their laws and had drawn their theories. But the manner and methods which they adopted for their research were all foreign. Their perseverence and tolerance, their ways of procuring positive information and concentrating on them, their detailed curriculums for education, their continuous observations and research experiments were absolutely foreign to the Greek temperament. In the old world during the times of the Greek Empire knowledge had got very close to no other city but Alexandria.

"But what we call knowledge today, only appeared in Europe as a result of the new spirit and new ways which themselves resulted from observations, experiments, tests, deductions and the development of mathematics in a way totally unknown to the Greeks. This spirit and these scientific methods were all bestowed upon Europe by the Arabs."

Dr. M. Iqbal has the following to say :

"Where did Rogers Bacon get his knowledge from ? He got it from the Islamic Universities of Spain. "Lepas Majus" which is dedicated to optics is in reality a part of Ibn Haitham's book "Kitab el-Manager" (Book on Optics.) The book of Bacon in general is a telling witness of his being influenced by Ibn Haitham."

What we have presented so far as realities of Arab Civilization, in methods and sciences, has become so popular and well-known among the judicious minded authorities, that there is no further need for any for any evidence in this respect.

The very inventor of the method of investigation, observation and tests has acknowledged the fact that Europe is indebted to Islam for the scientific method it has adopted. This is also acknowledged by all unbiased authorities. This, then, finalizes the conclusion and there is no room for any misgivings for anybody. With all this it must be pointed out that the Islamic method is by far much more complete, compact and accommodative. What Europe has taken from Islam is incomplete and deficient.

The experimental method only operates on matter and stops at the Natural Phenomena. This is an Islamic Method but it is not the complete method adopted by Islam. A Muslim does not stop at the Natural Phenomena as his goal and final object and does not limit his activities there. The aim and final object of this Muslim is what the Almighty has said,

"To Allah
Belongs the final End."

While Europe limits itself to the world of matter, Islam encourages humanity to another source of knowledge and enlightenment ; the heart or spirit or insight. Islam draws the attention of mankind towards inspiration, revelation and intuitive enlightenment. In this way Islam combines the modern science with the poet al-Bosairy said,

"The eyes, ears and heart
All are responsible
To know the Truth."

The eyes and ears are the basis of experimental knowledge which consists of observations, tests and calculations while the heart is the basis of spiritual knowledge. God induces the Muslim to seek knowledge through observation and experiment and in the same way prevails upon him to draw inspiration from Revelation.

Islam encourages a Muslim to elevate himself by following True Guidance and the spiritual light of the heart. This he should do by imbuing himself with noble attributes and exercising them in his morals. God-conciousness, sincerity, love for mankind and assisting people in all virtuous deeds.

Since Islam, in its scientifice approach is wider, more accomodative and by far more penetrative than modern civilization, it is therefore obvious that it differs from it fundamentally and basically in its intentions and motives and objects and goals.

Modern civilization advocates the idea that knowledge has no relation with ethics and morals. In other words, it shows that knowledge and morals have nothing to do with each other and so it has no relevance to virtue and evil.

Islam, on the other hand, brands the foundations of knowledge with virtue and morals its objective soaked in nobility. According to Islam knowledge brings you closer to the Almighty and imposes upon man to worship Him. Knowledge in Islam is an attribute of God and in an Islamic atmosphere it means the "Reading, chanting and remembering in God's Name."

In conclusion we would like to summarize our discussion by brief points :

1. In Islam, knowledge is part of the object for which the Divine Message was revealed. The mission of the Messenger of Allah, as defined by the Quran is education and purification.

> "He teaches them
> The Book and Wisdom
> And purifies them."

2. From its very inception commencing with the first revelation "Read," Islam was an ally to knowledge.

3. The encouragement to pursue and seek knowledge as propounded in the Quran and the Sunnah of the Prophet (P.B.U.H.) is above compassion. There is no inducement of this kind both in honour and dignity, in the highest literature of the world.

4. The knowledge propounded by the Quran and Sunnah is knowledge of everything beneficial in the physical and metaphysical worlds and in the sphere of faith and morals.

5. The scientific methods adopted by modern civilization is taken from Islam as acknowledge by Rogers Bacon ; the true father of the modern method.

6. There is no contradiction between religion and science because of the two different spheres they operate in. The sphere of religion is faith in God and the sphere of science is matter and substance. It is our fervent hope that the Muslim Nations respond to the Call of the Almighty and His Messengers and acquire knowledge, the basis of their revival and their motto in performing their duties and fulfilling the objects of their mission.

(Revised and edited)

2

The Inspiration Islam Gave to Cultivation of Knowledge and Learning

ABDUL ALI

(Abstract: If there is any reason for the lagging behind of the contemporary Muslims in science and technology, this can be nothing other than the difference between the true religion and the mere formal religion, that prevailed, in past and present, repectively).

Islam is not at all a dogmatic religion confined to the four walls of the mosque, but rather it is a scientific way of living which aims at the full efflorescence of all the spiritual, mental and other inherent faculties with which God, the Creator had endowed man, giving him the status of being the noblest creature in the universe. It cancelled the past based on superstitions and false notions. This is undoubtedly an unparalleled revolution brought about on earth in a most peaceful manner.

Islam inspired man to unravel the secrets of nature more than any other religion or school of thought could do with the purpose of making him believe in the existence of Almightly God, because of the more he knows about the universe, the more conscious he is bound to become of the Creator of the universe, provided he has a sound reasoning power. This is exactly what God Himself has said in the holy Book:

> [It is the scholars among His servants who fear God alone. Lo:Gos is Mighty, Forgiving](35:28).

The above verse makes it quite clear that if man wants to become a faithful servant of God, he must first of all become of the scholars. In other words, he must apply his intellect and power of observation, instead of superstitions and false notions in his comprehension and appreciation of the manifestations of nature in order to feel in his heart the immensity and greatness of the Wisdom, Might, Knowledge and Creative Power of God. Since God has chosen to be worshipped by man by keeping Himself veiled from his sight, there can hardly be any other way of feeling (His existence effectively except through acquiring knowledge of Him by reflecting and meditating on the Wisdom and Power with which He has created the infinite universe out of nothing.

It is with the explicit purpose of instilling in man the spirit of worshipping God with full awareness of His existence that Islam has put the greatest possible emphasis on the pursuit of knowledge and learning. It is the only religion in the world which has made the acquisition of knowledge and learning one of the unavoidable ordinances of God incumbent upon His followers. And therefore the cultivation of knowledge is considered in Islam as a sacred act of worship to Almighty God.

Both the holy Qur'an and the traditions of the Prophet (peace and blessings of God be upon him), the two main sources of Islamic thought, are full of such expressions as emphasize the importance of knowledge in the life of man on the one hand and stimulate him to cultivate it on the other. A brief account of such Quranic verses and the apostolic traditions is given here in support of this point.

First of all, it is important to note in this connection that the word *'ilm* (knowledge) and its derivative have occurred 805 times; the word *albab* (minds) has occurred 16 times; and the word *'aql* (reason) and its derivatives have occurred 49 times in the holy Quran according to a survey made by Prop. Darwish Mustafa, Director of National Museum at Qatar in his article, History of Science in Islamic Civilization. This clearly indicates that man has been repeatedly asked in the holy book to apply his brain and reason to attain knowledge.

Again, it is also equally important to note that God made Adam superior to the angels by giving him more knowledge than He gave to the latter, as is clear from the following verses :

And He taught Adam all the names, then, showed them to the angles, saying : Inform Me of the names of these if you are truthful.

They said: Be glorified : We have no knowledge saving that which Thou hast taught us. Lo ! Thau, only Thau art the Knower, the Wise.

He said: O Adam ! Inform them of their names and when he had informed them of their names, He said: Did I not tell you that I know the secrets of the heavens and the earth? And I know that which you disclose and which you hide. And when We said unto the angels:

Prostrate yourselves before Adam, they fell prostrate except Iblis, who refused, boasted and become of the disbelievers.

Two important conclusions can be drawn from the above verses. First, by ordering the angels to prostrate themselves before Adam, God has clearly demonstrated the dignity of the high office of knowledge. Here it is worth mentioning that they were ordered to do so only after it was proved that they possessed less knowledge than that granted to Adam. Secondly, it is also made quite clear that true wisdom consists in complete surrender to the Will of God. Therefore, the action of the angels in prostrating themselves before Adam on the order of God was based of wisdom. But, on the other hand, Iblis, who refused to abide by the order of God considering himself to be superior to Adam, was discarded and condemned as a proud infidel. In other words, it can be said that in these verses God had demonstrated the triumph of knowledge over ignorance and warned against the evil consequences of not practicing wisdom in life which consists in complete surrender to the Will of God. And it is only in the light of this fact that the following saying of the Prophet can be properly understood.

The sources of wisdom is the fear of God.

Besides, many of the early verses of the holy Qur'an were revealed to raise the banner of knowledge. They heralded the ushering in of the age of knowledge providing man with the incentive to cultivate it. The very first five verses which were revealed to the Prophet commanded him to read and learn:

> Read in the name of the Lord who created;
>
> Created man from a clot.
>
> Read: And thy Lord is the most Bounteous who taught by the pen.
>
> Taught man that which he know not.

At another place God has again highlighted the value and dignity of the pen by swearing buy it while upholding the lofty character of Prophet Muhammad:

Nun. By the pen and that which they write, thou art not, for thy Lord's favour unto thee, a madman.

God's swearing by the pen in those days and particularly among the Arabs who always boasted of their swords and attached little importance to the pen being ignorant of it, might have sounded very strange and insignificant. But now history has proved beyond any shadow of doubt that the pen is mightier than the sword. Today nobody denies it.

Some of the Qur'anic verses in which man has been asked to assert his reason, intellect and senses in order to develop a right conception of live as well as to see the clear signs of God's existence which pervade everything He has created are given below :

Have they not then observed the sky above them, how We

have constructed it and beautified it, and how there are no rifts therein?

And the earth have We spread out, and have flung firm hills therein and have caused of every lovely kind to grow thereon.

A vision and a reminder for every penitent slave.

And We send down from the sky blessed water whereby We give forth unto gardens and the grain of crops,

And lofty date palms with ranged clusters,

Provision (made) for man : and therewith We quicken a dead land. Even so will be the resurrection of the dead.

In these verses the disbelievers who rejected the theory of life after death outright calling it a remote possibility were asked to contemplate on the possibility of the same by observing the laws of nature around them.

Say (O Muhammad): Travel in the land and see how He originated creation, then God brings forth the later growth. Lo God is Able to do all things.

In this verse man has been exhorted to travel far and wide in the world in order to be aquainted with God's unique power of creation.

Besides, in the following verses God has highlighted the importance of knowledge for success in life in a more direct manner which cannot be ignored while assessing the role of Islam in inspiring the Muslims to cultivate knowledge:

1. Say (O Muhammad) : Are those who know equal with those who know not?
2. And say: My Lord : Increase me in knowledge.
3. He gives wisdom unto whom He wills, and whosoever is given wisdom, he truly has received abundant good. But none remember except men of understanding.

4. God will exalt those who believe among you, and those who have knowledge, to high ranks. God is informed of what you do.

Similarly the Prophet of Islam whose life is a living commentary on the holy Book did not lag behind in emphasising upon his followers the importance of knowledge and learning. Some of his saying in this regard are quoted below.

1. To seek knowledge is incumbent upon every Muslim.
2. Whosoever treads a path is search of learning, god makes thereby easy for him the way to paradise.
3. The superiority of the learned man over a mere worshipper is like the superiority of the full moon on a night over all other stars.

Is was from such Qur'anic verses and apostolic traditions that the Muslims both Arab and non-Arab, received a great incentive, travelled far and wide in search of knowledge and contributed a great deal to human thought and progress. Arabic soon become the language of natural sciences, medicine and philosophy. And between the beginning of the eight, and the middle of the thirteenth centuries the Arabic-speaking peoples were the main bears of the torch of culture and civilization throughout the world and Arabic translations were the instrument whereby the ancient sciences and intellectual legacies of Greece, Iran and India were preserved, supplemented and transmitted to the west, which made possible the ranaissance of Western Europe.

Here it should be remembered that had the Muslims done nothing apart from saving and preserving the ancient sciences of the then civilized world, even then they would deserve the appreciation of the twentieth century scholars for this reason alone. Preservation and transmission of knowledge is no less important than making original contributions, otherwise, as Hitti has put it, "had the researches of Aristotle, Galen and Ptolemy been lost to posterity the world would have been as poor as if they had never been produced."

In short it can be rightly said that history does not know any other nation which has contributed so much in a comparatively brief span of time to the cause of knowledge and learning as did the Arabs and Arabic-speaking peoples. The famous Muslim capitals like Cairo. Damascus, Baghdad and Cordova etc, became the chief centre of spreading education and conducting scientific researches. An idea of the Muslims' contribution to human thought the progress can be easily gained from the fact that when misfortunes befell the Muslim world in general and the Arabs of Spain, France and Italy in particular, the most precious booty treasured by the Europeans was a large number of valuable Arabic books and manuscripts. Prof. Umar al-Dasuqi has mentioned in his book entitled that the Europeans collected more than 2,50,000 valuable Arabic books and rare manuscripts and decorated their libraries with them. For example, the libraries of Berlin, Paris, London, Leipzig, Leiden, Oxford and Mudrid etc., are still very famous for having a large number of rare Arabic books and manuscripts on different branches of learning cultivated by the Muslims.

The Muslims made valuable contributions, especially in historical, geographical, philosophical, mathematical and medical studies. Although here it is not possible to enter into details of their achievements in these fields, a passing reference to a few Arab scholars may be made in this connection. For example, Ibn Khaldun, the greatest historical thinker of Islam, is admired in the West as founder of the modern sciences of sociology and historiography. And as R.A. Nicholson has observed, "his intellectual descendants are the great medieval and modern historians of Europe—Machiavelli and Vico and Gibbon." In the realm of geography the names of Ibn Khurudadhbih, Ibn Hawqal, Yaqut, Al-Bakre and Al-Idrisi are very famous. The great mathematician, Al-Khwarimi wrote the oldest work on algebra with over eight hundred examples known as *Hisab-ul-Jubr wal-Muqabalah* (the calculation of integration and equation). It is remarkable to note that the Latin version of this book was used until the sixteenth century as the main mathematical text-book by western scholars. Of the original writers on medicine Ibn Zakaria al-Razivi the author of *al-Hawi,* an encyclopaedia of medicine, and Ibn Sina, the author of the *Canon of Medicines*, are very famous. Upto the sixteenth century the works of theses authors constituted the basis of the lectures on medicine in the European universities. Similarly, the Muslims' contribution to the development of philosophical studies can be judged from the fact that Islamic philosophy continued to be taught in the universities of Europe upto the middle of the seventeenth century and that Aristotle was understood in European only through the commentates of Ibn-Rushd for a long time. Besides the Muslims achieved considerable distinction in Chemistry, Meineralogy, Botany, Fine Arts, etc.

In the light of the glorious past history of the Muslims as well as the inspiration which Islam gave and continues to give to the cultivation of knowledge it is quite clear that Islamic teaching are not averse to modern sciences. They only encourage their cultivation for the welfare of humanity at large. It is therefore, absolutely baseless to blame Islamic teaching for the current intellectual and cultural decay of the Muslims all over the world, while, on the contrary, the fact remains that whatever scientific progress has been achieved so far, it is only because there has been the domination of Islam in the world for a considerably long time which made man thoughtful and reflective and filled him with the spirit of scientific enquiry, which is the very life and soul of modern sciences.

In this connection it may further be mentioned that if there is any reason for the lagging behind of the contemporary Muslims in science and technology, this can be nothing other than the difference between the true religion and the mere formal religion, as has been admirably pointed out by Dr. Ahmad Amin in the following words:

The scholars and historians tire themselves in turning over the pages of books on history in order to find out the reason as to how the Muslims in their early days could perform miracles in making conquests and establishing their sovereignty as vicegerents of God on earth and how in their later days also they performed miracles in bringing about their downfall in such a manner that they soon became weak, humiliated and lowly, while the holy Qur'an and the teachings of Islam etc., continue to be the same. The scholars arrive at different conclusions in their analyses of it, but in my opinion there is only one reason for this and that is the difference between the true religion and the mere formal religion.

The formal religion according to the author consists in performing the formal acts of the religion without abiding by its teachings in the practical life and therefore it does not produce any big results in the life of the Muslims, while the true religion of Islams, if implemented in both letter and spirit, enables the Muslims to make all possible sacrifices in the path of God and ensures full efflorescence of all the creative faculties man has been endowed with.

(Revised and edited; originally published in *Islamic Culture* July 1979)

3

Islam's Solution of the Basic Economic Problems

E.A. POLIAKOVA

The Position of Labour

There is an innate contradiction in *Laissez-faire* Economics, consisting in a conflict between social welfare and individual welfare in the majority of cases. For individuals acting freely (from purely economic motives) for their private gain cannot be assumed to sacrifice their private gain for general welfare as only too often becomes necessary.

Moreover *laissez-faire* Economics errs in assuming equal or adequate competing power in case of each factor of production. Under "organized production" the working class does not have sufficient power to insist on claiming remuneration equal to its "specific production." The supply of labour cannot be withheld to an appreciable degree for any length of time, that of land an appreciable degree for any length of time, that of land on the other hand cannot be increased at all considerably. The two agents possess very unequal competing power, and economic freedom will very soon destroy the *laissez-faire* assumptions even if the conditions are perfect to start with.

The non-fulfilment of these assumptions is chiefly to the disadvantage of the working classes which constitute the majority of mankind. As soon as the conditions become unfavourable to them their condition begins to grow worse. The effect is cumulative; they are reduced to utter poverty. The exploiters grow overrich.

Laissez-faire has been the rule of the world through the ages, and through the ages poverty like a tragic spectre has haunted the ceaselessly toiling humanity in ironic contrast with the riches of the leisured few. Free operation of this system renders one part of mankind "not in a position", and another "not in a mood" to attend to any thing other than wealth. From time to time religion and statecraft have revolted against such a condition. Islam embodies one such revolt. And it is at this point that religion first touches the Science of Economics.

Religion has to promise and secure something more than mere subsistence for its followers and those to whom it is addressed before it can be properly attended to. Islam proceeds to secure this by a new economic system. It declares destitution or utter poverty as unthinkable in human society. Our Prophet defined the poor man as one "who finds not the wherewithal to make himself independent" (economically); and the Islamic State guaranteed subsistence to this class (removing thus the intrinsic weakness of labour). On this point I shall dwell later. But extreme and widespread poverty comes to exist by the side of excessive and concentrated riches because, as I said, private gains (from a purely Economic point of view) are only too often inconsistent with maximum social welfare. And the method which makes private gains maximum, namely, private enterprise, makes impossible the method which maximises the social welfare arising from a given output namely, equal distribution of wealth.

Economic thought has constantly emphasised the one method or the other. The novelty of Islam's contribution to Economics consists in an adjustment of the two in a way which eliminates the defects of both and combines their virtues. Thus Islam gives an economic system that : (1) is automatic, which is what the purely equalitarian or socialistic systems are not, (2) tends to equalise distribution which the *laissez-faire* system cannot, (3) provides a method of production which leads to maximum output with minimum disutility which the equalitarian systems do not, (4) provides stable business and industrial conditions which the *laissez-faire* economics cannot (5) and maximises both the national dividend and the social welfare arising from it to a degree which neither of the two can. In it private enterprise does not interfere with increasing equality of distribution; rather each promotes the other.

We shall now consider some features of this system which reveal its essential nature and have a direct bearing on our basic economic problems.

In the first place the Islamic system guarantees ample subsistence to the poor. Religion cannot make a complete case for itself unless it brings deliverance from economic anxieties and leisure for other things. According to Islam, it is for God to provide livelihood to every creature and so His law specifically contains the provision for it. God has ordered: "Slay not your Children, fearing a fall to poverty, We shall provide for them and for you," Again "We have apportioned among them their livelihood in the life of the world." And "We have given you power in the earth and appointed you therein a livelihood. Little give ye thanks." So in Islamic economics the State undertakes to fulfil this guarantee on behalf of God through the institution of *Zakat* or "Growth"-tax.

This is a tax on all property owned beyond a certain maximum and is meant, as the Prophet said; "to be taken from the rich among them in order to be given to their poor."

"Zakat literally means growth and increase,. and according to some purity. The tax has been named Zakat with respect to the first meaning because its giving leads to an increase of prosperity in this world and growth of religious merit in the next."

There are two important divisions of this growth-tax, Sadaqah and Tithe. The one takes away a large portion of actual or potential interest arising from capital goods and the other of the surplus produce arising from agricultural land.

The cause of Sadaqah being due is "the possession in full ownership of a productive Nisab (minimum) of property; and its rate is 2½ of the value of possessions other than land."

The tithe is a growth-tax on the produce of the earth. It is a charge on economic rent. In the Qur'an there are the verses, "And on the day of its harvest given its rights"; (VI. 142) and, "Bestow alms from the choice part of that which you have earned and that which we have made grow for you from the ground." (II. 269). Its rate is determined by the Prophet's saying: "In what has been irrigated by Heaven one-tenth and in what has been watered with buckets or water-wheels, one-half of one-tenth" *(Mishkat).*

The growth-tax is quite separate from other financial taxes of the State and goes exclusively to the poor in such a way that the prayers do not derive any direct benefit from it. It is because its beneficiaries are exhaustively enumerated in the Qur'an. "The growth-tax is only for the poor and the needy and those who collect and those whose hearts are to be reconciled and to free the captives and the debtors, and for the cause of God, and for the wayfarer; a duty imposed by God."

The immediate purpose of this institution is to relieve the poor and to help them to grow in prosperity by giving them better resisting and competing power. The tax is collected in kind and distributed locally; so it is more economical and provides good quality of food to the poor. For the Qur'an commands: "Bestow alms from the choice part of that which you have earned and that which we have made grow for you from the ground." The tax in these two ways increases the productive efficiency of the workers and thereby the prosperity of the whole community. It is a kind of protection to the labourers, and gives them an opportunity to improve their condition.

The tax tends to guarantee subsistence and thus eliminates one intrinsic weakness of *laissez-faire* economics. It introduces an important modification into that system by enabling the workers to claim and secure a remuneration equal to their "Specific production." For if the labourers are exploited they can go on strike. The employers will have to yield. The institution takes away their absolute resting strength. It makes it uneconomical for them to try and defeat the workers by closing the works. The State will automatically tax them down if they try to defeat the workers by closing the works. For the tax being on the property owned, their property will begin to be taxed and distributed. So in practice they will readily give to the workers wages equal to their contribution to production.

Here we may also note how much emphasis of the tax lays on production and productive employment of wealth. It regards all superfluous wealth as productive and taxes it as such, irrespective of whether it is so used or kept idle. It thus compels it to be so used. The Prophet once said "Are there those among you who are the guardians of orphans who possess property? They let them trade with it and not leave it uninvested, so that the growth-taxes due on it do not swallow it up."

Lastly it needs to be pointed out how fundamental this institution is in Islam. It is Islam's solution of a vital social problem and is of the essence of the religion. It is a cardinal principle next in importance only to belief in God and offering prayers. Many a time does the Qur'an repeat "establish worship and pay the growth-tax." No rich man can be or remain a Muslim without paying the growth-tax. It is an ordinance ("Fard").

But the growth-tax is only a second best thing. It is repulsive to human dignity to take even State aid. Moreover, the emphasis that Islam lays on an earned livelihood necessarily implies the undesirability of living constantly on State aid. Also, Islam gives, as we shall see, a technique of production which, if adopted, would lead to so much increase of output and to so good a distribution as to make the institution of the growth-tax obsolete except as a potential measure. The Prophet said "Give Sadaqah for a time is to come when people will offer Sadaqah and there will be no-one to take it."

So the permanent importance of the institution is as a potential measure of guarantee against the falling of workers below or even down to the subsistence-level so long as there are people with "superfluous" wealth around.

II

The Capitalistic Institutions

Another feature of Islamic economics is that, through it provides the greatest initiative to production by recognizing private enterprise, private property, the institution of the family, inheritance, and a high standard of living, it yet contrives completely to eliminate the harmful influences of each of these. Thus it solves the economic problems connected with these institutions. Under a "Let alone" policy private enterprise makes impossible any approach towards an equal distribution of wealth; and family affection, supported by inheritance provisions, blinds men to other considerations, and leads to an exploitation of labour by the other agents of production. Communistic economics therefore has revolted against these institutions blaming them for the accumulation of riches in the hands of the few and the consequent destitution of the many.

But the abolition of these institutions would kill individual initiative; and the disutility of producing a scientifically determined amount under State compulsion in an impersonal way may be enormous. Any scheme of arbitrarily distributing the wealth in equal amounts to maximise the welfare arising from a given output is bound to kill the incentive to production and thus decrease the amount of output. We cannot, therefore, be sure that by the abolition of these institutions the social welfare will increase. One thing is certain: the disutility incurred in producing a given amount will be very much increased.

Moreover, much of the innocent joy and charm of life, much of the education in gentler sentiments will be gone with the institution of the family, as also much of the brave endeavour and brave sacrifices of man. And with Private ownership will be gone the moral development which the exercise of personal choice in connection with private property makes possible.

All this will react on the psychology of man and through it on his productive efficiency. The communistic system only emphasises distribution. It neglects production. Islamic economics, having them both in view, finds itself unable to sacrifice these institutions. It approves them with limitations.

In Islam God has appointed the institution of the family, "And He it is Who hath created man from water, and hath appointed for him kindred by blood and kindred by marriage." And God counts it as of value to man, "We aided you with wealth and children." And they have rights over him, "Give the kinsman his dues." And their rights are prior, "And those who are akin are nearer one to another in the ordinance of God." Yet family affections are a partial value and a subordinate value. Devotion to family should never blind man to the ultimate values. There are vigorous limitations, as we shall see later.

Concerning private property, the Prophet declared;: "Verily your blood and your wealth and your property are sacred (and inviolable)." But its value is emphatically as a means.

Then Islam also approves private enterprise in business, the reward of which the Qur'an constantly calls the "the bounty of Allah." The permission is plain. "Allah permitteth trading and forbiddeth usury." Yet there are serious injunctions to honesty in business. "Give full measure and be not of those who give less (than due), and weigh with the true balance. Wrong not people in respect of their goods." And further see the chapter entitled "Defrauding." They are more elaborate in the sayings of the Prophet. From these the Muslim jurists have derived a large body of market laws.

Islam also appoints inheritance, "And unto each we have appointed heirs of that which parents and near kindred leave." "Unto the men of a family belongeth a share of that which parents and near kindred leave, and unto the women a share of that which parents and near kindred leave, whether it be little or much....a legal share." Yet the shares in inheritance are so many that far from leading to accumulation of big fortunes they cause a dispersal of wealth and tend to equalise it. They provide capital to more and more people and so give chances to others. In spite of property rights the individual cannot, by will, bestow more than one-third of his property on anyone except the State or the Cause of God.

The incentive to production is further increased by the religion's injunction to a better standard of living. Here Islam had to raise its voice against the ascetic in the contemporary religions and strongly to assert the values of this world. "Say: who hath forbidden the adornment of Allah which He hath brought forth for His bondmen, and the good things of His providing."

Again, "O ye who believe! forbid not the good things which God hath made lawful for you", Yet the high standard of living has also its limits; extravagance is reproached. "Lo! He loveth not the prodigals." These institution thus modified are retained and supplemented by the growth-tax to promote economic welfare.

III

Industrial Fluctuations

Within the above limits, Islam allows full-fledged private enterprise. How then would it solve the technical problem of industrial fluctuations which has arisen from "private-enterprise-economics" in the 19th and 20th centuries and so greatly affects the welfare of communities.

The most important feature of Islamic economics is that its operation eliminates these fluctuations altogether. The fundamental cause of them, as advanced by many writers, is that prices are pegged high and not allowed to fall by the same percentage as the increasing supply would require if it were all to be consumed. The causes for the initial rise in prices are not themselves so disturbing. Even climatic causes such as the various astronomical, meteorological, and physical cycles do not case much disturbance; they partially tend to cancel each other, and with economic speculation, storage, and specially with the growth of the world market they would sink into insignificance if not aggravated by other factors. Whatever the cause of the initial rise in prices, it is these aggravating factors that work the havoc. They are :

(1) Lending of capital on interest.
(2) Overproduction and underconsumption.

(3) Increasing inequality.
(4) Overspeculation.

The most important of them is the institution of lending on interest. With a good harvest or any other initial cause such as increased supply of gold or governmental inflation, industrial prices rise, bringing more profits to the entrepreneurs. People begin to produce more with borrowed money and to start new concerns, again with borrowed money. For a time there are profits. A wave of optimism spreads. Lending institutions become overconfident and lend more and more to the speculators and to the less competent enterprisers coming into business. Very soon the credit bubble expands to its full capacity. More money gets involved in production and comparatively little is left with the consumers, so there is a shortage of purchasing-power and pressure on the prices to go down. We shall see later that this situation is brought about in some measure by the other factors too, and it always causes fluctuation. But the fluctuations are enormous only when the enterpreneurs or the merchants are running their business with borrowed money, and money borrowed at interest. They find themselves in a fix. They cannot with-hold supply for they have debts to discharge and they cannot lower the prices to be able to sell more, because a slight fall in prices leads to a considerable increase of the rate of interest and of the amount of principle in terms of goods. As Prof. Fisher has said the very effort to pay the debts increases the debts. Moreover, they can sell comparatively less goods at this time for they have no discharge labour, which act further shortens the purchasing-power of the consumers. To sell more, prices will have to be considerably reduced, which means an enormous increase in the real value of debts. They begin to be unable to discharge their obligations.

Here the essential duality of interests between the money-lenders and the borrowers for productive purposes comes into open conflict and with it the inherent weakness of an industry based on this institution becomes obvious. Just when the vital interests of the *enterpreneurs* demand that they should have financial resources to cope with the situation, the interests of the lending class demand a payment of the loans and are against their renewal. As a consequence, the entrepreneurs are deprived of their resisting strength; they cannot withhold supply. Distress selling results with a cumulative effect, leading to bankruptcies and bank failures. The institution of lending on interest causes the whole trouble. It makes the lowering of prices so harmful and withholding of supply impossible. This institution is responsible for the fluctuations in a number of ways. On the one hand it facilitates the investment of much unjustified capital in an industry; and on the other hand, as Marshall says, "the danger of not being able to renew his borrowings just at the time when he wants them most, put him (the borrower) at a disadvantage relatively to those who use only their own capital much greater than is represented by the mere interest on his borrowing. And the failure of this renewal", as Marshall again says "may cause him to succumb to what would have been a passing misfortune if he had been using no capital but his own." It causes a slight rise in prices in any industry to lead to a great demand for the products of constructive industry and so it connects the fluctuations in the particular industries with the fluctuations in the constructive industry which by the nature of the commodities it produces fluctuates much more violently. And lastly, through bank failures, it spreads the distress of one industry to all the others and thus brings about a total breakdown in more serious cases. Thus the trade depression on the crisis and its resultant troubles are mostly due to this institution and the socialists have wrongly attributed it to capitalism. Mr. Jawahar Lal, for instance, says in *Whither India"*. "This is the crisis of capitalism.....And the disease seems to be of the essence of capitalism." The disease is only of the essence of the institution of lending on interest. Islamic capitalistic economy eliminates lending on interest but retains capitalism and thus gets rid of all crises.

The institution means a duality of interest in business. It causes an intrinsic weakness in industry and not only leads to a total breakdown of industry when a point of maladjustment of purchasing-power is reached, but is the fundamental instrument in helping the industry to reach that point. It is the only instrument which makes overspeculation possible. The prosperity that it brings comes quickly but goes quickly too. Islam considers this prosperity as sham and warns against it. "Although interest brings increase", said the Prophet, "Yet its end tends to scarcity." And the Qur'an says, "That which ye give on interest in order that it may increase on other people's wealth hath no increase with God; but that which ye give in "growth-tax" seeking God's countenance hath increase manifold" (XXX. 39). The Prophet positively said that it was destructive: "Avoid the seven destructive things", he said, and the third he mentioned was "interest." (*Bukhari, Muslim and Abu Daud).*

The great part played by the institution in causing industrial fluctuations has been clearly shown by Pigou, Fisher, and some other economists. Yet its justification has so far been taken for granted.

IV

A Digression on Interest

There is a tendency to regard interest as of the same nature as the shares of the other factors of production, i.e., the reward for a service rendered. It is never examined how doubtful is this service. "They say trade is just like interest-taking; whereas God permitteth trading and forbiddeth interest." Islam tends to be highly in favour of joint stock companies; only the denture-holders and commercial loans are ruled out as destructive. Partnerships were very popular in the days of the Prophet and were even extended to agriculture. If you have spare money you can become a partner or purchase a share and partake of both positive and negative profits. You are not allowed to give a blow to the entrepreneur in his worst moment and destroy his resisting power and not only ruin him but create social havoc. There is the huge injustice in the institution of interest and the strong tendency to get out of control.

In fact there is no argument for interest. If you say that you charge it because the borrower makes a profit out of it, then you should charge it only when the borrower makes a profit out of it. And the poorer his success or his chances of success the less should be the rate of interest charged. Contrary to modern Economics it should vary inversely with the risks. The productivity argument leads to a commercial heresy.

The point is this; either you have nothing to do with the fortune of the borrower or you have a share in it. You cannot share his fortune and leave him his woes. The bargain is loaded with iniquity, and we have seen its harms. According to Islam you can only become a partner.

Islam secures the capitalistic enterpriser and rules out the pure capitalist (if we may so call the money-lender) thus providing a very sound footing for industry, the growth of whose prosperity, although somewhat slow at first, is very rapid afterwards, and very sure and stable throughout.

Regarding the nature of interest, Professor Marshall very well begins by identifying saving with "the habit of distinctly realizing the future and providing for it" and correctly emphasizes that "men labour and save chiefly for the sake of their families, although sometimes they save from an acquired habit." The difference is here: Islam does not allow the separation of the functions of saving or waiting and risk-bearing. It does not allow a separate abstinence theory of interest. It is strictly what may be called the "Investment theory of interest." In the sense of an income from an investment in an enterprise interest is both necessary and legitimate. In this sense it is a sound inducement for accumulation of capital on which all progress depends. In the sense of a reward for mere lending it is a different thing. The elimination of such interest will not hinder accumulation of capital in the least while it will contribute to the stability, simplicity and morality of business. For, as Clark says, men save for a definite future income, "The Standard of living which needs to be maintained is the all important element in the case." Prohibition of lending on interest will only compel people to depend for this future income on direct investment.

V

A Digression of Agriculture

Abolition of lending on interest may not appear so beneficial in the case of agriculture. The resources of the tenants are scanty, the fruitation of their enterprise takes a long time. Without loans many of them cannot carry on production.

Yet it is in agriculture that the benefits of this abolition will reach farthest. For the institution is itself the cause of what it is supposed to remedy. But for this, people had not depended on those small holdings by working on which their labour is remunerated at less than half its worth. But for this, methods of production had taken an entirely different form in agriculture, and insufficiency of working capital had led to the development of joint-stock companies in agriculture.

Than joint-stock companies in agriculture no simpler solution is possible for our agrarian and humanitarian problems.

In them shares may be made to consist of areas of land as well as of sums of money, and the land-shares may be classified according to the quality of land. (Even this classification of land-shares, as I propose to show in a separate article, need only be a transitional measure.

The advantages of such companies will be very great, and I shall discuss them in a separate article for the matter is likely to raise some controversy. A few points however, may be mentioned in passing.

1. The agriculturist will no longer be kept tied to his land. Better mobility of labour will be secured.
2. With the development of "Land Exchanges" perfect transferability of land will be achieved. A world market for land will grow up and equality of prices be secured.
3. All the resources in land which cannot be utilized by individuals will be brought under the tractor. Food and raw materials will become much cheaper.
4. The universal handicaps of the agriculturists regarding finance and marketing would be very easily removed.
5. Employment of powerful machines and adequate chemical

manures may overcome Nature's resistance, and indefinitely postpone the operation of the law of diminishing returns.

6. Joint-stock companies in agriculture will be the missing link between the present form of agriculture and the "factory farms" or "chemical manufacture of food" and will have an optimistic bearing on the population question.
7. Large numbers will be freed from their uncertain, irregular employment and, by becoming workers in other industries, may make possible three-hours shifts in manufactures. What Hobson calls the "social surplus" and which in our case will be much greater because no deductions will be necessary for interest, may now be devoted to providing leisure to workers by employing larger numbers for shorter hours and on adequate wages.
8. With proper education this leisure will spell "life." Only thus can man become master of the machines: Only thus can open the way for a humane civilization from the stagnation we are in.

It is easy to see how much these benefits exceed those promised by the familiar innumerable partial solutions of agrarian problems.

This development in agriculture will overcome many of the caprices of nature; and it will more thoroughly balance the good against the bad harvests and so eliminate an important initial cause of business fluctuations.

The science of Biology is developing man's control over soil, seed and season. Chemical manures, Mendel's law, vernalization processes are all there to help agriculture. Physics is also aiding with such inventions as photo-periodism. An industrial counterpart is needed and we shall not have to wait long for it.

Highly mechanized farming aided by the above and similar inventions will ultimately conquer the differences in fertility of soil and with the consequent even distribution of population one result would be the disappearance of Rent. (This point too will be further dealt in a separate article). Only two factors would remain to share the national dividend: labour and investment.

Overinvestment, increasing inequality, changes in the value of money and inventions are some of the other factors which, combined with the institution of lending on interest, bring about a crisis in much the same way. With the abolition of this institution their harmful effects will very much diminish. They will have even then some power to cause unstable conditions. Islamic economics therefore eliminates them.

Overinvestment, oversaving, or overproduction is almost the same factor which in connection with the recent crisis has been described by the Pollak institute scholars, Foster and Catchings, as the shortening of purchasing-power by more and more of money being devoted to productive enterprise and less being given out to society to purchase the output. This is brought about by either not spending sufficiently on consumption-goods or by not paying enough in wages. This tendency may be called the second factor.

By emphasising the just and prompt payment of wages and by establishing the institution of the growth-tax, Islam has strengthened the position of the workers. It has made it possible for them to claim and have adequate remuneration. Unduly low wages are rendered more or less impossible, and so one of the causes of the shortage of purchasing-power is eliminated.

Secondly, Islam plainly saw that the efficiency of the everyday business of mankind depends upon the everyday habits of men, and it went on to emphasise spending. The religion expresses much contempt for miserliness and accumulation for its own sake. This prevents the critical situation that might have resulted from its emphasis on production. Wealth miserly accumulated can either be kept hoarded which means a wastage of productive resources and has been heavily taxed in Islam, or it may (to the neglect of consumption) be devoted entirely to production which will cause maladjustment of purchasing-power and may bring about a serious crisis. Islam rules this danger out too by emphasising spending.

In Islam two broad divisions of spending are on self and in charitable ways. For the present problem both have the same advantage; they help to increase the demand for industrial produce and prevent maladjustment of purchasing power. The Qur'an warns, "Spend your wealth in the way of God, and be not cast by your own hands to ruin" (II. 795). All that was said about Islam's emphasis on a better standard of living is a plea for spending on consumption goods. The great and repeated emphasis in the Qur'an on spending in charitable ways, the institution of the growth-tax, and the warning against accumulation—all these in effect combine to keep the purchasing-power of the community intact.

Against accumulation and oversaving it has been plainly said, "Let not those who hoard up that which God has bestowed upon them of His bounty think that it is better for them. Nay, it is worse for them." And hoarding and miserliness are again and again rebuked. "And let not thy hand by chained to thy neck....lest thou sit down rebuked." The emphasis on spending against a lust for hoarding, along with the emphasis on production and "work", constitutes ample provision for an economic distribution of purchasing-power to be steadily maintained. This eliminates the second factor.

A third factor that may cause fluctuations is a tendency towards increasing inequality of wealth. It was pointed out that this tendency is inevitable in *laissez-faire* economics. For under that regime the worker's position is intrinsically weak. For this reason people at the top of the concerns begin taking progressively greater proportions of the national dividend. This fact is clearly established by a study of the causes of the recent crisis, especially in America and Professor Thompson regards it as a very important cause. Islamic economic specially eliminates this tendency through a modification of the inheritance-provisions and some other measures, as we shall presently see.

The tendency is harmful in three more ways : (1) The people who begin to grow rich generally develop a greed for money. They cannot spend their wealth. They want it to multiply. So they overproduce. (2) Those who inherit large fortunes often spend on luxuries, diverting the community's resources to less stable industries. (3) Those who know that they are to inherit a large fortune very often come to lack ability and industriousness. When the business comes into their hands it generally fails. This also disturbs economic stability.

As we have seen, Islam, by emphasising spending and providing competing strength of workers, exercises the first danger. It condemns the outlook that leads to overproduction. For bringing the two ends of society nearer together it has three means. The first is the institution of the growth-tax. It assigns a part of the economic rent and of the interest (actual or potential) arising from the ownership of capital goods exclusively to the poor. This improves their condition and thereby helps them to improve it further and so to move towards the upper end. As the velocity of money in the poorer classes is very great, the effect of this transference is very considerable.

Somewhat similar in nature are the *rikaz* and the *kharaj* taxes. *Laissez-faire* economics gives the land-owner a monopoly and excessive advantage. All the economic rent, and often more, goes to him. According to Islam, land is a free gift for all. Yet all cannot own land. Its ownership is left to free competition, the rent arising from it is however distributed to all. The land is not socialised, the rent is. The growth-tax, the rikaz tax, and the kharaj tax, are the instruments to socialise rent. The rikaz tax assigns one-fifth of the output of mines exclusively to the poor. The kharaj is a levy of about 2½ per cent on the output of land. It is due irrespective of whether or not the owner cultivates the land. It is devoted to general welfare. Thus though all cannot share in the ownership of land, all share in the use of rent. This too removes the weakness of the labouring class and improves their condition.

The third means which Islam uses to eliminate increasing inequality is the Islamic law of inheritance, which distributes the big accumulations amongst a large number of close or even distant relations. This gives them a chance and stimulates their initiative. Thus, it not only brings the upper end of society nearer the lower, but also leads to a stimulation of enterprise and increase of prosperity. Now the business comes to be owned by a number of partners. So there is less risk of its being spoiled through incompetence and idleness.

It is easy to see that the general prosperity resulting from these arrangements should have a cumulative effect.

The fourth factor causing fluctuations is overspeculation. Abolition of commercial lending gives a death-blow to this.

Another cause of fluctuations is the introduction of new investions themselves which account for all progress. Professor Pigou has pointed out that it takes capital to make inventions practical. He argues that they are put in use only when capital is available, i.e., when credit is expanding. So he considers that they do not cause fluctuations but only aggravate them. Under Islamic Economics there is no such thing as expanding credit. So inventions are possible only when there is "expanding prosperity" and so when society is really best able to bear the slight disturbance caused by their introduction.

Another factor that causes or accentuates crises is changes in the value of money. These, however, assume social importance only in connection with loans on interest. Islam disallows such loans and so they lose their significance.

Islam thus eliminates fluctuations and with it the anxiety of the workers due to the uncertainty of employment.

VI

Some Other Questions

In one more way Islam tends to eliminate unemployment. For unemployment, in some measure, is also due to the unequal distribution of leisure. Islam, by assigning a limited value to the ordinary business of life, by providing prosperity and by emphasising a fuller life and specially a life in the interest of the Hereafter, diverts people's attention to other uses of time—learning, prayer, service—and makes them compete for leisure.

There is no use in quoting verses on this point. It is enough to remind ourselves that Islam is a religion and not an economic organization.

Another feature of Islamic Economics which goes to solve our problems is that it eliminates the central defect of *laissez-faire* Economics by prohibiting all economic practices which yield a "private net product" at the cost of the "social net product." For instance our Prophet said, "Do not sell singing slave-girls nor buy them." He also said, "Whoever holds goods for excessive prices is a sinner." We have already seen how Islam has forbidden false measures and weights, hoarding and interest. It also forbids other socially harmful practices such as begging, stealing and indolence. It lays down the general principle disallowing even the cases that are at the margin.

Islamic Economics of production thus takes a definite position between *laissez-faire* and socialism and so gets rid of most of the problems attached to them.

A last feature to be noted in this connection is that Islam is a great movement towards internationalism. The unity of religion is far greater than the unity of class, colour, or country. Muslims, the world over, tend to form one State. There does not arise the question of national self-sufficiency. Perfect territorial division of industries is possible. Nothing could further augment production.

VII

Economics of Distribution

Islam's Economics of distribution, then, maximises the welfare arising from this output by bringing about, as we have seen, a more equal distribution of wealth. The professional money-lender is eliminated. Rent is socialised. The only claimants to national dividend left are the entrepreneurs and the workers. Islamic distribution is conspicuous by the absence of the so-called "parasitic classes.' But to maximise welfare complete equality is not the means. Theoretically it may maximise the welfare arising from a given output: in practice it leads to a diminution in that output. There will be loss of initiative if unequal labour is equally rewarded, and loss of efficiency if it is standardised at a low level.

Complete equalisation thus destroys its own purpose, and fails to maximise social welfare. The correct position seems to be to move towards equality only so far as it is consistent with maximum social welfare, and to retain inequality to some extent as a reward for greater service and a price for liberty. This is exactly the position in Islam.

The Islamic plan of distribution has appeared communistic to some who have, perhaps, been misled by the operation of the institution of the growth-tax on a large scale under the Caliphs, because the growth-tax distributes wealth according to needs. Thus Von Kremer remarks "Omar's communistic theocratic system of politics is one of the most remarked phenomena of history.....All Muslims were to enjoy perfect equality of rights, the entire State income as well as the conquered land was to be the common property of the Muslim community and every member of the brotherhood of Islam was to receive a fixed annuity from the State chest", and Mr. Khuda Bukhsh has assigned a decisively democratic and socialistic conception to the "original Islam."

Yet the Islamic system is neither communistic nor socialistic. The Islamic formula of distribution seems to be: to the poor according to their needs, to the rich according to their services. More useful economic talents are higher placed and better rewarded. God himself makes this arrangement and guarantees the Economic hierarchy: "We have apportioned among men their livelihood in the life of this world, and raised some above others in rank so that some of them may take labour from others." And "He enlargeth the providence for whom He will and straiteneth (it for whom He will)."

Yet economic ranks and occupations do not affect the position of the individual in society. "The believers are nought else than brothers." The classes are just a matter of economic division of labour. They do not denote the value of men. Islam, destroying the money-illusion, substitutes an altogether different standard of distinction and valuation. This brings us to the fundamental feature of Islam, which controls the "ordinary business of life", declaring that it is a limited value subordinate in importance to love and altruism and thus strikes at the fundamental problem which is the fountain-head of all economic troubles. According to Islam "God has set a measure for all things, and the way of the growth of the individual personality is in adhering to that measure. A disproportionate devotion to any one value injures its growth. A study of what this measure is with regard to some values closely connected with economic problems clearly reveals that, if it is adhered to, some of the basic economic problems would be easily solved.

In spite of all that was said in praise of family and riches, they are only a part of the values of this world and not very much in themselves. "The comfort of the life of the world is but little as compared to the Hereafter."

Their value is more as means than as ends in themselves. They do not figure in the ultimate valuation. "The day when wealth and sons avail not (any man) save him who brings unto God a whole heart." They serve their purpose in this world. They help or harm the man. Islam completely disillusions man concerning family and riches. The Qur'an says, "O ye who believe, lo! among your wives and your children are enemies for you, therefore beware of them." "Let not your wealth nor your children distract you from remembrance of God. Those who do so, they are the losers." "They who hoard gold and silver and spend it not in the way of God, unto them give tidings of a painful doom.

This must be enough to destroy a disproportionate devotion to family and to cure money-madness.

In the ultimate valuation only the deeds figure. "Every soul is a pledge for its own deeds." And the good deeds which endure are better in thy Lord's sight for reward and better for resort."

Islam completely destroys the idea that wealth is an end and is of intrinsic worth. Hence its possession in itself confers no distinction. Instead, the distinction goes to those who do good and useful deeds. "Lo those who believe and do good works are the best of created beings." "And the pious deed doth He exalt." The Prophet said, "And the best of you is he who is best among you to his people." (At-Tirmidhi and Abu Da'ud).

The beneficial effect of substituting such a constructive standard of distinction is obvious. It is by such education that Islam solves the central economic problem to which prof. Keynes refers as follows: "At any rate to me it seems clearer every day that the moral problem of our age is concerned with the love of money, with the habitual appeal to money motives in nine-tenths of the activities of life, with the universal striving for the individual economic security, the social approbation of money as the measure of constructive success, and with the social appeal to the hoarding instinct as the foundation for the necessary provision for the family and for the failure."

And it is by such education that Islam fulfils the hope...."A revolution in our ways of thinking and feeling about money may become the growing purpose of contemporary embodiments of the ideal."

These are some of the features of Islam's Economic system whose simplicity, so long, concealed is profoundness. The world to-day is in a better position to appreciate them. After costly experiments it has found out the inadequacy of Socialism and *laissez-faire. Laissez-faire* has come to a complete end. In the war and post-war period all the countries of Europe have, one by one, given up the idea. The U.S.A. has suddenly gone in for wholesale Planning. The same change is noticeable in China. Thus Article 17 of the Provisional Constitution for the period of Tutelage, adopted on may 15th, 1931, states that the exercise of the right of ownership of private property, in so far as it does not conflict with public interest, shali be protected by law. The Fascist movement, on the other hand, has arisen as a demand for moderation of scientific socialism. Both for its life and efficiency it depends upon its sense of limit.

Economic History has plainly demonstrated that both *laissez-faire* and Socialism are untenable extremes. For efficient and equitable Economics the elimination of their defects and a proper balance of the two, such as Islam offers, seems well worth considering.

4

Some Aspects of Muslim Education and Culture

ZIYA-UL HASAN FARUQI

(Abstract: Outlines the story of the great intellectual activity with a survey of essential features of the formative period, culminating in almost standardization of Muslim education and culture).

Islam originated in Arabia and expanded very rapidly beyond its bounds. Lands where its first impact was felt in full intensity included Egypt, Syria, Iraq and Persia, each of which had once been the seat of a highly developed civilization and the centre of a rich culture. Naturally, the Arab conquests in these areas created tensions which is, turn, were responsible for great intellectual activity and the birth and the flourishing of the classic Arabo-and Perso-Muslim culture. The following in brief, the story of this great intellectual activity together with a survey of essential features of the formative period, culminating in almost standardization of Muslim education and culture. This would bring us to a point where the establishment of *Madrasahs* further augmented this standardization and led to a sort of intellectual stagnation that has deprived the Muslim societies of the vigour and dynamism which enable a society to readjust itself to new situations and circumstances.

The foundation of Islamic culture is religion, and hence, naturally, it is the basis of Muslim Education. The Muslims were inspired by the many verses of the Qur'an as well as the Prophetic traditions and sayings which exhorted them to seek knowledge as a religious duty and cheerfully bear hardships, if any, in its acquisition. The Qur'an says :

1. God will raise up in rank those of you who believe and have been given knowledge. And God is aware of the things you do.
2. Say : 'Are they equal—those who know and those who know not ?
3. It is not for the believers to go forth totally ; but why should not a party of every section of them go forth, to become learned in religion, and to warn their people when they return to them, that haply they may beware.
4. 'O My Lord, increase me in knowledge.

Moreover, the Qur'an does not discourage life in this world. Whatever and however short the wordly life may be, it declares :

1. 'Who has forbidden the ornament of God which He brought forth for His servants, and the good things of His providing ?
2. And others there are who say. 'Our Lord, give to us in this world good, and good in the world to come, and guard us against the chastisement of the fire.
3. "and forget not thy portion of the present world ; and do good, as God has been good to thee"

God created the universe and the mankind and put in Man a natural quest to know, because of which he studies and strives to learn what exists in the universe so that he could benefit by it and be grateful to his Creator.

1. We have established you in the earth and there appointed for you livelihood; little thanks you show.
2. Have you not seen how God has subjected to you whatsoever is in the heavens and earth, and He has lavished on you His blessings, outward and inward?

The sayings and the traditions of the Prophet and those of his companions, their followers (*tabi'in*) and the followers of their followers (*taba' tabi'in*) abound in number in regard to the point under discussion, but only a few are herein to illustrate it. These mentioned at appropriate given places in works like Al-Ghazali's *Ihya' al-'Ulum.* Al-Isfahani's *Muhadarah al-'Udaba'* and Haji Khalifah's *Kashs al-Zunun* etc.

No matter, some of them may be of weak *isnad* (authority) but they certainly indicate the place of pride Islam accords to the learned and knowledge in Muslim societies.

They are :

1. "The Prophet preached the value of knowledge, because who acquires it in the way of the Lord, performs an act of piety ; who speaks of it, praises the Lord ; who seeks it. adores God ; who dispenses instruction in it, bestows alms ; and who imparts it to its fitting objects, performs an act of devotion to God. Knowledge enables its professors to distinguish what is forbidden from what is not ; it lights the way to Heaven ; it is our friend in the desert, our society in solitude, our companion when bereft of friends ; it guides us to happiness ; it sustains us in misery ; it is our ornament in the company of friends ; it serves as an armour against our enemies. With knowledge, the servant of God rises to the heights of goodness and to a noble position, associates with sovereigns in this world, and attains to the perfection of happiness in the next."
2. Learned people are the heirs of prophets.
3. The ink of the scholar is more hloy than the blood of the martyr.
4. Valueless is the Muslim who is not a teacher or student.
5. Seek knowledge from cradle to grave and search for it even if you are to go to China.
6. He dies not who gives his life to learning.
7. Acquire knowledge as it will be an ornament if you are rich and a source of wealth if you are poor.

It is no less inspiring, in this connection that the very first revelation that Prophet Muhammad (peace be upon him) received was a command to read and write, and the praise of pen which is the only means or custodian of human knowledge :

Recite : In the name of thy Lord who created, created Man of blood-clot.

Recite : And thy Lord is the Most Generous, who taught by the Pen, taught Man that he knew not.

Commenting on this surah (Blood-clot), the famous medieval commentator of the Qur'an and the author of a mu'tazilah commentary al-*Kashshaf,* al-Zamakhshari (d. 1144), has emplained the meaning of the said surah, which is so true and has been vindicated by the glorious academic investigations an scientific inquiries made by the Muslims under the inspiration of the religious exhortations in this regard :

Zamakhshari Comments

"God taught human beings that which they did not know, and this testifieth to the greatness of His beneficence, for He has given to His servants knowledge of that which they did not know. And he has brought them out of the darkness of ignorance to the light of knowledge, and made them aware of the inestimable blessings of the *knowledge* of *writing,* for great benefits accrue therefrom which God alone compasseth; and without the knowledge of writing no other knowledge ('Ulum) could be comprehended, nor the sciences placed within bounds, nor the history of the ancients be acquired and their sayings be recorded, *nor the revealed books* written (*Italics ours*) : and if that knowledge did not exist, the affairs of religion and the world could not be regulated."

Islam produced an urban civilization which means organisation, administration and skill. With the expansion of Islam, the Arabs, within a miraculously short time, conquered Syria (including the land of the Phoenicians and the Philistins), Iraq, Persia and Egypt-lands which in the past had been the cradle of brilliant civilizations. It was all during the reign of the four pious Caliphs. When the Banu

Umayyah (the Umayyads) took over, they shifted the capital of the Arab empire from Madinah to Dimashq (Damascus)—a very significant event with far-reaching consequences. Besides the old urban centres, the new army camps and military settlements gradually developed into towns and cities with their own organisation and institutions.

These new lands and pastures with which Islam came into contact, had developed cultures, meritorious institutions, and brilliant academic and intellectual traditions. The Muslims were exhorted by the Prophetic traditions to acquire knowledge wherever they found it as, in fact, it was their own treasure lost to them. They were fully entitled to it. The Qur'an mentions ancient peoples and their rise and fall, and strongly induces the believers to learn from the histories of these peoples, and even from the ruins which were once flourishing cities. All this led the Muslims to fully participate not only in the organisation of newly created empire, but also in meeting the challenges of all sorts, no matter from where they were presented-whether from the social and politico-economic sides or from the intellectual and spiritual fronts. As our purpose here is not to make an assessment of the contributions the Muslims made to art and sciences, we would be contented only to remark that a new life-active, vigorous and pregnant with immense possibilities—was generated by them. The consequences that followed would certainly be dealt with but in a different context and with relevant implications. Presently, we would see as to how the Muslims organised their education in the first two centuries, i.e., mainly before the establishment of *Madrasahs.*

In is sad to not that a branch of art (education) so much praised, lauded and enjoined upon the Muslims almost as a religious duty (and this was one of the most attended and cared for aspects of cultural life of the Muslims), was completely neglected by the Muslim historians and writers. Social and educational aspects were paid so little attention that till 1709 when Burhan ad-Din al-Zarnuji's brochure entitled *Ta'lim al-Muta'allim-Tariq al-Ta'allum* drew the attention of the European scholar, this field was considered as completely barren although there was abundant material scattered in all sorts of books. Early and the medieval Muslim scholars had never taken the trouble to sort out the material and write books on the science of Education as such and particularly on the system of education that could in spite of local and environmental differences, be at least termed as a 'system' in terms of syllabuses, organisation of studies and the method of teaching and learning, even after the establishment of *Madrasahs* in the tenth century of the Christian era.

The main sources in respect of education during the middle ages are scanty and one may find Abu Hanifah, Imam Bukhari, Ibn 'Abd al-birr, Imam Ghazali, Zarnuji, Qazi Ibn Juma'ah, Muhammad Ibn Abu Zayd and Ibn Khaldun, giving the situation existing in their times or collecting and synthesizing the ideas of scholars and sages who had preceded them. All these writers taken together represent a long period and different regions. Hence again we can not talk about a 'system' of education having at least some concurring features in it, except one or two, and that also is here and there.

The present writer will not make an attempt to summarise what these learned men had said about education. Their views and statements, if relevant and necessary, might be stated at appropriate occasions in this paper.

It was not so that the Meccans were totally ignorant of reading and writing. Mecca had been a centre of trade and there were people, and particularly in Madina the Jews and Christians, who knew the art of reading and writing. The advent and then the consolidation of Islam gave an impetus to the idea of learning, apart from revolutionizing the whole life and the total attitude of the Muslims who, at least after the Hijrah, believed that they and their religion were now safe.

The spread of Islam first in Madina and then within a very short period (even) in the prophet's own lifetime) in Arabia necessitated the teaching of the Qur'an to a large number of Arabs who used to visit the capital and those who lived in far-off areas. Moreover, alongwith the revelation of the verses of the Qur'an it was also necessary that if the verses had to be protected and preserved in their original form, they required to be written down. The Prophet was fully aware of how previous peoples had distorted their book in order to suit their worldly desires, and also for other reasons had made changes in the teachings of their Prophets. He, therefore, immediately appointed 'Abd Allah bin Saeed bin 'As to teach the Muslims the art of writing and sent some of his Companions Hazrat Ibn-i-Maktum and Hazrat Mus'ab bin 'Umayr to Madina, in order to teach the Qur'an to the Medinese Muslims. At Madina, after the Prophet had settled down there, its scope was enlarged to such an extent that after the battle of Badr the prisoners of war (the Meccans) who knew the art of writing, were given an option to teach the Muslims of Madina the art of reading and writing in lieu of getting themselves released by paying the *fidyah* (ransom). Then, there was a group of persons in the Prophet's mosque at Madina, known as *ashab-i-Suffah.* Besides their other characteristics, one was the *halqah'-i-dars* in which one of them recited the Qur'an and others listened to him with attention. The new *muhajirin* were gradually added to the same circle for the learning of the Qur'an. But, the whole of Arabia could not join this circle; nor was it possible for all the Arabs (settlers) to go to Madina to learn the Qur'an and the Islamic way of life. Hence, the following verse which infused the Arabs with enthusiasm and exhorted them to go, in groups and by turn, to the centre of Islamic religious activities, learn what they could and on return teach that to their own people:

> It is not for the believers to go forth totally; but why should not a party of every section of them go forth to become learned in religion, and to warn their people when they return to them, that haply they may beware ?

These non-Medinese Arabs, when they reached Madina, stayed with *ansars* who taught them the Qur'an and the Sunnah. In *Musnad ibn Hanbal,* Wafd 'Abd al-Qays has been quoted as to have remarked :

> "Ansars taught us the Book of our Lord and the Sunnah of our Prophet.

When the Prophet died (633 A.D.) he left Arabia as a United Arab State, the main cities of which had imbibed the Islamic teachings to such an extent that the Arabs were fully equipped to try new lands and pastures with enthusiasm and confidence. The Qur'an had told them that they were the best community and they considered it incumbent upon them to preach what was permissible and what was forbidden in order to give a new shape to human life and lend it more comprehensive and much wider dimensions. Every Muslim, in his own place, was a missionary, but the greater responsibility lay particularly on those persons who had a good knowledge of the Qur'an and the Sunnah. Islamic State, i.e., the *Khulafa* had to make a section of such honest and learned persons and send them to the newly conqured lands beyond Arabia. For these lands administrators were sent and alongwith them teachers (in the context of the *Tablighi jama'at,* the *muballighin*) were also appointed to accompany them to their new assignments. For example, when Abu Musa Ash'ari was made the Governor of Basrah, Hazrat 'Imran bin Hisin was asked to be with him to instruct the people there in the Qur'an and the Shari'ah. The same was done in respect of Syria. Hazrat 'Ibadh bin Samit stayed at Hums as a teacher of the Qur'an. Hazrat Ma'az bin Jabal went to Palestine and Hazrat Abu Darda stayed for sometime at Dimashq. They and others like them (almost all of thems were Companions of the Prophet) established centres (*halqahs*) in Arabia and in those towns and cities which had fallen to Muslims. By the newly converted and by those Muslims who had not seen the Prophet or his time, his Companions were much in demand, from whom the people heard the Qur'an and learnt the *Hadith.* The early period of the Umyyad reign was very crucial in the sense that false traditions were fabricated in order to justify one party or the other. At this juncture the *Sahabah* (Companions) played the most important role in falsifying the fabricated *ahadith* attributed to the Prophet and telling the genuine ones to those who were desirous of knowing them.

Here a class of persons known as Qass (pl. Qussas) is to be mentioned. The people of this class were not officially appointed, but, in the beginning, it seems, their services were considered useful, which, later, because of thefear of the spread of false traditions, were strongly disapproved and finally suspended. However, they continued to exist as profane or gossip-tellers of anecdotes in the streets. The fifth chapter of Ignaz Goldziher's *Muslim Studies,* bears the title as 'The Hadith As a Means of Edification and Entertainment. In the earliest times of Islam the name *qass* did not carry an unfavourable connotation. "The Prophet himself (Sura 7:175, 12:3) used the name *qasas* in respect of his own message, and in traditional stories he is quoted as speaking favourably of pious preachers who bore the name of qass." On the authority of Ibn al-Jawzi, Goldziher says : "According to the Muslim account the development of this profession reaches back to the earliest period of Islam. 'Umar is said to have given express permission to tell stories to people, to the pious Tamim al-Dari or (according to others) to 'Ubayd b. 'Umyr, the first real qass. Upto the Umayyad times under Mu'awiya, especially the well-known Ka'b-pious men are named, who with the approval of the orthodox authorities practised freelance preaching and endeavoured to strengthen men in the beliefs, virtues and hopes of Islam by means of pious tales." Later in the Umayyad period the *Qussas* were sent along with the armies in order to exhort the fighters. It seems that in some areas, particularly in Iraq, the *Qussas* themselves undertook the task of expounding the Qur'anic verses to the popular gathering which assembled to listen to them. Goldziher has freely referred to *Kitab al-Aghani* and *Kitab al-Bayan,* but these are to be read cautiously. However, a close observation and analysis of these books give abundant information about the socio-religious life of the people during those days. The class of *qussas,* nevertheless, existed and flourished. But "in so far as the *Qussas* served serious religious ends, whether as homiletic exegetes or as tellers of sacred stories, they were left alone and undisturbed in their pious work ; official theology gladly tolerated these free preachers and popular theologians, who in streets or mosques condescended to the level of the understanding of the people, and spread amongst them ascetic beliefs which were not fostered by official theologians, who were chiefly bound up in the study of law, but which were publicly represented by these circles. Al-Jahiz gives extracts from the sermons of such men and we do not hear that they were hindered in the exercise of their profession, *which constituted a complementary element in the religious life of Islam.*"

Now we will briefly mention places where education, was, more or less, formally organised before the *Dar al-'Ilm* in Cairo and *madrasahs* in the eastern part of the Muslim world were established.

1. *Kuttab.* They were known as *maktab* also, and were meant to teach the children the art of writing, the Qur'an and some elementary subjects. (The very root of the word *Kuttab,* i-e. *taktib* signifies that teaching the art of writing was also included). It should be kept in mind that, unlike the current practice of to-day, in the early period of Islam, emphasis was not laid on reading the whole of the Qur'an without understanding its verses. It was very rare, during those days, if some one learnt the whole of the Qur'an. The Quranic verses are to be understood and meditated upon. Early Muslims, particularly the Companions, fully understood its implications. As mentioned in al-Suyuti's *al-Itqan fi'ulum al-Qur'an* (II) and *Musnad Ahmad Ibn Hanbal* (III), each of them (Companions) did not proceed, after learning ten verses until he knew their meaning and practised what had been demanded by them. Thus Ibn 'Umar spent eight years learning the Surah *al-Baqarah,* and the Companions are stated to have said: "The man who was able to read *al-Baqarah* and *al'Imran* seemed a great man amongst us."

Thus, the sort of *Kuttab* or *maktabs* we find to-day in the Muslim world, is entirely different, both in contents and purpose, from what it meant to be in the earlier period of Islam, particularly in the period of the Pious Caliphs and the Companions. The following passage will testify to this point :

> "The curriculum drawn up by `Umar ibn al Khattab and issued to the people in various Muslim countries was: `Teach your children swimming, horsemanship, famous proverbs and good poetry."

It was perhaps understood that the parents, particularly those who had themselves learnt the Qur'an, would take upon themselves the responsibility of teaching the Qur'an to their children. Thus, gradually the Qur'an became the pivot around which the elementary education revolved. "Learning the Qur'an then preceded everything, and next came religious instruction." After this with some poetry which mainly concerned manners, good be haviour, honesty and integrity, elementary grammar and arithmetic, the primary education came to an end. The statement given in *Shorter Encyclopaedia of Islam* that "the main subject taught was *adab*, so that the schools of children (meaning, perhaps, *Kuttab*) were called *madjalis al-adab"*, does not seem correct as the authentic sources, other than *Aghani* have been completely left out.

The curriculum, however, differed from place to place and this continued throughout the centuries before the establishment of *madrasahs* and even after that in the various *madrasahs* spread over from Nishapur and Delhi for example, in the east to Qartabah in the west (*the Maghrib*). In this connection Ibn Khaldun (1332-1406) has given a very vivid description of the 'instruction of children and the different methods employed in the Muslim cities. The present writer will quote extensively from this part of his famous *Muqaddimah*, a monumental work of his, which has rightly claimed for him the title of being the Originator of the Philosophy of History in its real sense. Ibn Khaldun says :

"It should be known that instructing children in the Qur'an is a symbol of Islam... .....The Qur'an has become the basis of instruction, the foundation for all habits that may be acquired later on......The character of the foundation determines the condition of the building. The methods of instructing children in the Qur'an differ according to differences of opinion as to the habits that are to result from that instruction.

"The Maghribi method is to restrict the education of children to instruction in the Qur'an and to practise during the course (of instruction), in Qur'an orthography and its problems and the differences among Qur'an experts on this score. The (Maghribis) do not bring up any other subjects in their classes, such as traditions, jurisprudence, poetry, or Arabic philosopy, until the pupil is skilled in (the Qur'an), or drops out before becoming skilled in it.....They use it [the same method] with old people who study the Qur'an after a part of their life is passed. Consequently, (Maghribis) know the orthography of the Qur'an, and know it by heart, better than any other (Muslim group).

Then, Ibn Khaldun tells about the method followed by the Spaniards. They have the Qur'an as the basis, but they bring in other subjects also "mainly poetry and composition, and they give the children an expert knowledge of Arabic, and teach them a good handwriting." According to him stress on the teaching of the Qur`an is not more than that on any other subject...It, (however), "prepares (them for further studies), in the event that a teacher (of them) can be found."

"The people of Ifriqiyah combine the instruction of children in the Qur'an, usually, with the teaching of traditions. They also teach basic scientific norms and certain scientific problems. However, they stress giving their children a good knowledge of the Qur'an and acquainting them with its various recensions and readings more than anything else. Next they stress handwriting. In general their method of instruction in the Qur'an is closer to the Spanish method (than to the Maghribi or Eastern methods), because (their educational tradition derives from the Spanish *Shaykhs* who crossed over when the Christians conquered Spain, and asked for hospitality in Tunis....."

About the people of the East, Ibn Khaldun's knowledge was very limited and he himself admits it. He had heard only this much that when the children grew up, the teaching of the Qur'an and other religious subjects was combined. They did not lay much stress on handwriting. "Those who want to learn a (good) handwriting may do so later on (in their lives) from professional (calligraphers), to the extent of their interest in it and desire."

"In his *Rihlah,* Judge Abu Bakr b. al-'Arabi made a remarkable statement about instruction, which retains (the best of) the old, and presents (some good) new features. He places instruction in Arabic and poetry ahead of all the other sciences, as in the Spanish method, since, he said, 'Poetry is the archive of the Arabs. Poetry and Arabic 'philology should be taught first because of the existing corruption of the language. From there, the (student) should go on to arithmetic and study it assiduously, until he knows its basic norms. He then should go on to the study of the Qur'an because with his (previous) preparation, it will be easy for him.' (Ibn al-'Arabi) continued: 'How thoughtless are our compatriots in that they teach children the Qur'an when they are first starting out. They read things they do not understand and work hard at something that is not as important for them as other matters.' He concluded: 'The student should study successively the principles of Islam, the principles of jurisprudence, disputation and then the Prophetic traditions and the sciences connected with them.' He also forbade teaching two disciplines at the same time, save to the student with a good mind and sufficient energy."

Ibn Khaldun seem to be in favour of the method presented by Judge Ibn al 'Arabi. But he also knows that the customs will not change. (The reason is the belief in the blessing and reward in the other world, of teaching the Qur'an even from the very beginning when the child is mentally not equipped to understand a word of it.) Another point that he has tried to make out is that it is, perhaps, under the yoke of the parental authority that the children, before growing to manhood, may learn the Qur'an. He Says : "If one could be certain that a child would continue study and accept instruction (when he has grown up), the method mentioned by the Judge would be the most suitable one ever advised in East or West." But he forgot that this advice of his may be meant only for those children who will stop and not go for further studies after learning the Qur'an. A curriculum, however, should be comprehensive and complete in the sense that the talented students who want to go in for higher education and really understand the Book and the Wisdom contained in it, find it useful as well as meaningful.

2. Besides the *Kuttabs,* in some of which only reading and writing was taught while in others the Qur'an and elementary subjects were also taken up, there was, in earlier times, a tradition of elementary education in palaces. The tradition persisted in succeeding centuries also with not only elementary education but also with the study of a higher course, and in some cases, the whole course in higher religious and secular sciences. In palaces the courses of study would also vary in view of the future career of the student. According to Al-Jahiz, the teachers, some of whom even lived in quarters provided in palaces, were known *Mu'addib* (in India *ataliq*). "The Fatimids went further in the matter of having a special elementary curriculum in the palace. Under them, the palace had a boys' school where the youth of the upper class were taught and prepared for the Caliph's service."

3. In Muslim societies bookshops and booksellers have always enjoyed a distinguished place. The sons of nobility and intellectual elite were always advised to make the bookshops a den of theirs if they went to the bazar at all. Bookshops appeared early under the Abbasids. It had its good results, and, because of the patronage the Abbasids gave to learning and sciences, very soon a large number of them came into existence in almost all the important towns of the Islamic world. It resulted in the development of paper industry and in the fast growth and flourishing of the profession of *Warraq* and *nassakh.* The booksellers were usually men of letters. This is confirmed by *al-Fihrist* of Ibn al-Nadim and yaqut's *Mu'jam al-buldan* and *Mu'jam al-'Udaba'.* The function of booksellers at that time extended to an important intellectual service. It were they who had the best books copied and placed them in the hands of the public at the average price of one dinar. "It was in their shops that a man such as al-Jahiz would pay for the privilege of being locked in all night in order to read and copy what he wanted."

In the contemporary literature there is abundant material, particularly in the biographical notes of celebrated scholars, about the bookshops having been the resort of students and the learned. But we cannot afford here to go into details. *Mu'jam al-Fihrist,*

Wafyat al-A'yan, al-Khitat and *Manaqib-i-Baghdad* (by Ibn Jawzi) are the source material which one, if interested, can look into.

4. Private collections of books and houses of learned men were also the places from where literary sparks and intellectual flames illuminated the minds of these who were interested in education and culture. These houses were a repository of cultural values as well as cultural goods that filtered down, unfelt and unseen, even to the lower strata of the Muslim societies.

It is well-known that Ibn Sina (980-1037) worked for sometime on an administrative assignment under Shams al-Dawla, the Buwayid ruler of Hamadan and Kirmanshah. But his evenings were spent in the promotion of learning. "He used to sit in his house to read from *al-Shifa* and from *al-Qanun* to a large number of groups." Likewise "Abu Sulaiman al-Sijistani Muhammad b. Tahir b. Bahram who died shortly before the close of the 4th century A.H., was a leper and one-eyed, so he ceased to appear in public. But his house was a resort of students and scholars who devoted themselves to the cause of learning and who flocked to attend his lectures." We are familiar with Al-Ghazali's (1058-1111) abandoning the Madrasah Nizamiyah of Baghdad and wanderings, visiting places and contemplating for about eleven years and then returning to Tus, his home town, engaging himself in teaching at Madrasah Nizamiyah of Nishapur only for a short time. Finally, at Tus he busied himself, in his own house, to teach theology. Such examples are innumerable and one can read about them in almost all the biographical works, where the life-sketches of individual 'Ulama' of all types, whether secular or religious, have been given.

5. Literary salons were also characteristic places where knowledge was disseminated. As the number of palaces grew and palace-life became the nerve-centres of varied activities, literary salons came into existence and with the ascendency of the Abbasid these salons, in the true sense, reached their zenith, and regular meetings were arranged not only in the Caliphs' palaces, but in the palaces of their ministers and *amirs*. "Reading about these literary salons, one can imagine the splendour and magnificence of these

meetings which exemplify the prosperity and the many-sided culture of the period," The tradition continued even when independent and semi-independent dynasties were established. Their rulers vied with each other in their patronage of learning and their courts and palaces became centres of culture.

6. Mosques, however, remained the main place for Muslim education till the establishment of Madrasahs. Even then they were indispensable and some of them had prominent *halqahs* even in the beginning of the twentieth century. (Al-Azhar is well-known in this respect.) Mosques were the places of worship around which, during the earlier period, social and political activities of the Muslim communities revolved. Although schools spread during the Umayyad period, and, as already stated, instruction was also given at home but mosques continued to be used as places of instruction in not only religious sciences but also in secular subjects, particularly those which developed along with religious *'ulum* or were intrinsically related to them.

In the mosques, the Qur'an was taught and learnt, then came *Hadith.* It was the Sunnah of the Prophet and then of his Companions to answer the questions of the devotees and give proper advice in respect of a good and commendable religious conduct. It was this very tradition, out of which arose schools of higher learning through the *halqahs* of learned teachers who attracted students even from far-off places. Historians and biographers have preserved the description of the intellectual activities in such mosques and the disputations and debates which sometimes led to events that subsequently proved historic and of far-reaching significance in the intellectual and cultural development of the Muslim peoples. We have already seen that "the first teachers in the mosques were the *Kussas*———whose discourses dealt with the interpretation of the Qur'an and the proper conduct of divine service. Their *mawa'iza* was the direct continuation of the moral instruction given by old Companions (cf. *Eukhari 'ilm,* bab 12). The instruction started in the mosque of 'Amr was continued for centuries. In the third century A.H., al-Shafi'i taught various subjects here every morning till his death (d. 820 A.D.) (Suyuti *Husn al-muhadara,* i, 134; Yakut, *Udaba,'* VI. 383)." Such examples are numerous. They provide ample proof of the use of mosques as great centres of learning. (See footnote above.)

The well-known traveller, Ibn-Battutah (d. 770/1368-69) while in Shiraz, attended lectures on *hadith* in the city-mosque, and before his arrival at Shiraz, he had done the same in Jami' Mansur of Baghdad even though during his days at Baghdad there were a number of good madrasahs. Similarly, *madrasah* and *masjid* remained interchangeable for a long time throughout the Muslim lands. Even the tombs and *Zawivahs* of *Zuhhad,* Khanqahs of Sufis and, at some places, the inns, too, were used as places of instruction. Hospitals or *Bayt al-Adwiyah* (Houses of medicines) and observatories were also utilized respectively for teaching medical sciences and mathematics and astronomy. In Sistan (a part of the eastern Islamic empire), in the first century Hijrah, the Irani historians tell us, the Arab Governor 'Abdur-Rahman bin Samarah had a *Jami'* constructed, in which Hasan al Basari (642-728) gave, for quite sometime, lectures on religious matters. At Bukhara, widely known at that time as *"Qubbat-ul-Islam",* there were some mosques used for the instruction of sciences related to the Shari'ah. Ibn Faqih has told us that in Sistan, Fars, Balkh and Herat, mosques were the centres of learning where *Fuqaha'* were engaged in imparting knowledge of *fiqh* to its seekers. Nishapur, one of the foremost educational and political centres of Khorasan, had great mosques like Jami' Mani'i, masjid-Matrizi and the old masjid, which were also used for teaching and learning.

Some Aspects of Muslim Education and Culture

No educational system can function without the proper arrangements and provision of libraries. The same spirit which worked among the the Muslims in the acquisition and dissemination of knowledge, also induced and exhorted them to have books written, collect them, build up libraries, private and public both, and made them available to scholars and other seekers of knowledge. In this learned venture of theirs the Muslims were at great advantage, as they had learnt the art of manufacturing paper from the Chinese as early as 751 A.D., when they first came in contact with them in Central Asia and made Samarqand the *First centre* of paper-making in the Muslim world.

Khalid bin Yazid (d. 85 A-H.) is said to be the fore-runner in the building of libraries. He was known as Khalid bin Yazid *Hakim,* because he was an able and learned man. He got a number of books on various crafts translated into Arabic from the Greek and Coptic languages. He was himself an author. This establishes the fact that it were the Umayyads who laid the foundation of a brilliant tradition of learning. As civilization and sedentary culture developed and the Arab empire expanded, or later, various (powerful) Muslim dynasties sprang up, and royal authority increased and stable administration maintained a high standard of law and order, particularly in cities and towns, sciences were cultivated, books were written, copied and transcribed in large number and bound skilfully. Consequently, this process helped and made easy, according to the contemporary standard, the establishment of libraries, generally known as *Khizanah al-Kutub.* Along with this development the craft of book production attracted the attention of not only scholars but patrons of learning and the learned also, and, in course of time, reached, with all the minutae, a high level of skill, perfection and excellence. But we shall deal with it shortly. First, let us know, at least briefly, what was happening in the realm of the establishment of libraries in some of the important places of the Muslim world.

1. Baghdad

Caliph Mansur (d. 775. A.D.) was a great patron of learning and he got hundreds of books in other languages translated into Arabic. Harun al-Rashid (d. 808, 809 A.D.) went further and founded the famous academy known as *Bayt al-Hikmah,* and here translation work reached its zenith. It had two sections, one library and the other translation bureau. It was a sort of public library for which a good number of books of Arabic, Persian, Sanskrit, Greek, Coptic, Syriac and Chaldean languages, were obtained. "Ibn al-Nadim states that the Persian scholar Abu Sahl al-Fadl bin

Nawbakht was a translator, in Khiza-nah al-Hikmah (*Bay al Hikmah*)...Many Persian books were introduced through him to the Arabic tongue." From lands Harun conquered, came along with other spoils of war, the libraries of those lands and their books were translated into Arabic. In the battles of Ankara and 'Ammuriyah Harun was victorious; and the defeat of the Byzantines gave him a considerable number of Greek books which he sent with full safety to Baghdad. For the translation of these books Harun's Christian tabib (*doctor*) was apointed as the translator-supervisor. Under Harun's son and successor, al-Mamum (d.833 A.D.) who was a good scholar, the intellectual activity received his full attention. During his reign the number of books increased considerably and he employed Iranian scholars as the administrative officers, and scholars like Ibn al-Batriq, Hunayn b. Ishaq and Salam al-Hajjaj b. Matar as translators who, alongwith their translations, made useful comments also. Mamun's mother and wife were Persian and he had a bias for Irani shu'ubi. His vazir, Fadl bin Sahl, to whom he was obliged for his ascendency to power, was also Persian. But, in spite of the Persian environment around him, Mamun was quite liberal in acquiring books of other languges also. He made temendous efforts to get Greek books on almost all the important sciences translated. He also collected valuable material as *qasa'id,* poems, letters, business-documents and contracts belonging to the Jahili (pre-Islamic) period of Arab history. Thus Mamun was instrumental in making the library section of the *Bayt al-Haikmah* as one of the wonders of his age. One can well understand and make an estimate of the greatness and splendour of this library that, in spite of the frequent devastations and destructions that Baghdad had to face, quite a good number of its books survived the holocausts till the seventh century Hijrah. Some of them were possessed by Ibn Abi'Usaiba`h, which he mentioned in the biographical sketch of Hunayn bin Ishaq and indicated that they bore Hunayn's signature and Mamun's toghra.

From amongst the large number of private collections only two will be mentioned here. One was that of 'Ali bin Yahya Munajjim (d. 275) known as *Khizanah al-Hikmah,* to which scholars travelled from distant places in the Muslim world to study the valuable and rare books. Olga Pinto who wrote a learned paper on the subject of *Islami Kutubkhane,* quoting Yaqut's *Mu'jam al-'Udaba'*, tells us that people who visited this library were provided with accommodation and food. "One of its famous students was Abu Ma'shar al-Munajjim who had seen it on his way from Khurasan to the Holy Places. When he entered the library he marvelled at its magnitude so that he abandoned the pilgrimage and stayed there to learn astrology which he succeeded in mastering." The other *Kutub-khanah* (library) was the achievement of Muhammad bin Husayn Baghdadi. It was something like an academic museum which contained rare books, valuable manuscripts and ancient documents and writings. On this account this collection had hardly any parallel. Ibn al-Nadim confessed that he had never seen such a valuable collection of books and documents. Muhammad bin Husayn was a bit miserly, and too cautious to allow any one access to it. Certainly, its richness had made him so. Ibn al-Nadim has laid down that it was with great difficulty and also when he was sure of his being an honest person that he showed him treasures consisting of ancient literary pieces written on leather and on Khurasani, Chinese and Egyptian paper. Almost all of them were authentic as they bore the signatures and certificates of great scholars. The Prophet's letters written to various sultans and tribal chiefs were there in their original form. A number of written statements of Hazrat 'Ali and Hazrat Imam Hasan and Imam Husayn also added to the richness of this treasure. *Rasa'il* of great grammarians and the writings of persons like Sufyan Thauri and Awza'i who had collected *ahadith,* were also there to add to one's bewilderment. The same author states that it was here that he came to know that the science of *nahw* (Arabic syntax) was first introduced and developed by Abu al-Aswad Dauli (d. 688).

2. Samarqand

We have noted that the Arabs established the first paper-making industry in the Muslim world at Samarqand. This historical development paved the way for the quickening of writing activity and the establishment of libraries throughout the Islamic lands, and

Samarqand became famous and widely known for its paper. This city remained a centre of learning for a long time, in the Samani, Khawarazmshahi and later in the Mongol period. It was the capital of the great empire that Timur (1369-1404) had built up. He also constructed an observatory at Samarqand. His grand son, Ulugh Beg (1394-1449) was also interested in 'stars' and built in 1421 in this great city "his celebrated observatory, where in collaboration with four eminent men of learning, Salahu'd-Din Musa, called Qadi-Zada-i-Rumi ("the Turkish Judge's son"), Mulla Alaudin 'Ali Qushji, the commentator of the *tajrid,* Ghiyathuddin Jamshid and Mu'inuddin of Kashan, he compiled the notable astronomical tables known as the *Zij-i-Ulugh Beg,* or *Zij-i-Jadid-i-Sultani,* which were probably completed in 1437-38." During those days there used to be a library adjacent to each observatory, as it is well-known in the case of the observatory at Maraghah, which was built in 1257 by Nasiruddin Tusi (1200-1274) with the assistance "of a number of men of learning, whose names he enumerates in the *Zij-i-Ilkhan.*" Halaku, the destroyer of Baghdad in 1258, held him in high esteem. It is said that he accompanied "the Mongol army which destroyed Baghdad and profited by the plunder of many libraries to enrich his own which finally came to comprise, according to Ibn Shakir (*Fowatul-wafayat,* Vol. II, p. 144) more than 400,000 volumes."

3. Bukhara

Bukhara occupies a unique place not only in the Muslim world, but in the hearts of the Muslims, particularly, the Sunni Muslims, as there lived the great *muhaddith,* Imam Bukhari (d. 869), the compiler of the most authentic *hadith* book known as *Sahih Bukhari.* Ibn Battutah, when he visited the graves and tombs of the once famous 'Ulama' of Bukhara, where he saw their names along with the titles of their works, was wonder-struck and could easily and rightly guess what a great centre of learning this city, known as *Qubbat-ul-Islam* would have been during the preceding centuries. During the Samani regime it was made the capital and, because of this, to this distinguished place poets, writers, learned men and skilled artisans and craftsmen flocked and flourished. Ibn

Sina (980-1037) was attracted to Bukhara and had started living there. Here the *Kutubkhanah* of Nuh bin Mansur (regd: 976-997) had great fascination for the learned. Nuh was a great monarch and a patron of learning. Ibn Khallikan recorded (*Wafyat-al-A'yan*) that his *Kutubkhanah* possessed books on almost all the arts and sciences and a good deal of them were so rare that they were hardly to be traced anywhere else. Ibn Sina also spoke highly of this *Kutubkhanah* and confessed that it contained "many books the very titles of which were unknown to most persons, and other which I never met with before nor since."

4. Ghaznah

During the reign of Sultan Mahmud of Ghaznah (970-1030) men of letters flourished and he had gathered around him learned persons like Al-Beruni, Fair-dawsi, Unsuri, Asjadi, Farrukhi, Abul-Fath al-Busti, 'Utbi and Bayhaqi. "It was, indeed, a time when literary men were highly esteemed and eagerly sought after, each more or less independent ruler or local governor striving to emulate his rivals and peers in the intellectual brilliancy of his *entourage.*" Mahmud also did it and built a library and a museum. He established a great *madrasah* in Ghaznah, to which he really lent lustre and brilliancy worthy of the capital of a great empire. But the author of the article 'Nakhustin Kutubkhanah-i-Ghaznah dar 'Asr-i-Islami (the first library of Ghaznah in the Muslim period) tells us about the existence of a precious library in Ghaznah almost two hundred years before Sultan Mahmud, which contained rare books, even of the Christians.

Apart from Samarqand, Bukhara and Ghazanah in the east of Baghdad, there were a number of centres of learning, like Herat, Marv, Balkh, Tus, Nishapur and Shiraz, etc., where, according to historians, knowledge flourished and men of letters were honoured and rewarded. Naturally, these centres had valuable *Kutubkhanahs,* some of which attracted students from beyond Baghdad and Cairo. It is difficult to give a detailed account of each one of them, and it would suffice to make a mention of a few of them. For example, in Herat, under the patronage of Sultan Husayn b. Mansur b.

Bayqarah (d. 1506) and his minister Mir 'Ali Shir Nawa'i (1440-1501), there was great enthusiasm among its men of letters and members of the royal family to build libraries. They themselves established large *Kutubkhanahs* for the benefit of scholars, among them *Kutubkhanah Gauhar Shad Begum, Kutubkhanah Madrasah Husayn Mirza, Kutubkhanah Jami' 'Ali Shir* and *Kutubkhanah Madrasah lkhlasiyah* etc., were known far and wide for being the repository of a large number of books, some of which being very rare.

Marv and its libraries are well described by Yaqut Hamavi (1179-1228) in his *Mu'jam al-Buldan,* because he used quite a good number of them while compiling this book; of these libraries, according to him, *Kutubkhanah Nizamiyah, Kutubkhanah Aziziyah* and *Kutubkhanah ad-Damriyah* were very important and contained precious books. Scholars were allowed to use the books of these libraries freely and many of them could have the books issued also. Balkh, before the advent of Islam, was famous for its fire-temple *Naw Bahar.* The Bermecides of the Abbasid period originated from its priestly family. But this city and its suburbs produced great men of learning and letters, among them Mawlana Jalaluddin Rumi (1207-1273) is still venerated throughout the world. He was really the pride of his age.

Another city of fame, particularly in connection with its renowned 'Ulama', poets and men of letters, was Tus which the Arabs had conquered during the period of Caliphate of Hazrat Uthman. Muhammad 'Abdur-Razzaq of Kanpur (India) has written a comprehensive biography of the Saljuq *Wazir* Nizam-ul-Mulk Tusi, in which he gives a list of renowned persons whom Tus produced and who had far-reaching influence upon the course of cultural and intellectual development during the succeding centuries centuries in the Islamic world. Tus continued flourishing along with the progress and prosperity of the Islamic empire and there came and there came to be established, in course of time, a number of *madrasahs* and *Kutubkhanahs.* The greatest and best of all the *Kutubkhanahs* of Tus, perhaps, is that which has been associated with the tomb of Imam Rida (765-818) and is known as *Kutubkhanah Mashhad Muqaddas.* Established in (*Circa*) 1030 A.D., fortunately, this *Kutubkhanah* escaped all devastations through which Tus had to pass from time to time and it is now more than one thousand years that it has been the centre of attraction for scholars and men of learning and letters. The catalogue of books that it contains has been published with the title *"Fihrist Kutubkhanah'-i-Astanah'-i Quds Ridvi"*, and gives an idea of what a precious treasure it is.

How the Buwayhids came to wield influence and made the Abbasid Caliphate a protectorate of theirs is not our concern in the present context. We have to see only their achievement in the field of patronage of learning and letters and their encouragement of sciences. "The Buwayhids were Persians and Shi`ites....They were generous patrons of literature and science. Philosophy especially, which had been stifled by Turkish ascendency and Hanbalite fanaticism, as well as by the growing strength of al-Ash`ari's doctrines, was once more revived, and it scon found expression in the formation of that remarkable fraternity of encyclopaedists known as the *lkhwanu's Safa.'*, or "Bretheren of Purity", who summed up the physical and metaphysical sciences of their time in a series of fifty-one tracts...." Among the Buway hids, however, 'Adud al-Dawlah (949-982), himself a poet, litterateur and a lover of all sciences, possessed a wide and extensive area from Fars to Musal and *Jaziratul-Arab* and was so powerful that his name was read in the *Khutbah* at Baghdad. He built a *Kutubkhanah* at Shiraz, in which he saw that all the books written from the time of the advent of Islam right upto his own times, were acquired and collected for it. Al-Maqdisi in his *Ahsan al-Taqasim fi Ma`ri-fat al-Aqalim* (Leiden, 1906 has given a vivid description of the library of 'Adud al-Dawlah at Shiraz. He says: "The library consisted of one long gallery with store-rooms off it. Along the wall of the gallery and the store-rooms book-cases were placed which contained many shelves. The books were arranged on the shelves and for every branch of learning there was a separate section" and to each section of the library there were catalogues in which the titles of the books were written. To administer and supervise the library

Wakils, Khazin and *muhasib* were appointed and only the learned and the people of status had access to it.

So much about some of the important libraries of Baghdad, the seat of the Abbasid Caliphate, and a few centres of learning in Iran, Khurasan and Central Asia. Now we have to note that along with the spread of learning and the establishment of centres of learning and *Kutubkhanahs,* a number of related professions also grew and flourished. For example, calligraphy, transcribing and bookbinding where honoured professions in which the Muslims not only took interest but made them so perfect that it all shing along with the progress and prosperity of the Islamic empire and there came to be established, in course of time, a number of *madrasahs* and *Kutubkhanahs.* The greatest and best of all the *Kutubkhanahs* of Tus, perhaps, is that which has been associated with the tomb of Imam Rida (765-818) and is known as *Kutubkhanah Mashhad Muqaddas.* Established in *(Circa)* 1030 A.D., fortunately, this *Kutubkhanah* escaped all devastations through which Tus had to pass from time to time and it is now more than one thousand years that it has been the centre of attraction for scholars and men of learning and letters. The catalogue of books that it contains has been published with the title *"Fihrist Kutubkhanah'-i-Astanah'-i Quds Ridvi,"* and gives an idea of what a precious treasure it is.

How the Buwayhids came to wield influence and made the Abbasid Caliphate a protectorate of theirs is not our concern in the present context. We have to see only their achievement in the field of patronage of learning and letters and their encouragement of sciences. "The Buwayhids were Persians and Shi`ites... They were generous patrons of literature and science. Philosophy especially, which had been stifled by turkish ascendency and Hanbalite fanaticism, is well as by the growing strength of al-Ash'ari's doctrines, was once more revived, and it scon found expression in the formation of that remarkable fraternity of encyclopaedists known as the *Ikhwanu's Safa,'* or "Brethren of Purity," who ummed up the physical and metaphysical sciences of their time in a series of fifty-one tracts...." Among the Buwayhids, however, 'Adud al-Dawlah

(949-982), himself a poet, litterateur and a lover of all sciences, possessed a wide and extensive area from Fars to Musal and *Jaziratul-Arab* and was so powerful that his name was read in the *Khutbah* at Baghdad. He built a *Kutubkhanah* at Shiraz, in which he saw that all the books written from the time of the advent of Islam right upto his own times, were acquired and collected for it. Al-Maqdisi in his *Ahsan al-Taqasim fi Ma'rifat al-Aqalim* (Leiden, 1906) has given a vivid description of the library of 'Adud al-Dawlah at Shiraz. He says : "The liberary consisted of one long gallery with store-rooms book-cases were placed which contained many shelves. The books were arranged on the shelves and for every branch of learning there was a separate section" and to each section of the library there were catalogues in which the titles of the books were written. To administer and supervise the library *Wakils, Khazin* and *muhasib* were appointed and only the learned and the people of status had access to it.

So much about some of the important libraries of Baghdad, the seat of the Abbasid Caliphate, and a few centres of learning in Iran, Khurasan and Central Asia. Now we have to note that along with the spread of learning and the establishment of centres of learning and *Kutubkhanahs,* a number of related professions also grew and flourished. For example, calligraphy, transcribing and bookbinding were honoured professions in which the Muslims not only took interest but made them so perfect that it all became a fine art. Special and learned studies have been made on Islamic calligraphy.' Book binding and even on painting, and one, if interested, may go through them.

There were public, semi-public and private libraries. As for the public libraries, it is difficult to trace their existence till the last quarter of the 4th century (A.H.). To the best of our knowledge we can say that Shapur b. Ardsher built a *dar al-'ilm (Khizanah ash-Shapur)* in the Karkh quarter of Baghdad in 382 (A.H.), collected about ten thousand select books and endowed it for public use. He provided funds for its maintenance, and it is recorded to have been a centre for eminent and learned men. Then, in 305 (A.H.) the Fatimid ruler, Hakim bin amr-Allah, built a public library on a grand scale, which has been recorded by the historians as the *Dar al-'ilm* or *Dar al-Hikmah.* Afterwards when the *madrasahs* were established, the founding of public libraries came in general vogue.

Now a word for the staff of the *Kutubkhanah.* One is really amazed to learn how the Muslims organised and administered their *Kutubkhanah* in the medieval times. There were different sections in a *Kutubkhanah,* each of which was assigned a particular function and alongwith it suitable staff. The staff, however, depended upon whether the *Kutubkhanah* was large or small, public or private. Generally, it consisted of a librarian, translators, scribes, binders and attendants. The librarian was called *Khazin (al-Kutubkhanah)* or *muhtmim.* He was in charge of the administrative and intellectual affairs of the library; but the main function which he had to perform was the acquisition and collection of books. The sources for the most part, from where the books were acquired or, of themselves,arrived in the library, were the following :

1. The rulers and their *'Umara'* (pl. of *amir*) used to receive books as gifts.
2. Books were purchased.
3. The scribes were appointed to prepare copies of books borrowed from other persons who sometimes, happened to live at distant places.
4. Books came to the rulers as *spoils* of war (*mal-i-Ghanimat*) after victory in battles.
5. Travellers and emissaries brought books from their lands and in exchange took back books needed at home.
6. Books were acquired through the good offices of the Hujjaj (pl. of al-Hajj).
7. Bequests were made by scholars and rich persons. Through bequests school and mosque libraries, in particular, gained very notworthy collections of books.

The intellectual aspect of the librarian's function was fully recognised and, therefore, learned men and reputed scholars were appointed as librarians. In *al-Fihrist, Tadhkirah al-Huffaz, al-Aghani, Mu'jam al-'Udaba'* and a number of other works one can find that great scholars served as librarians in notable libraries and they felt proud of it.

Translators enjoyed a unique position. It is well-known that foreign learning was transferred into Arabic through a number of translators, Muslims and non-Muslims both ; but here translators of a different category are meant and have to be noted. It has been already mentioned that "with the name of Khalid b. Yazid (d. 85 A.H.) the earliest collection of books is associated. Khalid devoted his life to the study of Greek sciences, particularly alchemy and medicine, and according to Ibn al-Nadim, Khalid employed a certain Stefanus to translate books on these subjects for him and for the supply of the library." The practice established by Khalid b. Yazid was continued on a large scale, when the *Bayt al-Hikmah* was founded. Besides, other libraries also had translators to enrich themselves with their activity. But there came a saturation point, and also took place certain historical events and intellectual developments, as a result of which, "translators seem to have disappeared from the libraries shortly after that [about the middle of the 3rd century], probably because the most useful works had already been translated and also because this immense activity had enabled Muslim scholars to evolve their own philosophy and science upon which they later relied."

It was necessary for all the important public and private libraries to employ *Katibs* (scribes) who, also known as *Warraqun*, worked in the book-producing section of the library, where the work of copying the books continued day and night. This necessitate the employment of clever verifiers (*mushih*) who did their job quite efficiently by going through the books that were copied with great care and detailed caution. In some of the libraries there used to be *mustamlis* (amanuenses) who wrote from dictation and the expert among them produced more than what a copyist could do; however, with *mustamlis,* there always remained more chances for omissions and mistakes.

As for the calligraphists and book-binders, we have already written and referred to valuable sources for further study. The job of the attendants (*munawilun*) was to help the readers and find out the books they needed from the library. Mention of attendants is found in connection with all the important libraries. In *Risalah al-Ghufran* al-Ma'rri, a girl, Tawfiq, is reported to have worked as attendant in the library of Shapur Ardsher at Baghdad.

Madrasahs are Founded

It is generally said that it was the Saljuq Wazir Nizam-ul-Mulk Tusi (1017 or 1019-92 A.D.) who established the first *madrasahs* in the Muslim world. But actually it is not so. We are told that several *Madrasahs* did exist before the advent of Tusi as the consolidator of the Saljuq Empire under Alp Arsalan (regd. 1063-73) and Malik Shah (regd. 1073-92). The Sunni madrasah-building movement had already begun in the second half of the tenth century A.D. "It was a response first to the challenge of Mu`tazili thought, and subsequently to the Fatimid institutions meant for training Shi`i *da`is* or propagandists: i.e., the Azhar mosque of the Fatimid general Jauhar and the Caliph al-Mu`izz (founded in 359/970), the *Dar al-Hikmah* ("House of Learning") of the Caliph al-Hakim (founded in 395/1005), and the various local *dar al-da`was,* or rallying-places and centres for propaganda. The Buwayhids also helped the propagation of Shi`ism, and some of them even tried to impose their religious views upon their subjects. As a reaction to this, the sunni rulers who followed, established centres or *madrasahs* for the protection of what they thought to be the right belief. Ibn al-`Imad al-Hanbali in his *Shadharat al-Dhahb* wirites that a *madrasah* was founded by al-Imam abi Bakr bin Faurik al-Isfahani (d. 405/1014) who himself taught various sciences in it. This was, perhaps, the first *madrasah* ever established in the traditional sense. Then the people of Nishapur built a *madrasah* for Abu Ishaq Ibrahim Asfara'ini (d. 418/1027) to teach the principles of *fiqh.* He was succeded there by Allamah Baihaqi (d. 458/1065), once a student of Asfara'ini, who taught hadith and *fiqh* and was comparatively a very staunch supporter of Shafi`i *madhhab.* Very soon the *madrasah* came to be known as *Madrasah Sa`diah.* In this very city Imam Abu Mansur 'Abdur Rahim bin Muhammad al-Bayshaki (d. 453/1061) and his *madrasah* also flourished. He was a rich person who left a large and valuable property as endowment for his *madrasah.* Amir Nasr bin Subuktagin, brother of Sultan Mahmud, during the period of his governorship at Nishapur, built *Madrasah Sa`diah.* Besides these, there were other *madrasahs* also at Nishapur which, because of the intellectual atmosphere that prevailed there, had gained the reputation of being the second important city after Baghdad in the eastern Muslim world.

As the *madrasahs* at Nishapur were controlled by the Shafi'i Sunnis, it, consequently, became a centre of Sunnism, particularly the Shafi'i shade of Sunnism which carried its crusade against the Shi'i institutions and their influence on the social and religious life of the Muslims. Thus, we can conclude that the Shafi'is were the founders of the *madrasah* system of education in the world of Sunni Islam.

Now the question is whether this madrasah-building movement among the Sunnis was meant only to check the growing Shi'i and Mu'tazili influences and turn the table on the anti-Sunnites. To the present writer it seems only partially correct. Partially, it was to fulfil the need of a society in which demand for education, both religious and secular, was growing. The mosques where the *halqahs* were main characteristic, could not provide ample space for both worship and instruction, particularly when along with the increase in the number of students the number of circles also increased. Moreover, by the close of the 10th century (Christian era) a new class, the class of the learned (to be known later as 'Ulama'), had come into existence. It was gradually assuming the position of a professional class which, while engaged in imparting knowledge, wanted a permanent source of income in the form of salary or stipend. Von Kremer does not agree with the view that it was the want of room in the mosques that called into being the *Madrasahs.* He is, however, of the view that the "progress and diffusion of knowledge created a body of men who found it difficult to make a decent living through their abstract learning. It was to promote further study and to provide sufficient stipend for such men that the Madrasahs were really established."

Besides, able administrators required loyal and reliable personas to implement their administrative policies. There was always a need for educated and trained personnel. We should also note that an administrator like Nizam-ul Mulk had to build a network of *madrasahs* so as to always have reliable personnel for continuously strengthning his own position as well as the structure of Saljuq empire. This he did also by encouraging the progress of the Sunni revival. These *madrasahs* naturally became the citadels of Sunni orthodoxy.

The *Madrasahs* built by the Nizam-ul-Mulk are known as the *Nizamiyah* and represent the new turn that the mad rasah-building movement in the eastern world of Islam assumed with the advent of the Saljuq Wazir. This was the beginning of the state-supported educational institutions in Islam. As indicated above, Nizam's objectives in building madrasahs were "a mixture of the desires to emulate the Fatimids, to gain favour with the *`Ulama'*, and in practice to provide his administrative reforms with the necessary personnel, especially judges and clerks." He also aspired to play and he did play a decisive role in rehabilitating Ash`arite Sunnism and creating a stable political and social order out of the chaos wrought by the Buwayhids both in politics as well as in religion. Goldziher has very rightly observed that "....for a long time it was not possible for the Ash`arites to teach theology in public. It was not until the middle of the eleventh century, when the wazir of the Saljuqids, Nizam al-Mulk, created *public chairs* in the great schools founded by him in Nishapur and Baghdad for the new theological doctrine, that Ash`arite dogmatic theology could be taught *officially* and was *admitted into the system of orthodox theology;* its most illustrious representatives could have chairs in the Nizamiya institutions. It is, therefore, here that the victory of the Ash`arite school was decided in its struggle against Mu`tazilism on the one hand, and *intransigeant orthodoxy* [Hanbalism], on the other. The era in which these institutions flourished is, therefore, important, not only in the history of education, but also in that of Muslim dogmatic theology."

The Ash'arite school was vehemently supported by the Shafi'is who had their own theory of education. It seems, therefore, reasonable to know what it was before we make a study of the method of teaching followed and the sciences taught at the Madrasahs. It is also to be noted what the Hanafi theory of education was. According to both the schools, education is basically meant for understanding the relation of man with God as revealed in the Holy Qur'an. However, the difference of approach remains there. In his *Ta'lim al-Muta'allim* az-Zarnuji quotes Imam Abu Hanifah (699-769) as having said: "The purpose of learning is to act by it while the purpose of action is the abandoning of the perishable for that which lasts for ever. It is necessary for man neither to neglect his soul nor what helps or injures it in this life and in the next life. Hence man should try to provide what is useful while avoiding what is harmful to the soul, lest his intelligence and his knowledge become weapons [arguments] against him and his punishment be increased. May God preserve us from His wrath and His punishment.

Moreover, the role of intellect is not ruled out and a Muslim is again exhorted to understand and control the forces of nature for the progress and betterment of human life. Development of the qualities of head and heart, both, should be the aim and aspiration of true education; and "with this object in view the Hanafi school aims at the spiritual as well as intellectual development of human nature. Ibn Sa`id says, 'We are in need of developing both the theoretical and the practical capacities of human beings since this is the only way of achieving blissful life, and when it is admitted that this object is gained through knowing the nature of the things which lead us to believe in God and do the right, it becomes obligatory that we should acquire knowledge, for it helps us to understand the nature of things and enables us to choose virtues and avoid evil deeds.' The emphasis by the Hanafi school on the use of reason to acquire knowledge along with the belief in revelation as a source of knowledge also is one of it chief characteristics. This is further elaborated by az-Zarnuji who says:

"And it is meet for the student in his quest for knowledge to strive for the good will of God, the future life, the removal of ignorance from himself and from the rest of the ignorant, the conservation of religion, and the survival of Islam. For the survival of Islam depends on knowledge and the ascetic life and piety are not perfect where there is ignorance.

"The professor, the venerable Saih, the Most Illustrious Imam, Burhan ad-Din, author of the *Hidaya,* recited a poem by an unnamed author:

'1. An immoral man of learning is a great evil, but a greater evil still is an ignoramus leading a godly life.

'2. Both these types of men are a great trial everywhere to him who clings to both knowledge and godliness in his religion.'

And again :

"One should also select what is essential according to the stage reached in one's religious development and finally one should choose what will be necessary for one in the future. And thus the individual perfects himself in the knowledge of the unity of God and learns about Almighty God through logical evidence. *For the faith of him who blindly follows authority, even though it may be correct in our view, still is defective because of his failure to ask for proofs."* (*Italics ours*)

Imam Abu Hanifah's views on use of reason and his interest in the scholastic studies are well-known. It is equally well-known that Imam Shafi'i (769-819) was a traditionalist and hence not in favour of scholasticism. This had its bearing on the approach of the Shafi'is to education. "In the opinion of this school, knowledge was of little importance, and an intellectual approach to the realization of divine wisdom was supposed to be misleading. Education according to Ibn Juma'ah was a medium for drawing people nearer to God and for spreading and reviving divine law. Teachers, in the opinion of this school, are the torch-bearers of prophetic revelation and it is their duty to illuminate the minds of their pupils with divine inspiration. To these educationists (unlike the Hanafis) faith in God as taught by the Prophet required no confirmation by human intellect. They, therefore, disliked philosophical studies and dogmatic theology ——— Imam shafi'i is said to have mentioned that it is far better that God should see his servants plunged into all sorts of sins (except polytheism) than that He should see them indulging in dogmatic theology." But dogmatics was much in demand and scholasticism was a branch of learning which could not be ignored in view of the philosopher's attempts to prove the fundamentals of Islam on the basis of pure reason. Morever, there were people among the Shafi'is, who could not reconcile themselves with the extreme position which Imam Shafi'i and some of his adherents had taken in regard to scholastic studies. Hence there came a time when Shafi'is adopted a balanced view and wrote on Islamic scholasticism. Among such Shafi'is Imam Ghazali (1058-1111) was a real *mujtahid* and he won followers from among both the Shafi'is and the Hanafis. He advised one to learn all the arts that could be useful in one's striving for a good moral life and understanding the nature of his relationship with God. He protested against the total denial of usefulness of scholasticism and declared that students should not leave any useful art or a branch thereof untouched. He also pointed out that different sciences, seemingly at variance, in fact, comliment each other and are inter-related. He was, as a matter of fact, neither for blind faith nor for placing too much trust on human intellect as a source of true knowledge. In order words, he tried to achieve a synthesis between *tasawwuf* and *kalam;* and he was, to a great extent, successful in this attempt which was subsequently adopted by orthodxy and confirmed by *Ijma'*. "Imam Nawavi", as Dr. M. A. Mu'id Khan lays down, "also differed from Imam Shafi'i in this respect, for he says : 'Our Imam ash-Shafi'i has exaggerated in showing the study of dogmatics as forbidden and has gone too far to make it a sin for which severe punishment will be inflicted on its adherents."

The difference of opinion between the Shafi'is and the Hanafis in regard to the sources of knowledge in general and hence to their approach to education in particular, was reflected and clearly marked in the classification of subjects to be taught and the courses of studies to be followed in their *madrasahs*. Even their methods of teaching differed from each other. These points have been, on the authority of reliable sources, very ably elaborated by Dr. M. A. Mu'id Khan in his learned article so extensively quoted by the present writer. At the end of discussion under 'classification of subjects' he compares and points out the basic differences between the two schools in these words:

Hanafi

1. Faith in Allah and the Prophet should be rooted in the mind and based on firm intellectual grounds.

2. Compulsory education at the elementary stage should consist of all those religious and non-religious subjects which one requires daily in practical life.

3. The higher stage of education provides a vast choice of subjects for study; intellectual studies are combined with the religious, and selection of the subject is made according to the taste of the student.

Shafi'i

1. Faith in Allah as revealed in the Qur'an should be accepted unquestioningly.

2. At the elementary stage such religious subjects are compulsory as children will require for devotional services when they are grown-up.

3. The higher stage of education includes deeper knowledge of the different branches of religious studies and some non-religious studies like mathematics, medicine, history, literature etc., but purely intellectual and scholastic studies were discouraged.

Now, we will see what non-religious or secular subjects were taught in the Islamic *madrasahs.* Among them Arabic language and literature naturally enjoyed a favoured position, because it was the medium of intellectual communication among the learned and the medium of instruction at *madrasahs.* In short, it was the language of the Arab civilization. Moreover, the literary excellence of the Qur'an was unsurpassed and this had established relationship between *din* and *adab* (religion and Arabic literature). This is why it became a prerequisite for every *mutakallim, faqih, mufassir* and *muhaddith* to be well versed in *adab* and rhetorics in order to be able to fully comprehend the essence of the Prophetic message of Muhammad (Peace be upon him). Renowned scholars like Abu Zakariya al-Khatib at-Tabrizi (1030-1109), Ali bin Muhmmad al-Fasihi (d. 516/1123) and Mawhub bin Ahmad al-Jawaliqi (1073-1145) occupied the chair of Arabic language and literature at the Madrasah at Baghdad, and were the centre of attraction even for those who aspired to especialise in *fiqh* or any other branch of Islamic learning.

Arrangement was also made for the teaching of mathematics in the *Madrasahs.* It is said that Abdullah bin Ahmad bin al-Khashshab (1099-1172) learnt *adab* at the feet of Mawhub al-Jawaliqi, mathematics and *fara'id* at the feet of Ibn 'Abd al-Baqi al-Ansari and al-Marzuqi respectively. All of them were teachers at the Nizamiyah of Baghdad. They usually consulted with each other and discussed academic matters among themselves. It can, therefore, reasonably be conjectured that the teaching of mathematics was not banned in *madrasahs.*

History was not one of the basic subjects taught at the *madrasahs.* It depended upon the personal inclination of the teachers themselves that, if they wished, they gave some lessons in history to their students who were, otherwise, admitted there to especialise in some other field. Besides, history could not find a place in the courses of studies because of the preponderance of the science of *hadith* from which *sirah* as a special subject was deduced. And along with *sirah* attention was gradually concentrated on the history of the first century of Islam. In the beginning, with the exception of a few, *muhaddithing* generally considered it below their dignity to show interest in *akhbar* (history). Some of them even expressed their strong disapproval of it if they found any student or teacher interested in it. But afterwards, when the compilation of *hadith* was completed, history gradually came to be recognised as worthy of attention by the *muhaddithin* themselves, some of whom made significant contributions to the field.

Study of *Falsafah* (Philosophy—translations of Greek philosophical works — was greatly encouraged by some of the Abbasid Caliphs, but it did not find a place in the *madrasahs* and *masjids.* Still more, Muslim society, in general, frowned upon it and considered it as something obnoxious. There were, however, scholars who made a thorough study of *Falsafah.* They kept *din* and *falsafah* at their proper places. Some of them even made an attempt to bring about a reconciliation between the two. But they did not succeed in producing any thought-system out of their intellectual pursuits in this field. Had they been able to do this, they would have certainly created a climate, at least to some extent, favourable to its study.

Now why this inimical attitude towards *falsafah* among the Muslims ? Apart from the main reason that it created skepticism among its students, its lovers consisted of the Sabaeans, *Zanadiqah* and other like-minded elements who manoeuvered to use it against Islam which, they considered, was undermining their own faith. Non-Sunni Muslims, like the Isma'ilis, for example, took special interest in *falsafah.* But this interest of theirs was disorganised and oriented to non-academic motives. Al-Ghazali, in his *al-Munqidh min al-Dalal,* has referred to the corrupt form of *falsafah* which these heterodox groups were propagating in order to achieve their mischievous motives.

The Isma'ili and other political movements, by showing keen interest in the study of *falsafah,* themselves rendered great disservice to the cause of *falsafah* as such. They were not interested in the philosophical ideas and concepts of Greek philosophers like Plato and Aristotle. They took out things, at random, out of their teachings, which suited their political motives and called them *falsafah.* This was misleading and the misunderstanding caused in this way was handed down from generation to generation and it prevalent even to-day.

Falsafah, though not taught in *madrasahs* and *masjids,* was not completely banished from the Muslim society. It enjoyed a place of pride in the discourses of the learned who had real and purely academic interest in it and whose house had become the centres of philosophical studies. It was from these centres that Ibn Sina (980-1037), al-Farabi (874-950) and Ibn Rushd (1126-1198) drank deep and subsequently flourished with the title as *the Muslim falsafah.* They studied *falsafah* with devotion and great sincerity and never used it for any ulterior motive. The hostile attitude towards *falsafah* attributed to Muslims as a community is, therefore, not correct. And even if there was one, it was mainly due to the misuse of *falsafah* by the Isma'ilis and the Zanadiqah for their political ends. These were the people responsible for the banishment of *falsafah* from the *madrasahs.*

The orthodox theologians, because of their vested interests, supported and sided with the rulers who always expected trouble from the heretical and heterodox groups, some of which were, no doubt, politically motivated and which always looked for an opportunity to organise themselves to lead an uprising against the established authority. As indicated above, some of these heterodox groups also had philosophical background and, in their zeal to opposed and combat orthodoxy further encouraged the forces of disintegration in the society by propagating pseudo-philosophical ideas. Thus, the ruler and the theologian, considering orthodoxy as defence strategy, conspired against the *falsafah,* in general, and vehemently discouraged the study of philosophy in *madrasahs* which turned out to be the citadels of orthodoxy. It should, however, be kept in mind that the *falsafah* devoted much of their attention to the metaphysical concepts and it was this aspect of philosophy which could not reconcile with the fundamental articles of Islamic belief. Otherwise, other aspects of rational sciences like logic, medicine, astronomical sciences, geography and arithmetic, were not forbidden and, as Qazi Sa'id (1029-1070) has mentioned in his *tabaqat al-'Umam* the people of Andalus were not opposed to these branches of learning and the Umayyid Caliphs generally patronised the scholars of these sciences.

"The natural theology of the philosophers....posed a potential threat to the revealed content of Islam. The very point of its original achievement in religious thought became the target for orthodoxy's suspicion and attack, i.e., the point where it had sought deliberately and consciously a liasion with orthodox dogma and had hoped for acceptance as a valid interpretation of Islam." Imam Ghazali, therefore, rejected the position taken by the *falsafah* and pointed out to the right course of thought and action in his works, *al-Iqtisad fi`Ilm al-I`tiqad, Tahafut al-Falsafah* and *al-Munqidh min al-Dalal.* The refutation as formulated by al-Ghazali won recognition from the renowned *Ash'arite* theologians and in course of time came to be accepted as the true basis of intellectual exposition of the religion of Islam and, by implication, as the backbone of the *Shari'ah.* The fourteenth century theoretician-historian Ibn Khaldun speaks on behalf of almost the entire orthodox world of Islam of his time when he says: "Thus, as one has seen, the science (of logic) is not adequate to achieve the avowed intentions (of the philosophers). In addition, it contains things that are contrary to the religious laws and their obvious meaning. As far as we know, this science has only a single fruit, namely, it sharpens the mind in the orderly presentation of proofs and arguments, so that the habit of excellent and correct arguing is obtained.......Such is the fruit of this craft (of logic). It also affords acquaintance with the doctrines and opinions of the people of the world. One knows what harm it can do. Therefore, the student of it should be aware of its pernicious aspects as much as he can. Whoever studies it should do so (only) after he is saturated with the religious law and has studied the interpretation of the Qur'an and jurisprudence (*al-tafsir wa'l fiqh*). No one who has no knowledge of the Muslim religious sciences should apply himself to it. Without that knowledge, he can hardly remain safe from its pernicious aspects."

Experimental sciences, namely, alchemy, medicine (*tib*) and physics were studied; particularly medicine was taught in *masjids* and *madrasahs.* In hospitals, along with instruction in theories, arrangements were made for practical and clinical training. The teaching of alchemy was not generally encouraged at the *madrasahs.* This was not due to any religious prejudice, but, perhaps, due to the current view that it was a science that studied the substance through which the generation of gold and silver may be artificially accomplished, and commented on the operation leading to it. There were people who did try to find out the substance to produce gold and silver. But this was all based on misunderstanding. Jabir bin Hayyan (-815) who is considered the chief systematic writer on al-chemy, had it undoubtedly as his special reserve. He wrote several treatises on al-chemy. All of them read like puzzles.

Medicinal chemistry (alchemy) was in vogue, but it is not known whether it enjoyed the status of an independent discipline or it was taught as a part of the syllabus of medicine. There were, however, people like Abu Bakr al-Razi (865-923) who was well-versed in *tib* and chemistry and taught in hospitals of Ray and Baghdad. Probably he gave lectures on alchemy also. Some *madrasahs* were known for *dars* in physics, and Ibn al-Haytham (*965-circa* 1038) was unsurpassed in this field. He was as a matter of fact, the Newton of the middle ages. He lectured at al-Azhar and wrote more than seventy treatises.

Arabic was the language of the Arab civilization and hence, the medium of instruction at educational institutions. But the doors of these institutions were not closed to other languages. There were teachers who knew languages other than Arabic and explained the difficult portions of the lessons to their non-Arab students in their (students') own languages. Abu Bakr wajihuddin al-Darir an-Nahwi (1140-1215) was a teacher of *Nahw* at the Nizamiyah of Baghdad. He knew Turkish, Persian, Greek, Armenian and Ethiopian very well and helped his 'Ajami students through the medium of their own languages. So was the case with Abu Hayyan al-Gharnati al-Nahwi (1256-1344) who taught *Hadith* and *tafsir* at the Madrasah Mansuriyah (Cairo), knew Turkish and Persian and wrote books in these languages. However, it has not be ascertained whether these languages were taught also in the *madrasahs* or there were only some of the teachers who knew them. Yes, the study of *tib* required knowledge of Syriac and Greek and this is why we find that, generally, scholars of *tib* during those days knew at least one of these languages.

Nizamiyah Madrashas

As stated above, Nizam-ul-Mulk Tusi was the pioneer in founding state-supported educational institutions in Islam to which endowments were made to provide stipends to teachers and students. Subki, in his *Tabaqat al-Shafi'iya al-Kubra* (Vol. III), describes him as one of the greatest reformers and personalities in the world of Islam. He was undoubtedly in agreement that after Yahya Barmaki (737-805) and Sahib ibn 'Abbad (938-995) no other wazir may be said to have been equal to Nizam-ul-Mulk in his versatility of knowledge and qualities of mind. He was wellversed in the science of *Fiqh* and *Hadith*. He had mastered a number of subjects specially *Hadith* at the feet of scholars like Muhammad bin Ali bin Muhammad bin Mahrayazd Adib (976-1067), Abu al-Qasim Qushyri (986-1072) and Abu al-Khattab bin al-Batr (1002-1084) at Isfahan, Nishapur and Baghdad respectively. He himself held well-attended circles for *Hadith* in different *Majalis-i-Imla* of Jami'Mahdi 'Abbasi and other places in Baghdad. Towards the end of his student life he went to Bukhara in order to complete his study of *Hadith.* Imam al-Haramayn (1028-1085) held a very high opinion of him and eulogised his intellectual achievements, his steadfastness in matters of religion, his generosity and obliging nature and his love for justice and charitable acts. He not only patronised the learned and the writers, but also himself wrote books. Although he does not have any Arabic work to his credit, his Persian writings are of high quality. His *Wasayah* (or *Dastur-ul-Wuzara'*) and *Siyasat Namah* bear testimony to this.

Such was the personality of Nizam-ul-Mulk who joined the Saljuqs' service about (400/1048). At their court his ability and sincerity put him in a position to overshadow all his opponents.

Later he won the confidence of the Saljuqs to such an extent that "he was given a free hand to deal with all affairs of the empire according to his own initiative and without consulting the Sultan—, Malikshah—, called him his father and granted him the title 'Atabik' which was used for the first time and which means the prince-father. [He] became the real monarch of the empire and his ministry, indeed, surpassed the Sultanate." It was because of this that he left the impact of his initiative and freedom of action not only on matters of politics and administration, but also on the intellectual life of the period and the year that followed it. And the latter he did by establisting *madrasahs* in almost all the important cities of the empire. These known as *Nizamiyah Madrasahs,* some of which became quite famous and attracted students from distant places. As the Nizamiyah of Baghdad acquired a legendary character and began to be considered a model institution, we will deal with it in detail.

The Eizamiyah of Baghdad

> "In the month of Dhu`l-Hijja [of the year 457] work was begun on (the construction of) the Nizamiya College in Baghdad. The remainder of the riverside palaces located on Mashra`at al-Zawaya, on the Furda (Lower Harbour), at Bab al-Sha`ir and on Darb al-Za`faran. were torn down (and their materials were used) for is construction.

This is the announcement made by Ibn al-Jawzi (1114-1201) in his monumental work *al-Muntazam fi tarikh al-Muluk wa al-`Umam* (Vol. VIII). "Almost exactly two years later, in the year 459/1067, the construction of the Nizamiya was completed." Here is a report about its inauguration, as Makdisi says, given by Sibt Ibn al-Jawzi in his *Mir'at al-Zaman fi Tarikh al-a`yan* (MS arabe Paris, 1506). Makdisi also says that "all additions in square brackets are from *Muntazam*, VIII, 246-7."

On Saturday, 10th Dhu'l Hijja (459/22 September 1067), the 'Amid Abu Sa'id al-Qashi invited the people, according to their various classes, to meet in the Nizamiya College. Nizam al-Mulk had founded it [in Baghdad for the Shafi'ites], placing it in the charge of Abu Ishaq al-Shirazi [after having obtained his consent in the matter].

On the day in which the people had gathered at the Nizamiya, [waiting in anticipation of the arrival of Abu Ishaq.] he faild to come. They sent after him, but no trace of him was to be found.

The reason for this was that a young man, meeting him (on the way), had asked him: "O Master, is it your intention to teach *fiqh* in the (Nizamiya) College ?" And (when Abu Ishaq) said "Yes", he pursued: "But how can you teach (*fiqh*) in a place unjustly appropriated?" This decided (Abu Ishaq al-Shirazi) to change his mind, and he did not make an appearance.]

The choice then fell upon Abu Nasr b. al Sabbagh, the *Shahid* notary [who was given his place.] Abu Nansur bin Yusuf assured him that he would not allow him to be superseded [and that it would not be possible for Abu Ishaq to cause him damage.] (Ibn al-Sabbagh) relied on his assurances [and occupied the chair (of *fiqh*). A session of disputation (in *fiqh*) took place], (after which) the people dispersed.

Ibn al-Sabbagh was troubled by Abu Ishaq's absence. He allotted to each of the *fiqh* students a daily ration of four *ritls* of bread.

Abu Ishaq appeared in his mosque college in the quarter of Bab al-Maratib, and carried on his teaching (of *fiqh*) there as usual. The people joined him (there), invoked the blessings of God upon him, and praised him. They had already received word that he had made the following statement: "I could not bring himself to assume the chair (of *fiqh*) in this college, because of what I had heard concerning its furnishings, and that Abu Sa`id al-Qashi unjustly appropriated most of it, tearing down a part of the town (in order to provide the materials) for its construction."

However, the followers of Abu Ishaq began to show signs of

disrespect and discouragement. They sent him a message in which they intimated that they would leave him in order to join Ibn al-Sabbagh "if you do not comply and give up your rude manners." So he satisfied them by complying with their desire in order to appease them and put an end to their estrangement, and in anger against Ibn al-Sabbagh for having taken his place. And they plied their efforts in regard to this affair, he too joining them in so doing, until Ibn al-Sabbagh was dismissed.

Nizam al-Mulk, upon receiving the news of Abu Ishaq's refusal to teach in the Nizamiya reacted with a strong indignation against the 'Amid al-Qshi. He wrote him a letter in which he blamed, reprimanded, and threatened him, saying (among other things): "Whereupon (the 'Amid) Abu Sa'id went to Abu ishaq and showed him the letter. But Abu Ishaq did not comply. So (the 'Amid) went to Bait al-Nauba (in the Precincts of the Caliphal palace) and sent a message to the Caliph informing him about the matter. The Caliph then sent a message to Abu Ishaq saying: "You are fully aware of our situation with the foreigners." So Abu Ishaq (complying) went (to the college) carrying a large-zized brick which he used as a chair when he held his sessions at the college.

Abu Ishaq assumed the chair (of *fiqh*) at the college on Saturday, I Dhu'l Hijja (459/13 October 1067). At the appointed times of the canonical prayers, he was in the habit of leaving the college and going to one of the mosques to perform them there.

The tenure of Ibn al-Sabbagh at the Nizamiya had lasted for a period of twenty days.

Abu 'Ali al-Maqdisi said: "I saw Abu Ishaq al-Shirazi in dream after he had died and I asked him: 'What did God do with you? He replied: 'I was told to give an accounting concerning this building'—that is the Nizamiya College—'and had I not refrained from performing the required (prayers) there, I would have been among those who perish."

Such was the beginning of the Nizamiyah of Baghdad—a

beginning on a grandiose scale indeed! It is said that Nizam -ul Mulk spent more than sixty thousand dinars on its construction. Then an endowment was instituted to provide a permanent source of income to meet the expenses of the *madrasah.* There are people who believe that money for this *madrasah.* and for other *Nizamiyahs* came from Nizam ul-Mulk's private purse. But this is not correct "Nizam seems to have acted in this matter, as even in more important matters, as the highest administrator of the empire with the delegated authority of the sultan and ultimately that of the Caliph. For even in the era of the *madrasah,* the Caliphate failed to develop a state department devoted to *ta`lim.* Accordingly public educational institutions were supported not directly from the treasury but largely from the income of assigned *waqf,* properties. Administration of such educational *waqf,* as well as actual teaching, was left in the hands of the *`ulama',* with remote state control. They too seem to have acted with delegated authority. While their administration of the *waqf* was governed by the actual deeds in accordance with the sacred law, their teaching was on the whole free and subject only to mutual checks and balances within the learned community."

Shalabi states that inspite of his best efforts he was unable "to find any detailed or precise documents of the endowments allotted to al-Nizamiyyah." What Ibn al-Jawzi and others have given in their books, if put together, comes to about what has been described by Makdisi in these words. He says:

"On 26 Jumada II 462 (14 April 1070), a different 'Amid, Abu Nasr, invited the important persons of Baghdad and summoned Abu'l-Qasim b. Jahir, son of the Caliph's Wazir Fakhr al-Daula, the two syndics of the Hashimites and 'Alids, the nobles, the chief Qadi, and the *Shuhud*-notaries, to the Nizamiya, now in its third year of operation, where in the reading of the endowment charter, as drawn up by Nizam al-Mulk, took place. He endowed his college with books, cultivable land, and other property, and a market (*suq*) was set up in front of it. Its administration was kept in the hands of Nizam himself and in those of his sons according to conditions made explicit in the charter—Here they are in substance:

1. the Nizamiya constitutes an endowment for the benefit of members of Shafi'ite school who are Shafi'ite in both *fiqh* (positive law) and *usul al fiqh* (legal theory);
2. the possession with which the Nizamiya is endowed are also for the benefit of those who are Shafi'ite in both *fiqh* and *Usul al-fiqh:*
3. the following members of the staff must be Shafi'ite in both *fiqh* and *usul al-fiqh*:
   (a) the professor [incumbent of the chair of *fiqh*);
   (b) the preacher [Wa'iz];
   (c) the librarian.
4. the Nizamiya must also have a teacher of Qur'anic science to teach the Qur'an;
5. it must also have a grammarian to teach the Arabic language;
6. each member of the staff receives a definite portion of the endowment revenue."

These stipulations in connection with the endowment allotted to the Nizamiyah of Baghdad may suggest that its beneficiaries were to belong exclusively to the Shafi'i school of *fiqh.* But it should not necessarily mean that it was for this branch of religious knowledge alone. The teacher of the Qur'an and the grammarian were also among the beneficiaries and they could belong even to other schools. And there were Hanafis and Hanbalis among its empolyees both during the lifetime of Nizam-ul-Mulk and afterwards. If it is true that Nizam's objectives, by establishing the *madrasahs,* were to gain the favour of the *'Ulama',* to rehabilitate Ash'arism and propagate Sunni Traditionism against Shi'i and Mu'tazali "heresies" and to produce the necessary and suitable personnel for the implementation of his broad-based administrative reforms, then, it is certain that he, being a shrewd administrator and politician, could not exclude the non-Shafi'is altogether from the Nizamiyahs. And there appears to be no evidence that the candidates recruited both for employment in the *madrasahs* and the state-administration were exclusively Shafi'is.

It is not known what was actually taught in the Nizamiyah of Baghdad. That is, the content of the syllabus has not been mentioned in any of the historical sources dealing with the institution. But in view of the absence of the mode of specialisation that developed much later, it can be safely said that, barring *Falsafah,* the whole range of religious sciences ('ulum al-Din) was included in the syllabus. It is true that the principal teacher, although he had to manage the day-to-day affairs of the *madrasah,* was primarily entrusted with the task of imparting *dars* in the sacred law. Yet, it is equally true that "in the absence of the actual curriculum, there is no evidence that he was excluded from teaching all the other related religious and even auxiliary linguistic subjects. A fair indication of what was actually taught is to be found in the writings of teachers. The teacher of the Nizamiyah with the most numerous surviving works is, of course, al-Ghazali. His range is clearly that of a comprehensive scholar who digested all the religious sciences and more". As for theology as a branch of religious learning, there is again no evidence that Nizam-ul-Mulk established a chair of this subject. But he certainly saw that Ash'arite theology was propagated and a climate for its acceptance was created both in the premises of the Nizamiyah as well as outside in the city of Baghdad. This he did by employing learned Ash'arites as *Wa'iz* who delivered homilies, as the practice then prevailed, mixed with Ash'arite propaganda. It was on more than one occasion that irresponsible utterances of some preachers led to communal nots between the Ash'arites and Shafi'is on the one side and Hanbalis and other Traditionists on the other.

REFERENCES

1. Ameer Ali, The spirit of Islam, London, 1922.
2. Al-Ghazali, Ihya,
3. Al-Isfahani, Muhadarah al-ubada.
4. Haji Khalifah, Kashf al-zunun.
5. Arberry, The Koran interpreted, London, 1955.

6. Riyasat Ali Nadvi, "Islami Nizam-i-talim," Ma'arif, Jan. 1938, 34-.
7. Ignaz Goldziher, Muslim studies, vol. II, London, 1971.
8. Ahmad Shalabi, History of Muslim education, Beirut, 1954.
9. "Madrasa," in Shorter Ency. of Islam, Leiden, 1953.
10. Kh. Semaan, "Education in Islam from jahiliyya to Ibn Khaldun," Muslim World, Jan. 1966, 194-.

(Revised and edited; originally published in *Islam and the Modern Age*, May and Aug., 1979).

5

Some Reflections on Islamic Education

SYED H H NADVI

(Abstract: Islamic education aims at creating true viceregents of God on earth without divided loyalties between God and Ceaser. It is unfortunate that Islamic education has been losing sight of the happy combination of Reason and Revelation in the face of world-wide tendency in the contemporary scientific civilization to neglect spiritual values and in consequence to foster intellectual and cultural anarchy).

There are three basic attitude towards the cognition of 'Reality', namely the theocentric, anthropocentric and nihilistic. The approach of the first is ontological. God is a divine and supracosmic Person. He is a 'Being' and not a 'Becoming'. He is the fountainhead of the highest values and ideals, brilliantly revealed in His creation. Man's ideal goal, in this belief-system is to reflect divine attributes, through education or through social behaviour. Islam in its entire thinking, including its education, belongs to the theocentric group.

The anthropocentric school interprets the 'Ultimate Reality' as intracosmic and impersonal, that is, God is a 'Becoming' and not a 'Being', consisting of both natural and supernatural worlds. Man according to this belief is the centre in the cosmos, and his ideal is to efface his personality in order to attain freedom from the bondage of the natural. Since salvation lies in renunciation, man has to follow the same course with a negative outlook on life. Ascetic exercises and magical concepts form the parts of his worship. Its goal is to submerge human personality in the Impersonal Reality. This outlook is represented by Buddhism and Confucianism.

The nihilistic view of Reality is based on illusion where cosmos is no more than a mere accident and man an ephemeral speck of mechanical activity in a chance order. This school teaches its followers that power lies in cunningness. It ideal is the acquisition of maximum physical happiness. All human struggle ought to be directed towards this end in a world hostile to man. Its ethics or moral philosophy is based on expediency.

Can the philosophy or education in these three schools conform to each other? Can they teach their followers any concepts other than their own? The answer is in the negative. Each school of thought will and ought to teach its followers its own ideals.

In Islam normative education starts with its own ontological beliefs. The Quran, being the eternal Covenant between God and Man, teaches the mysteries of human life, and promises to show man the signs of the Lord, the world of nature and also the world within his own soul.

Despite intellectual controversies about the role of Reason and Revelation in Islam, the paramount significance of Revelation was never minimized. Throughout the ages philosophers tried hard to bring harmony between Reason and Revelation. During the ideological tension between the Mu'taziltes, the Ash'srtites and Sufism, when the Muslim world was torn between theological and phiosophical movements. Reveltion commanded the allegiance of Muslim public opinion. However, Al-kindi, Ibn-Sina and Ibn-Rushd, the great champions of Reason had small following their influence was neutralized, chiefly by al-Ghazali.

No Muslim Philosopher did ever deny the Quran as the basis of Islamic metaphysics. The Quran itself invites man to use his intellect for the cognition of the Creator of the universe and its wonders. Greeks ideas, exerting their influence from time to time, could not wean Muslim Philosophers from the teachings of the Quran. Al-Kindi, al-Farabi and Ibn-Sina, despite their Aristotelianism, believed in the harmony between Reason and Religion. Ibn-Sina's work *Tis' Ra-sa'il' Hikma wat Tabi'a* confirmed the idea of harmony.

In the Muslim west both Ibn Tufail and Ibn Rushd laid emphasis on harmony between the two. Ibn Tufail's hero, Absal followed Revelation while Salaman followed pure Reason but finally both agreed that Revelation protects mankind from errors. Experience convinced Salaman that education through pure reason was hazardous. Ibn-Rushds work *Fasl al-Maqual fi ma-bain al-Hikama wash-Shari'a min-al-Ittisal*, was a similar attempt. He proved that the use of intellect was not forbidden by the Quran or by the Hadith. Both Ibn -Rushd and al-Farabi agreed that Revelation was the real source of human knowledge.

The Muslim Philosophers were not unaware of the basic contradiction between the Aristotelean philosophy and Islamic beliefs. Islam taught that God know everything however minor it could be, while the Aristotaleans taught that God knew nothing beyond His own Being. God according to Islam was the Creator of the universe and the universe was changeable and perishable, while Aristotle believed that the world was eternal and unperishable. 'O Lord increase me in knowledge' has been the cornerstone of Islamic epistemology. Since God is the fountainhead of all knowledge, He alone is the Teacher. Adam gained ascendancy over the angels merely because God taught him what the angels did not know. God enhances the honour and position of those who believe in Him and equally those who have been endowed with knowledge.

Learning has ever been regarded in Islam as the source of divine beauty and divine perfection and its acquisition as one of the greatest human virtues. Man has been endowed with a curious and reflective mind to seek it. A virtuous teacher teaches the truth. The teaching of half-truth is dangerous, and there is no neutrality in Truth.

Islamic epistomology rejects the concept that all knowledge is derived from sense perception, for it can never represent the eternal entities quite distinct form spatial and temporal world.

Among the three sources of knowledge, that is, sciences, philosophy and Divine Revelations, the latter alone communicates the whole Truth. Science (which emerged as the rival of religion in Europe in the middle of the eighteenth century) was never in conflict with Islam as a religion. Unlike the Cartesian method wherein knowledge starts with doubt, Islamic quest for the knowledge, the First cause, begins with the certainties of the Revelation.

Take Ibn al-Arabi's *Wahdat al-wujud* (unity of Being). According to this doctrine, knowledge of the cosmos is the knowledge of God, for the archetypes of all things are aspects of God's Names and Attributes. Ibn al-Arabi explains in his *Fusus al-Hikam* that man acquires knowledge only when his entire being is illuminated by the intellect.

Thus the Islamic idea of education is rooted in the Islamic ideas of God, of the Universe, and of Man. It establishes relation between God and man so that he may realize a virtuous nature and aspire for the development of his personality on the model of divine excellence. The achievement of these virtues ought to be the ultimate ideal of Muslim education.

There is no denying the fact that evil exists, but has the freedom of choice. Despite this freedom, man's choice remains limited by the will of God and by the laws of nature. This relative freedom can be exercised within the terms of the Revelation and through Reason, the faculty given by God to man to distinguish between good and evil.

Consider two examples: The British code issued by the Department of Education defines the aims of education as 'habits of observation, clear reasoning living interest in the ideals and achievements of mankind, physical fitness, strength of character, development of intelligence and efficiency in the work of life.' The American Commission on the Reorganization of Secondary Schools emphasized 'vacation, citizenship, leisure health, and command of all the fundamental process of ethical character'.

The inherent tension between the different aims of education is quite obvious. None of these educational aims leads to the development of the viceregent of God who submits his will to the will of God in intergrating himself in the normative society.

Islamic education aims at creating true viceregents of God on earth without divided loyalties between God an Caesar. It is, however, unfortunate that Islamic education, has been losing of the happy combination of Reason and Revelation in the face of world-wide tendency in the contemporary scientific civilization to neglect spiritual values and in consequence to foster intellectual and cultural anarchy. The cure is surely in the philosophy enshrined in this passage:

> 'This single fundamental fact that determined the concept, dictated the content and governed the evolution of Muslim education is the belief that God's final message to mankind was revealed in its entirety through Muhammad and is in-shrined in the Quran. The divine revelation embraces not only the dogmas of the faith and the religious and moral duties of the believer, but also guidance on the political, social and economic organization of the community. This is the basis of the philosophy of Islamic education. Its content is of divine origin; its aim is to direct the conduct of the individual and the community according to God's commands.'

(Revised and edited; originally published in *Islamic Quarterly*).

6

Youth and Moral Education

M. MAHDI ALLAM

(Abstract: Today it is not the crime, in legal sense which bothers us, but sin in religious sense, which is worth considering and bringing in a moral sceince education system in the society is the need of the day).

Our youth is our human wealth. This wealth is made up of two important components, the spiritual value and the actual physical force or the manpower of our youth. Each part of this wealth is in need of care and insurance. Our care of this wealth is the method which we follow in looking after our young generation, and the premiums that are paid for the insurance of this wealth take the form of the effort which is taken to preserve it and enable it to do its utmost in life for its own prosperity and of its country.

A young person is like a traveller who goes into a new land full of unbeaten tracks and rugged terrain. Such a traveller should be provided with a chart of a map to guide him in traversing such terrain. The best way to prepare our youth for such a journey is to prepare them intrinsically for such travel so that they may have no need to turn to other persons save in exceptional circumstances.

Thus the care of our youth should take the form of bringing them up in such a way that they become their own supervisors. We should give every youth a spiritual battery, as it were, which would seldom need reacharging ; and if it needs to be recharged he would find among the people around him those who would be willing and able to recharge it for him.

Youth should be considered the most important asset in the budget of our people, and thus should have priority over other things for preserving and developing it, not only from the day of its birth, but even before that. Such care is to be directed towards the development physically, mentally and spiritually.

The preparation of youth for the future life is the natural duty of the family, of relatives, of friends, of teachers, and indeed of the state.

One important fact that should be noticed is that, thought those who are responsible for the direction of youth, may do their utmost for their guidance, youth frequently resent advice proffered to them. The curious fact is that those who most need advice are those who usually refuse it. But it is the natural feeling of parenthood which enables mothers and fathers to tolerate such behaviour and resistance on the part of their young ones. They are anxious to guard their children against mistakes which they, or indeed others, had made in their life.

We find an obvious example of this guidance among animals and birds; they train their young by giving them practical lessons in the way of life based on their own past experience. There is of course a great deal of difference, in this respect, between animal and man. Among animals, these lessons are few and limited in their scope, and the young ones accept them without disobedience or opposition, not out of persuation, of course, but of instincts which regulate animal life. As for the human child, owing to his superior intellignece, he usually takes his opportunity to stand out, showing his personality and self-assertion, as his intelligence continues to develop.

There is no doubt that this feeling, which parents have, that their children wish to have their own way, has brought about a large amount of literature, in which the Arabs take the lead, embodying “The recommendations and advice” that fathers and mothers have left for their sons and daughters.

One of our Arab poets has summarized the importance of the guidance that parents give thir young ones, calling it "The essence" of life's experience offered in a single hour.

> Musa Ibn Sa'id El Qansi says :
> Keep may advice to you in sight,
> And in your mind it be,
> For in a life mature and full
> In an hour you will see
> The lessons from experience gained
> When learnt, will help you so,
> For your intelligence is such
> 'Twill help you as you grow.

It is necessary that our method of guiding our youth should be practical, based on an understanding of their tendencies and instincts, relying on a minimum of verbal advice, depending mostly on our good example in conduct, and endeavouring to initiate them in an atmosphere of healthy habits which are based on their instincts in their sublimated form. Moral education should neither be inhibitive, nor loose, since either course is fraught with dangers which are too obvious to deal with here.

Life based on morality is the outcome of a well-founded faith. Faith is a light which guides its bearer on his way: Or again faith is a clear spring from which one quenches his thirst in the course of his life. Indeed, faith is a haven in which we seek shelter from the storms of life. Without faith youth cannot lead a life of happiness, nor would it be possible for them to cope with, and master, their problems and difficulties. On the countrary, a person with no faith would be easily drawn by currents wherever they run. Such person may sometimes be obstinate, or wasted, with little or no use to himself or to his community; his judgements being mostly unsteady and spasmodic.

The soundness of Muslim youth, in the early times of Islam,

was due to their up-bringing in a good environment, among Muslim parents who were honest, clean-living, and sincere in following the treachings of Islam. Faith was the strongest guarantee for their behaviour; it was the light that showed them the way; it was also a kind of brake which stopped any attempt at deviation from the right path.

The "Imam" which is the Arabic word for "faith" is derived from "Amn" which means "security", and is closely connected with "Aman" which denotes "tranquility". It is obvious, therefore, that "faith" fills one with a sense of security, tranquility, and self-confidence. It also fortifies one against "doubt", the Arabic equivalent of which is "Shakk" denoting in its origin "stabbing pain". A person with faith and conviction is, therefore immune against scipticism and indicision.

Faith in God and His Prophet and all that is holy may be likened to a shady oasis in which one seeks shelter from the troubles of life, from the conflicting opinions, from temptations. Youth have to have faith in their glorious past, in order to bind them to their ancestor and their rich history : they have to have faith in their present, for it is the field of their activities and constructive achievements; they have to have faith in their future which is the beacon that illuminates their way to real happiness; they have to have faith in their religious values and ideals which stand them firmly on the right path, guiding their conduct and safeguarding it from taking a false direction.

God has blessed man with life, and demanded that he should enrich this life with knowledge and action. Freedom is given to him but it is bound with the sense of responsibility that guards against its abuse.

"It is He who has made the earth manageable for you, so traverse you through the tracts and enjoy the sustenance which He provides."

Let us appreciate these blessings and express our gratitude by applying ourselves to the life which they prescribe. Any community that neglects these blessings, allowing corruption to get hold of it, would be similar to a body that grows in size from tumours that bring along diseases which may be undiscovered for a time, owing to the sheer power and stamina of the body, but the body is sure to succumb ultimately unless it is examined in time and given the proper treatment.

Our responsibility is grave towards society : any society resembles a great river which starts along its course, sometimes smoothly, sometimes in an unbridled torrent; in its course it may become polluted, carrying disease and causing epidemics; sometimes it would overflow its banks, it may pass through gorges studded with rocks hindering its progress. Yet the human hand can tame it and render it a source of life, strengthening its banks where they are weak, straightening its course where it meanders, building bridges and dams across it, making it ultimately a life-line for the land through which it runs, creating Civilization, better life and prosperity.

This picture resembles our human society. But I do not intend to enumerate the deviations that occur in society. This subject has been dealt with by two eminent members of our Academy, Professor Nadeem El Jisr and Professor Muhammad Khalafallah Ahmed. Suffice it for me to refer to the religious foundations which underline our plan of moral education, then to give a practical suggestion for the implementation of the scheme. If we go back to the root of the subject of the soundness of a moral life in society we find the secret of success in the obedience of the early Muslim society to the holy words of the Quran.

"O you who believe ! Give your response to God and His Apostle, when He calls you to that which will give you life." (Surah VII. 24) "Verily, this is My Way, leading straight : follow not other paths : they will scatter you about from His Path : Thus does He Command you, that you may be righteous." (Surah VI, 153).

Among the great examples that our forefathers had set before us for the purpose of guiding our society are those which are based on comprehensive Islamic principles, and based at the same time on psychological and sociological grounds. One such suggestion embodies some of the Sayings of the Prophet may peace and grace be upon him ! — it is a response to him when he called upon us to that which will give us life.

Abu-Dawood-God bless him !—says : Islam is based on four foundations which are embodied in the following Traditions :

1. "Deeds can only be judged according to the intentions which motivate them; and every person is judged according to his intention."
2. "The good Muslim is he who leaves alone that which does not concern him."
3. "He who does not wish for others what he wishes for himself is not a true believer."
4. "What is permissible is obvious, what is forbidden is obvious; but between the two there are borderline cases which many people do not discern. Those who avoid these borderline cases are saved from downfall and religious deviation. But those who practise the borderline cases would fall within the forbidden range, as does the shepherd who grazes his fold in the vicinity of forbidden ground, he may find himself trespassing. Let it be known that every king has his forbidden grounds, and the forbidden grounds of God are the impermissible deeds. And let it be known that the human body contains a small lump on the atate of which depends the life of the whole body; if it be good the whole body will be good, and if it be bad the whole body will be bad : this lump is none other than the heart."

In the presence of so learned a gathering I would hesitate to go into all the details included in these Traditions: But let me summarize what I understand from the idea of Abu-Dawood in his reliance on these sayings as a basis for moral education. My deduction is as follows :

1. That responsibility is closely bound to intention, which helps in the training of self-discipline, and the consideration of one's behaviour before hand ; thus saving such behaviour from being a mere response to a passing whim instead of being the result of a stable, mature and co-ordinated action.

2. Training man to respect the limits in his human relations, avoiding inquisitiveness. This comprises two important things : The first is the good relationship between one and his fellow men, for a good Muslim should not push himself into other people's affairs which do not concern him. The second is that a Muslim who keeps to himself, shunning all that does not concern him, will save the time and energy needed to go about his own business.

There is no doubt that it is understood from the phrase "What does not concern him" that it refers to what will be of no benefit to anyone; and it is here that it is left to one's discretion to decide what one may involve himself in, and in this way there is a moral and psychological method of training oneself.

3. In his decision about what concerns him and what does not concern him, a Muslim is guided by the other Tradition which declares that the soundness of his faith depends on wishing for his fellow-men what he would wish for himself. Thus his relation with others is defined as helping them without imposing himself upon them in matters that could be considered by others as interference.

It has been usual to speak of the virtue of unselfishness and the vice of selfishness. But in my opinion these two Traditions have introduced a moral degree which has been overlooked by writers on Ethics. This moral degree combines selfishness and unselfshness, or rather the love of self and the love of others. Indeed we should not depricate self-love to such an extent that we consider it altogether evil for most human activities spring from self-love Therefore, if we mitigate the love of the self by the love of others—not by giving priority to others — then we would reach that moral degree of which I speak, and which I believe to be meant by the well defined words of the Prophet — may peace and grace be upon him ! — "until he wishes for his fellow man what he wishes for himself." Here the soul would be nearer to satisfaction and closer to acceptance, than if it had been called upon to deny itself, and give complete priority to others.

It is hoped that what I have explained above does not, in any way, mean that I belittle unselfishness or that I claim that Islam does not approve of it. The Quran speaks of those who "give in preference over themselves, even though povery is their own lot." It also speaks of those who "give food in charity, thought they do like it, to the indigent, the orphan and the captive."

But it should be remembered that these two verses stand alone in contrast with some hundred verses which call for giving away in charity without any reference to unselfishness. Furthermore, these two verses do not demand, or openly urge, self-denial and unselfishness; they simply contain a statement about some people who practise such a high level of human conduct with obvious approval of their conduct. Thus, these two verses set before Muslims an ideal which attracts some individuals — not all the people — and even those who do so will vary in the degree in which they realize that ideal.

Let it, therefore, be stated that the practical and possible way for each normal person is to share his self-love with his fellow men, and not to give it up completely.

In the Tradition that declares that "What is permissible and what is forbidden are obvious" we find that the Prophet—may peace and grace be upon him ! — has placed the criterion of behaviour on a scale wider than that which governs the relation between man and man. This Tradition includes man's response to God's commands in every respect of life. It asserts that "what is permissible is clear and what is impermissible is clear" meaning—as I hope to be correct in understanding—that the question of the permissible and the impermissible is beyond doubt, and, having been finally defined, should not be a subject of discussion. Man, therefore, has to take his line of behaviour within the framework of what is permissible and what is forbidden. What is left for one's moral judgment — a judgment which is closely related to one's intention, and which constitues his responsibility— is his careful consideration of those marginal cases, the borderline cases which every Muslim has to avoid.

5. This Tradition also emphasizes the importance of the moral judgement that man makes as foundation for his action and for the shouldering of his responsibility. It is not a mere coincidence that the Prophet — may peace and grace be upon him ! — has used the word "heart" rather than such words as "mind", "brain" or any other word whose meaning would be limited to one kind of activity. Hope I am not mistaken in interperting the meaning of "heart" in this connection to mean the source of every consciousness, thinking, sentiment and volition.

There is no doubt that if these activities are right the whole life of man would be right, and if they are wrong then the whole life of man would be wrong. There is no doubt that all these aspects of life are related to the heart physiologically and psychologically.

It is also my view that what is meant by "the body" here is both the material and spiritual sides of man, since the context of the tradition is dealing with man's righteousness or unrighteousness, and not merely his physique.

Now I would like to refer to what we always hear about the cause of delinquency as being the excess of spare time. I do not think that there is a real vacuum which causes the mental and spiritual perplexity to our youth. A careful examination of the countries where youth demonstrated an upheaval of perplexity will reveal that there are good many ways and means for occupying spare time. Indeed it is difficult to imagine that youth cannot find some activities which absorb his leisure time. The fact is that there are so many diverse and conflicting activities, some of which are detrimental to the body, to the mind and to the soul. These evil activities are the cause of the confusion of youth, for they surround them as a sweeping currents dragging them along, and few of them have the power to resist these currents while most of them succumb to one or the other of these currents or shift from one to another in sheer submission and dispersion.

What can young people do, who have been deserted by those who are responsible for them, whether by virtue of their blood ties, by virtue of their relation as teachers, or by virtue of their affinity as spiritual leaders ? If parents abandon their offspring, contented with giving them food shelter and clothing ; if teachers only furnish their pupils with knowledge of science and art in the form of books and lectures; if religious leaders are content to deliver their speeches and sermons, once a week, to those who happen to come to them; then our youth will find themselves confronted with various temptations in what they see and hear in the theatre, the cinema and other organs of entertainment ; some newspapers and magazines add to the problem. What then can they do in the face of all this ?

Is not the natural result that they take the line of least resistance, and fall in with these sweeping currents. But what is worse is that they find, that those should have been giving them guidance as good examples, in addition to neglecting their duties, are ahead of their juniors in the indulgence in these diversions.

The power of the influence of the example does not need any elaboration. The father who claims that his work or engagements with his friends leave him no time to sit with his children every day, or nearly every is neglecting the first duty of fatherhood ; and the mother who is too pre-occupied with the life of fashion and society to share with her husband the company of their children is wanting in the most important function of motherhood. The teacher who considers himself responsible only for giving his pupils knowledge without acting as a spiritual father to them does not realise the full extent of his duty. The people of religious authority who wait for the public to come to them, and do not take the initiative to meet them and mingle with them, inviting them to open discussions and sharing with them their good and bad times—these people barely comprehend a narrow view of their spiritual obligation.

Let us now turn to those agencies that are interested in the welfare of youth, and have no small measure of directing them. These organisations, such as the press, the radio, the television—in so far as the Muslim world is concerned— are owned and controlled by the state (except in a very few cases). Their responsibility is therefore, very great in the guidance and the building up of a strong moral buttress.

I do not deny that in these organisations there are some programmes that are purposeful and answer the requirement; but these useful programmes become worthless when they are accompanied and even outnumbered by other programmes which lure the youth into a line of conduct that cannot be accepted by any standard of decency.

We do not advocate austerity or deprival of innocent pleasures and enjoyment; nor do we aim at a prim and rigorous life that becomes intolerable. But we ask and how often have we asked ! — about the goal of those programmes — whether they are specially perpared or taken from the cinema and the theatre. What is the point in insisting, time and again, on showing marital infidelity, the resort to alcohol on the silghtest provocation, and the glaring exhibition of indecent dancing even where there is not the least occasion to present it ?

It is true that every family in our society, whether Muslim or Christian, in Egypt or in any other Arab or Muslim country, hold such riotous parties in which bodies mingle and alcohol is drunk—whether there is a birthday of a member of the family or a marriage ceremony ?

There is a solemn duty for those in charge of these organisations to realize their responsibility towards a nation that wishes to lead an honest life in which it enjoys pleasure but shuns perversion.

The excuse that is given by some who supervise the cinema and the theatre, namely that they are giving the public what it wants, is indeed a poor excuse, for the public has been defrauded by what has been given to it; and, having seen nothing better, it thought that this was the only form of recreation. The real responsibility lies in giving the public what it needs, not what it wants.

Every father and mother has a duty in choosing what should be heard or seen by children.

Then there is another source that handicaps moral education. It is these wretched songs that have fallen to such a low level, both in word and meaning, that some, at least, constitute what amounts to a public indecency punishable by the law of the land, to say nothing of the religious legislation and the moral code of a decent society.

I return once more to the Islamic society in the past. As I was guided by it in its glorious past, I can find the diagnosis of the moral diseases in it corrupt intervals, which bear resemblance to those diseases that attack our society today. They spring from the same evil roots. Corruption began to creep into our Muslim society when fathers and mothers became lax in their moral life. Their sons and daughters grew up in homes where wine and vice were part of their parents' life, and they saw or knew of wanton deeds in their family circle.

Statistics are available which show the effect, on children, of families that have collapsed through immorality or disunion.

The most important danger to our youth, in my opinion, is not criminality in the eyes of the law, but sins in the eyes of religion, which do not fall within the jurisdiction of the criminal law, such as drinking, gambling, camouflaged bribery, sexual gartification and the betrayal of trust by an official in the discharging of his duty.

This is the real danger to our youth and this is what we first and foremost plan to correct. I am of the opinion that this Academy should undertake the study of these problems in a thoroughly scientific manner, and announce the results of its study in the next Conference. I suggest that all other bodies and organisations which are concerned with the youth movement should participate in this effort. As we have seen, the Ministry or Waqfs has, through its Minister made a valuable contribution about the education and training of the "imams" of the mosques. We have also seen the Ministry of Youth introducing a plan for the modern mosque and its social part in addition to its religious function.

We listened, likewise, to the president of the Young Men's Muslim Association giving up projects, cultural, economic and moral, to be the outcome of a general union of all Muslim Youth.

These studies should also have the collaboration of the following bodies :

The Ministry of Education, the Ministry of Higher Education, the Ministry of Culture, the Ministry of National Guidance, the Ministry of Social Affairs, the Universities, the religious Associations, foremost among them, the Young Men's Muslim Association, the Shar'iyyah Association, the Sheikhdom of the Sufi movement, the Syndicate of Teachers, the National Centre for Social and criminal Research, the Organizations of the Cinema and Theatre, the Arab Socialist Union and the National Assembly.

We must also include for these studies representatives of the young people themselves in order that they take part in putting forth their problems, and in shouldering the responsibility of the results of the study.

I am not putting forward an imaginary plan, I fully realize that the question is too serious to be satisfied with voicing some of our troubles in the form of speeches and talks, then console ourselves with chewing our chagrin over the downfall and deviation of our youth.

Indeed a coordinated and comprehensive line of reform must come into being, in order to give birth to a practical plan, which will guide our young generation to realize the true Islamic qualities:

Pride without arrogance
Obedience without servility
Modesty without humility
Generosity without extravagance
Independence without obstinacy
Patience without weakness
Competition without malice
Piety without fanaticism
Courage without recklessness
Knowledge without pretence
Progressiveness without renouncement of the Past.
Tolerence without looseness.

(Revised and edited)

7

Religion and the Protection of Youth from Misbehaviour and Intellectual Deviation

MOH. KHALAFALLAH AHMAD

Broadly speaking, youth covers that stage of life extending from the early teens up to the late twenties, the stage which marks the end of childhood and the beginning of adolescence and adulthood. The end of this stage of life is characterised by physical growth, mental, social and moral development, the development of one's consciousness of responsibility and independence, the craving for a suitable job or position, one's tendency towards stability and making a family, and the interest in playing an active role in social service.

The importance of the stage in so far as integrity or deviation is concerned, will be crystal clear if we bear in mind the characteristics and phenomena revealed to us by scientific researches. For this period of life is marked by physical and mental growth accompanied by emotional and biology disorder. Philosophical and spiritual questionings and problems find their way to one's mind; one harbours mixed feelings, of hope and despair, of security and restlessness, of failure and success.

From experience and study the human societies have come to realise that the preparation of the individual for a good life that is free from deviations should start at home with the very early years of childhood. Home, school and society should co-operate during the following stages of development especially in the child's teens. Many factors and influences should come to help in bringing up the individual and equipping him properly for social life. On top of these are the cultivation of religion, discipline, setting up of cultural ideals, psychological care, rewarding economic conditions, and a favourable social environment.

The ideal which the society sets for its young generations should be to make them live up to their responsibility and help them to be independent. This enables the individual to develop an integral personality and a philosophy based on personal and social principles whereby one becomes a good citizen, loyal to his people, faithful to the traditions of his society, ready to sacrifice oneself and one's property for the defence of his country's (sacred heritage) and capable of doing one's share for the welfare and happiness of humanity.

It is natural that the individual members of a society should differ in their endeavours to attain these ideals according to disposition, heredity, social environment, family conditions and educational, cultural, political and social systems. Much depends on the kind of spiritual and human heritage one's country has, its distinct character, its attitude towards alien influences and the tidal waves of world culture which sweep across one's country along the course of its historical development.

The teachings of all revealed religions and the laws of all positive systems have been concerned with such differences and with individual and social behaviour, in a bid to see how far people follow the right path, abide by laws, stick to principles and keep away from deviations. This is why religious, and positive systems have legalised invitation and intimidation regulations, and reward and punishment.

Reformers and educationists have been interested in the study of human impulses and directing these impulses the right way. Lawmakers and ulemas have been preoccupied with all sorts of deviations or offences and the necessary kinds of punishment or reform.

A look into human life would reveal to us that there are different degrees of deviation ranging from incidental mistakes, temporary whims, unpremeditated faults to great sins and crimes. Sins and crimes always result from rootless faith, lack of will and the failure to observe the teachings of God. God has given sinners the chance to turn to Him for repentance and He promised to forgive them. Prophetical traditions also emphasised this and raised the hope in the sinners for God's forgiveness if they sincerely turned to Him.

There is a kind of deviation which constitutes a chronic disease forcing the deviator out of the fold of believers and making him break away with the rules of society. This kind of deviation would be manifested in one's conduct and deeds or reflected in one's disrespect of religions and social values or the renunciation of a part of these values and even the attempt to pull them down and to substitute for them false ideals as a result of one's ignorance, improper education, bad logic or sheer prejudice.

First, I should confess that contemporary Muslim youth are on the whole young men of integrity; deviation in some of them does not constitute an incurable illness. We should also admit that the response of the great majority of our young people to the teachings of religion and their observation of its rites could be easily seen in all the stages of education, in youth camps in villages, and in sports clubs. This religious tendency is exemplified in the keeness of our young people, even our children, on fasting the month of Ramadan. We can cite as other examples of moral and social maturity in our youth their seriousness, interest in national affairs, willingness to render social services to their people, and their preparedness for sacrifice in defence of their country and the liberation of the lands of Arabism and Islam.

What are the main forms of deviation in the behaviour and thinking of some of our youth? There are some types of deviation common among Muslim youth in the stages of puberty and adolescence. These include their inclination towards being aggressive, their readiness to gratify sexual desires, their occasional disrespect of public morals, their attempt to use cheat or their breach of trust, their disrespect for religious values and their blind surrender to materialistic thinking. Some of these deviations may take the form of open treason and the offer of services to their country's enemies; sometimes they would even be led to commit suicide particularly in case of despair and failure in face of seemingly unsurmountable problems.

These kinds of deviation underly different forms of behaviour and bizarre thinking conductive to the violation of the dictates of social morals and the breaking away from the values of society. Such forms of deviation emanate from a number of social and psychological factors such as the tyranny of the instincts of aggressiveness domination, possession and sex. These instincts are at their peak in the early years of youth. If they are not elevated, and sublimated they lead to aggression and assault, or to drinking, addiction, and breach of trust. Sex, for instance, is sometimes extremely dangerous when unchecked not only in the stages of early youthhood but in the later stages of life; because it plays a major role in the conflict between vice and virtue, and has a great impact on the stability or the instability of family life. Modern life with its sophistication, luxury, arts, information media, social upsurge and the divorce of daily life from religion, has added new dimensions to the problem of Sex. Unfortunately, the Muslim East has only recently stepped forward to catch up with modern times when the Western world had already outpaced it in the fields of science and art, power and political supremacy. The East could not help but imitate his Western renaissance and was unable in many cases to sort out the harmful from the useful elements nor was it able to judge this alien culture in the light of its own religion, culture and traditions. This has had its impact on the behaviour and thinking of Muslim youth; led a few of them to a state of undecidedness, shook their belief and their loyalty to their culture, and forced others to adopt an attitude of indifference and renunciation of their own values.

The teachings of Muslims (urge them) to be decent in their dress and manners, to observe moral sanctions, to cast down one's eyes and avoid flirtation with women and to be chaste; they tell them to keep away from anything that could arouse in them lust and carnal desires. These teachings view sexual relations where they should properly be gratified; that is, in the form of marriage and for bringing up children. This is not so with modern life which is brimful of all sorts of irreligious customs. Now men and women unashamedly mingle and, women and scantily dressed. Art has been exploited to evoke sexual desire and not to evoke aesthetic pleasure. Society has become indifferent to the protection of youth from these tidal waves of corruption.

What aggravates the situation is the kind of life the youth all the world over are leading. Their life is featured with restlessness, indifference, aberrations, addiction to drugs, the feeling of not belonging and the domination of violence. Their inclination towards violence has plagued societies everywhere due to the facility of the means of communications. News media daily bring to us more and more about these behaviour anomalies. Educationists, reformers and rulers are worried over the young people's violation of moral sanctions and their indifference to discipline at school and in the university. The press daily publishes studies conducted by research workers explaining these phenomena.

I do well to refer to two items of news already published in the paper; one from Washington which appeared in the Egyptian Daily "Al-Akhbar", July 15, 1969. It said that the American president called upon the Congress to take the necessary measured to curb drug addiction, which he described as constituting a threat to the health of millions of American nationals. He defined the dimensions of the problem, and pointed to the fact that the number of youth arrested for drug addiction has increased to 800% in the last 7 years. The news item also revealed a statistical report showing the astounding increase in crimes in Washington last May, crimes ranging from murder and rape to robbery and theft. The other item is a letter from London which appeared in "Al-Ahram", July 15, 1969, and entitled: "British Society Whereto, Its Youth Being Obsessed With Sex, Drug Addiction, And Violence". The letter said that the British Government, thinkers, sociologists and psychologists were preoccupied with a major problem. It is that the British society has undergone a dangerous change. It has been swept by sex shown in their films, on the T.V., performed on the stage, and openly expressed in books and given ample room in magazines. It has become a society dominated by deviation among its young men and women, not to mention the widespread addiction (to narcotics) among young people even school girls who have not passed their teens, a phenomenon worrying parents and government. No less dangerous is the problem of violence which threatens the security of young people and is reflected on their behaviour particularly in the fields where they get together in clubs and for games. A great many thinkers lay the blame on parents because they left their children have their own way in order not to be accused of being too conservative and of failing to keep abreast with modern life.

Such deviations expressed in the two news items could be easily traced in other advanced societies. Newspapers and magazines publish daily and weekly reports about them; films and books are full of them. It is natural that they could be easily communicated to our society, leaving their harmful effects on our young people. Not only are these deviations transmitted to us but also youth could be liable to their immediate effect in their original environment in other countries where they pursue their studies. There they mix with the young men and women of advanced countries and stay long enough for them to be liable to suffer from distortions into their beliefs, values and their ways of thinking. When they come back home they in turn carry these seeds of distortion to their fellow countrymen.

Other factors which would lead to deviation should also be mentioned. One of these factors is the conflicting views adopted by specialists towards some aspects of modern life and how far they agree with the teachings of religion. This is best exemplified in the fields of economic life with all its methods and institutions.

Another factor lies in the achievements of other advanced nations in the fields of sciences, invention and technology, with the resultant achievements in terms of worldly power and domination to the detriment of the spiritual values where very little attention is paid to the cultivation of religion in their young people and (and much more time is given to) indoctrinate them in the materialistic aspects of life. A number of Muslim youth who had the opportunity to study in these countries have been led astray; and they come back with much doubt and misgivings. To meet this problem, some countries brought home a number of these students and organised for them seminars where they could meet with specialists in Muslim and national studies to discuss with them their problems and questionings.

A third factor is represented by the ideologies and trends in philosophical artistic, and literary works imported from abroad carrying with them the seeds of deviation reflected in the young people's indifference towards moral values and their disrespect of religious beliefs. The young, naturally inclined to adopt what is new and exciting, find themselves vulnerable to the impact of this alien culture unless they were protected by deeply-rooted religious convictions.

Such factors have made it incumbent on us to ensure intellectual security for the protection of our youth, so that they could be spared the fancied conflict between religious preachings and life interests. We should make them aware of the fact the Islam, the (religion of Allah is easy; it is) far from being a set of dogmas as it is the religion of all times and places, and that Islamic law is both original and flexible. It is not against progress, but it enjoins Muslims against corruption and urges the mind to inquire into the nature of things and the study of changing conditions.

The long history of human experience and the study of different educational systems have proved that the revealed religion is the only system that can combine the light of knowledge both the power of belief and the warmth of faith. which can give integrity to human personality, and maintain the strength of morale in society. If religion is properly understood and practised, it would be the basis of knowledge and social life. From its integral system emanate not only the principles of human morals but all the laws determining the relations between individuals and peoples. Thus, the maintenance of virtue and the abandonment of vice would be nothing other than a manifestation of abiding by religious teachings and constitute forms of worship bringing youth nearer to God.

Tracing the history of Islamic civilisation and the study of its achievements through the ages would emphasise the face that Arab efflorescence in the golden ages was due to Islam, and that our cultural traditions, our moral and psychological existence were greatly affected by religion. The need of our young people for a religious and spiritual revival to develop their personalities and to guide their conduct is no less necessary than their need for science and learning to help them build cities and towns and promote, industry, agriculture and economy. In order that religion could play its role in protecting young people from deviation, it should have the place it used to occupy in the glorious days of Islam when it breathed life in thought and beaconed humanity along the road of progress.

The comprehensive educational system was put into effect fourteen centuries ago and it met with success when it was properly applied. The effect of this success could be evident in the strength of the structure of Islamic society and the affluence it attained. History had proved that Muslims never failed unless they were unable to put into effect this educational system as the basis for bringing up their young people. The reformation and protection of youth from deviation lie in practising the teaching of our religion and the cultivation of religious values in the minds and hearts of our young people. These principles should be the basis of youth education all through the various stages of development. We should also protect them from everything that weakens their religious sensibility—they should be brought up in a suitable social setting where righteouness and purity rank highest and dig into our history for the Muslim hero representing Muslim glory, virtue and learning as the ideal to be followed by our youth. We should also help them by an unceasing and enlightened endeavour to dispel every shadow of doubt and restlessness of thought.

Where do we stand now? How far has modern Muslim society succeeded in following this heavenly system, and how far has it adopted its programme as the basis of protection from deviation and as the best measure for psychological health?

To answer this question we should conduct a comprehensive and thorough study of modern Muslim societies and communities in all their varying degrees of liberalism, progress and development, their political, social, and cultural struggle and their relations with modern civelised communities.

We do well to confine ourselves in this study to the study of the conditions of youth in the Egyptian society because it represents the centre of the Arab and Muslim world and because what is going on in the Egyptian society may have a bearing on the Muslim world as a whole.

In this country the majority of people believe in Islam. Egyptian scholars have had a long and fine record in Islamic studies. Since our modern awakening we have been trying our best so that Islamic values should remain the source of inspiration and the guidelines of our actions. Religious educational programmes have been always the basis of our educational system, propagated by information media and discussed in seminars organised by our rising generations. Our ulemas have taken upon themselves the responsibility of curing the ills of modern society and setting right its modern systems on Islamic basis. Our library daily receives new researches and dissertations which explain our cultural traditions, deal with problematic questions, criticise society and work out means for social reform. The fact that the Islamic Research Academy is preoccupied in its present conference with the problems of Muslim youth deviations, under the present conditions of an atrocious war of destinies is no more than an aspect of the interest in the application, of Islamic teachings and the deep awareness of the various weapons and the broad dimensions of the present battle.

Muslim youth, as I have already stated, are on the whole young people of integrity but they are subject to various types of deviations. As we have touched upon some of these deviation and pointed out the most sections of those social diseases, we should then try to translate this into a working philosophy, part of which should be dedicated to the environment and a part to the individual himself, though it is not easy to divorce the one from the other.

The close relation between the child and his environment starts as early as babyhood. In this stage the child comes to it equipped with his instincts, natural tendencies and heredity. The Prophet (peace and blessing of Allah be upon him) pointed to this relation when he said: "Select (fit) women (in respect of character) for your seed for ancestry is hard to detect". The Qur'an also testified: "And of His signs is this: He created for you helpmates from yourselves that ye might find rest in them, and He ordained between you love and mercy." (Surah, the Romans, 21). The respect of husband and wife for marital relations in the light of the Qur'an and their adherence to virtue have their impact on their offspring. The Prophet, referring to this relation said: "Would one of you go into his wife he should say: "In the Name of Allah O Allah, protect us from the devil, and protect that which Thou grantest us," then it offspring is decreed for them, it (the devil) will not harm it".

Islam's interest in establishing sound family relations is well-explained in the Qur'an and Hadith (Prophetical Traditions).

Educational and psychological studies have emphasised the importance of family environment on child personality and the way he is going to behave in future when he grows up. Hence comes the importance of religious education at home. Parents and grown ups should be devoted to their religion. They should practise their religious rites, keep away from sins, abide by virtue and decency, ensure security and kindness for their children, educate them, cultivate in them the basic teachings of their religion in a way suitable for their ages and instill in them the seeds of faith and belief.

As he grows up the child leaves the family environment for school. School and society will have their influence on the development of his personality and his attitude towards social and moral values. In this stage, education, religious instruction, moral example, social conditions and patterns of public life, all affect the young in different ways. Their ability to adapt themselves to the new environment is determined by natural instincts, hereditary and family background.

The growing-up children become distinctly different from one another in their behaviour and thought; they experience varying types of aberration and deviation which necessitate special care and treatment. These kinds of deviation are at their strongest in the stages of puberty and adolescence. In these stages they are in need of special religious education, suitable social setting and psychological care.

The cultivation of religion is essential to the growing-up child to awaken his conscience and go deep into his inmost soul, to arouse his sense of religion, to bind him with spiritual preachings and to bring him nearer to God through the study and learning of the Qur'an and following the teachings of the Prophet and his companions. They should be urged to keep in touch with authentic Islamic texts that help develop the right attitude towards life. The young should also be introduced to the basic principles of religion, the outstanding landmarks of the history and civilisation of the Muslim nation and the role it has played in the progress of humanity.

This kind of up bringing should necessarily be based on a careful drawn up educational and psychological programme. The Educational staff should set a good example to be followed by the young people. Schools, institutes and young centres should be equipped with all facilities to enable the young people to perform their religious rites. They should be taught to observe Islamic festivities.

To secure a suitable social environment for our Muslim youth necessitates from the government and individuals alike to observe public manners, wipe out moral and social corruption and purify arts, in all their forms, songs, motion pictures and literature, from all element that weaken the personalities of youth, excite their physical desires, and lead them to deviation. Scholars and those in authority should do their utmost to adopt religious principles as the basis of life in all its political, social and economic aspects, and to strengthen the nation, shedding light on its glorious history, with the purpose of making young people renounce subservient imitation of alien cultures and of their being proud of belonging to their nation.

Psychological care should aim at understanding young people and recognising the typical characteristics of their development in the various stages of growth, in order to help them solve their problems and get over their psychological and intellectual crises, and give them the chance to debate religious matters and intellectual questions related to life and death, extinction and immortality, matter and spirit, resurrection, reward and retribution, heavenly messages, human development and political and social systems.

Religious education, suitable social environment and psychological care, all grouped together, would protect the youth from the different types of deviation. And it is clear that the most important element of this protective programme is the cultivation of religious education in young people since babyhood that is capable of offering nourishment to emotions and developing in their conscience, devotion and self-control.

Through observation it has been established that the child who is brought up in a family where the Qur'an is recited, religious rites are practised, and a life of decency and virtue is led, could be more immune to all diseases of behaviour and through when he grows up. As he steps towards youthhood, he could exercise self-control, and never allow himself to be the slave of passion and carnal desires. This fact is also proved by Islamic researches and moral and educational studies. I do well to mention in this context one of the Muslim leading thinkers, namely, Imam Al-Ghazali who adopted religious principles as the basis of the educational programme. He referred to this is almost all his writings and particularly in his book entitled. "The Revival of Religious Science", (Ihia's Ulum Al-Din), wherein he dedicated a whole chapter to means whereby young people could exercise self-control as early as babyhood. Al-Ghazali said: "Parents are entrusted with bringing up the child whose pure heart is a priceless gem. He is vulnerable to all dictations, subject to all inclinations. If he gets used to doing good, and if he taught how to do it, it becomes a habit with him enabling him to be happy in life and after-life. Before reaching his teens, a child should be rebuked if he neglected prayers, and he should be ordered to fast some days during the fasting month of Ramadan. If deviation befell him in this stage of life, he would find protection in his religion whose teachings had already been inscribed into his heart as ineffaceable inscriptions engraved upon stones. And if he got used to deviation to the extent that he became corrupt, gluttonous, and boastful, his heart would never stick to right as walls would not hold to dry dust."

Some of the youth of past generations had a spiritual awareness which controlled their behaviour, an awareness that grew from their interest at home and in public life, in religious teachings, in the learning by heart of verses of the Qur'an and parts of the Prophetical traditions, in reading into Islamic culture and literature and in attending religious sermons and Arabic lessons at Al-Azhar and its institutions and in the various mosques along our villages and towns. When these young people were sent abroad and came into direct contact with European civilisation, they could resist temptations and find in their religious background a protection from deviation of thought and behaviour. And if they were sometimes subject to deviation they reasoned it out and turned to God for repentance. Only in this way were they protected from deviation and recklessness which befell those indifferent to religious teachings.

It is worthy of recording that the our society is trying to inculcate into our young people such religious values through the relay of religious programmes, the organisation of seminars on all national occasions and religious festivities, and the publication of simplified books explaining religious matters and Islamic legislation. By so doing we could protect our youth from deviation. And this system of education should be intensified as the only way to bring up Muslim youth here and elsewhere in modern Islamic societies.

The young people who devote themselves to religion, who practise its rites, who are described in the Qur'an as the "slaves of God, Most Merciful, in Surahs, "The Believers," and "She Is To Be Examined", and who follow the Prophet, peace and blessings of Allah be upon him, along the path of good conduct and deep faith, could lead a life of integrity were they to be brought up in such a favourable atmosphere. They would never be led astray, and they would set an example of how a good Muslim should be, a good Muslim who should obey God, defend his country, maintain good relations with his neighbours, make friends with others and do not harm to anybody.

After this sketch of some of the characteristics of youth, their development problems, some of their deviations of thought and behaviour and the role religious could play in protecting them, I may suggest the following recommendations:

I. The evolving of our religious education systems in all Islamic societies to be in harmony with modern life. As a result the mosque should be given its proper place as a centre of religious enlightenment and cultural and spiritual guidance. Youth should be encouraged to study and hold in high esteem their Islamic culture as it has originally been. We should draw their interest to religious books and pay more attention to educational and psychological studies on their problems and particularly in the stage of puberty.

II. We should call upon those in authority to do their best to make people observe public manners and practise the teachings of religion. They should take drastic measures to fight corruption which leads to deviation, mobilise all information media in all their different forms, books, papers, magazines, radio and T.V., to help in the guidance of youth, and avoid all that which would excite their instincts.

III. The Scientific circles should be their best to harmonize religious principles and systems of life in modern Islamic societies, and conciliate these systems to Islamic law. Islamic research scholars should trace imported ideas and ideologies which may tend to weaken the fervour of religious emotion in Muslim youth of shake their faith in their culture. The falsity of many of these ideas should be laid bare. This would ensure that our youth could be led along the right path, the path of Allah, who alone possess Heavens and Earth.

(Revised and edited)

8

Religion and the Youth

ABDULLAH KNOUN

The heading of the topic draws our attention to a thorny and grave problem that is too complicated and many-sided to be exhaustively dealt with in one single session, however long it may last.

Its complexity is due to the fact that considerable number of our youth have grown indifferent to religion. Hence, if you were to talk to a young man about religious matters, he would immediately think that you are making allusion to him and that you are intruding upon his own private affairs. He would become haughty and scornful, and then he would turn away from you. In certain cases, you might be confronted with what is distasteful and embarrassing to you.

Such is what these discussions would amount to, had the person, in question, not rejected religion altogether, and become boastful of being an atheist. In the latter case, he would be so roused as to cry out exasperation. Then, there would be no end to his violent outbursts and insolent retorts.

The issue is undoubtedly grave and perplexing, as it is entirely bound up with the future of the Community, since the youth and the rising generation constitute more than half the total number of Muslims. With the persistence of this trend in which the hold of Islam becomes increasingly shaken amongst the youth, there would hardly be anyone profession belief in God, after one or two generations.

The problem is many-sided, and as such, it required, to be fully dealt with, a precise definition of what is meant by the word "youth". The term is, of course, used, respecting the really full-grown; but it is also loosely applied, either to those nearing that stage from amongst the young, or to those approaching old age, who, so long as they are clean-snaven, push themselves into youth's ranks; so that they might be taken as belonging to them. This means that some of the old people or those who are considered as such, still retain youth's levity and light-mindedness.

Also does the full investigation of the problem require dealing with the religious attitude of all these sorts of people. We have to consider, as well, what is intended by religion in this connexion. Does it refer to a body of beliefs, to good works, or to both? All these points, which would extend the range of our discussion, might touch the feelings of a considerable number of people, to whom we do only wish welfare and moral uplift.

Therefore, we have to confine ourselves to what is positive and relevant to our topic without implying any disgrace or discredit. Our approach is just to make a bare exposition of the problem, and the formulation of an appropriate method, showing how to cope with it.

Let us suppose the concept of the two terms: "religion", and "youth", to be well-known to us, fully grasped, admitted, and needing no expounding nor explanation. There will remain with us the conjunction "and", joining the two terms together.

The problem is, thus, set; and its various aspects and dimensions are made clear in our minds. Hence, we have to direct our discussion towards the topic formed out of the combination of these two terms, and to avoid dealing with each apart from the other.

What we have to refer to, at outset, might be the fact that the issue, concerning youth in general, is markedly an universal problem, not specifically confined to the attitude of Muslim youth towards religion. The revolt that was tired up by the French youth in the spring of 1968, and was on the point of overthrowing the regime in France, had wide-spread echoes all over the world, where it was met with the response of youth in a considerable number of countries, including those of the Orient.

It is to be remarked that the outbreak of this revolt took place in university circles, and among the students of higher institutes. Then, it embodied the adolescents whose indignation was so vehement as to make them rebel against usages, and all sorts of ethical and social conventions.

There is at present a feature quite common in many countries, where you see hosts of young men who have become inclined to levity, and taken as their distinctive mark the loosening of their hair and dress in a shocking way.

As to the group of young men called "Hippies", they have bypassed that stage, and indulged in certain coarse obscenities. They have become addicted to narcotics, and pursued the practice of all sorts of depravity; thereby challenging their elders, and the usages of the society to which they belong, through their peculiarities, and frivolous behaviour they are merely expressing their contempt of all moral principles and human values.

The starting-point of such laxity among present-day youth is their rejection of all the established traditions and rules of public morality they found their fathers had been adopting, and which had been obtained in their environments. It is to be noted that such norms are the groundwork of modern civilization, and are not confined to religion, as supposed by the minority of our youth.

According to the viewpoint of present-day youth, religion is a nugatory trend they have been brought up to dismiss in anticipation; because their elders used to consider religion as something impracticable. Those elders had, for long, been shaking it off; thereby paving the way for the present attitude towards religion, as indicated in the youth's entire rejection of everything that is virtuous and righteous.

Such is the issue that is arousing our deep anxiety about the future of our Muslim youth amongst whom have become widely-spread, at present, atheistic trends which would cause far-reaching catastrophes and reverses to Muslim society, the grave consequences of which more none would ever know, save the Almighty.

This will certainly take place once the younger generation has been reared in the moral atmosphere of the present-day youth. Then, the new-comers will lack any restraint or deterrent imposed by religion and morality, and withholding them from relapsing in to the savagery for which had been noted the primeval usages of the Jahiliyyah (= the Days of Ignorance).

Yet, it is fair to admit the fact that youth, throughout the ages and in all countries, have always been given care and guidance, because of their inclination to act on instinctive impulse, to which a certain Arab poet referred by saying:

"If Aamer uttered anything out of folly, the motive for such impetuosity would certainly be the buoyancy and vigour of youth".

It is a commonplace remark that the youth have always been notorious for the frailty and flimsiness of their religious beliefs and practice; a trait that has been tolerated owing to the hope that with the advance of age, and the attainment of mature manhood, they would reconsider their views and rectify their attitude...

Had the Prophetic tradition not counted "the young man who had been brought up in the worship of God as one of the seven whom God had accorded protection, when there would be no refuge but His"?

This is due to the fact that such sort of youth is quite unusual and rare in accordance with the common run of young people.

The Prophet (P.B.U.H) is also reported to have said: "Your Lord had wondered at a young man who had been lacking youthful propensities". It is further assertion of the above-mentioned view that the youth are naturally swayed by passions, and cannot adopt right conduct, save after the lapse of sometime.

Such has surely been the bearing of young men and their attitude towards religion. Hence, we cannot hope that they be more righteous nor more religious, at the present time, especially when they are overwhelmed from all directions by queer ideologies and atheistic doctrines under the guise of scientific truth and free inquiry.

Modern technology, with its wonderful discoveries and inventions, has made the confusion worse confounded, because it has shaken to the core the Faith of young men, and nothing did it produce but psychical perplexities, mental restlessness and spiritual vacuum.

It is certainly a novel and unnatural feature. Yet, if youth's bearing, as previously described, be deemed inevitable owing to the vehemence of their passions during maturity, which rendered them excusably by the Shari'at, the issue proves to be quite dissimilar to the phenomenon, in questions, which is considered as one of the psychological ailments and social evils which has broken out amongst the youth on a large scale, owing to wanton neglect and failure to adopt the appropriate cure.

Therefore, we are facing a grave responsibility the greater part of which falls upon educational authorities which have to make plans for the building up of Muslim personality, in a way as to be well-adapted to the genuine spirit of scientific culture, and the same norms of modern civilization.

Thus, before striving to perform out duty towards our youth, it would be quite unfair to be prejudiced against them, and to heap reproaches upon them, because of their straying from true religion. We have to hold fast to the Book, before allowing the mainspring of the issue to slip from our hands.

In fact, Islam had made so deep an impact upon human culture as to realize, for the first time in history, such as well-balanced harmony between science and religion. It is to its credit that the belief in the existence of God has survived even in non-Muslim societies.

We have only to recall, in this respect, what had been written by Ibn Rushed (520-595 A.H.) (known in medieval Europe by the name Averrhoes), to prove the concord of religion with philosophy. His writings had exerted a great influence on Maimonides (1135-1204 A.D.), and later, on Saint Thomas Aquinas (1225?-1274 A.D.).

How is it possible, then, that the Muslim youth undergo such psychical disorders, and suffer so grievously from spiritual vacuum as to be tempted to indulge in sheer materialism, whilst their illustrious thinkers and philosophers of old had prescribed, hundreds of years ago, the cure that is most specific for the preservation and the maintenance of their Religious Faith?

The remissness is unquestionable our fault. But worse would be the outcome the more there would be delay in warding off the peril and in extirpating the evil, before these would come to be overwhelming.

Up to quite a recent time, Muslim philosophy has been studied in our institutes alongside ancient philosophy, since the latter came in touch with the World of Islam, during the movement of translation that took place in the second (and the third) century of the Hijrah.

No sooner had the works of ancient philosophers been rendered into Arabic than the heresies and atheistic trends they embodied were refuted by our scholars; a task they had so admirably carried out that (a later) writer (following in the footsteps of his predecessors), criticized certain false doctrines in a book he gave the sensational title: "Ijtima' al-Juyush al-Islamiyyah fi Ghazw al-Mu'attilah wal-Fahmyyah" (=The Mustering of Islamic Armies to Overcome Those Who Divest God of what Pertains to Him, And The Adherents of Fahm ibn Safwan).

Muslim scholars spared no pains in striving to preserve the Islamic creed. All the gaps that incited doubt and bewilderment in the minds of Muslims, through the study of ancient philosophy, had been dealt with by working out a counterbalancing Islamic philosophy which they called 'Ilm Al-Kalam, the science of theology or 'Ilm al-Tawhid, the science of God's Unity. Also had they worked out a science of ethics which came to be known as Sufism.

This had taken place when philosophical doctrines had only few problems to deal with. But much more would have been handled, once the scope of philosophical research has been widely extended, and novel systems of thought have been worked out, most of which are entirely materialistic.

Yet it is much regretted that we have not done anything in this field, since in our countries had been established numerous institutes and faculties where our sons (and daughters) are initiated into theories and ideas about ontology, the nature of the universe and philosophy of life.

As a result of such initiation, a group of them tended to deify science, and another to be agnostics. Anyhow they no longer have any faith in the ideals of Muslim ethics and morality which came to be looked upon with contempt and ridicule. Were there ideals to be moderately criticized, they would be dubbed as reactionary tendencies, backwardness, or obscurantism.

Yet in order to be fair, we have to admit that advocates of reform have spared no effort in confronting these challenges. So much had they been refuting the allegations levelled against Islam, is Shari'at, and ideals that their writings form a monumental corpus known to have greatly enriched modern Islamic thought. Thus, Islam came to be entrenched in a well-fortified position, provided with the competence of give and take, and rendered immune against any shock or relapse.

Nevertheless, it can be said, from an official standpoint that we have not yet introduced the study of Islam as a philosophy, system of thought, and a way of life, into our educational programmes. We still cast our children into foreign schools where they are taught by non-Muslim teachers, unqualified to impart any creed other than their own, if they had any. How would it be the case, were they downright atheists?

This takes place while we are neglecting to provide our children with sound religious education. Neither do we instruct them in the articles of the Muslim Faith, and the history of their illustrious ancestors who had made admirable contributions in learning and culture. No doubt then that we have done wrong to them, and made way for the deviations of which we, at present, bitterly complain.

This holds true respecting the system of public education which is in charge of instructing millions of pupils and students. As to students in religious schools, though decreasing in number day after day, the educational policy in force, as regard the primary stage is to cram the prescribed subject-matter with data that are too numerous for pupils to grasp or to recollect.

Thus, the boy who has not yet reached the age of puberty is still instructed in the fully-detailed rules of ritual purity, worship, zakat, fasting, and pilgrimage, as if he were going to be at come graduated as an imam qualified to conduct prayers in a mosque, or as a mufti, competent to give legal decisions in a certain town.

For instance, he studies more than sixteen acts and defile ritual ablution such as micturition, emission of wind, incontinence of urine, prostatic secretions touching and kissing (people of the other sex); a besides the rules respecting unmindfulness which are scarcely fully recapitulated by well-versed faqihs.

Şimilarly, the zakat is fully dealt with. In it are studied the nisab, stock, kinds of property, merchandise, and monopoly that are subject to the legal impost, the various rates to be applied, the assessment in case of debts, etc.

Thus, is aroused in our young pupil's strong aversion to what we think to be the entire fundamentals of the Islamic Religion.

In this preliminary stage of religious education, we should have instilled into their hearts deep affection for the faith, and developed their religious sentiments by acquainting them with the merits of Islam, and its praiseworthy traits. It would have only sufficed to teach the bare rules of 'ibadat, religious ordinances according to which the performance of worship is to be considered as valid; as had been done by the Prophet (P.B.U.H.) who used to instruct the unbelievers in the modalities of worship, besides the other Islamic injunctions without any further details.

No more was required of these sane adult unbelievers who had been so close to the paganism of the Jahiliyyah, just before their convertion to Islam. But the case of our children is quite different.

As to our pupils, we find that they have to grasp an extensive syllabus, embodying principles and branches of Muslim learning which are too numerous to be calculated. In one sole manual of "fiqh", jurisprudence, from amongst their prescribed school-books, there are one hundred thousand postulates and problems expressly stated; besides others, equal in number which are implied. Yet, this manual is called a summary.

Pupils, however, are not afforded any studies in the spirit of Islam, its Message to mankind, the political and social reforms it had introduced, and the part it is expected to perform to save humanity from darkness and oppression. Even the graduates who had mastered the prescribed courses do not believe in their adequacy, save those who had completed their studies and acquired more competence in Muslim learning through their own personal efforts.

This is an issue we ought to reflect upon very carefully. We have to recall, in this connexion, the well-known aphorism of Imam Malik in which he said: "Never can the later generations of this Community be reformed save by what had been effectual in reforming their predecessors." It is a maxim the purport of which still holds true after the lapse of twelve centuries.

Hence, if we want to be fully assured about the future of Islam by saving our youth from bewilderment and straying, and guiding them to rightousness, we have to introduce the study of Islam in the sense we have already stated, into all our educational programmes from primary up to higher schools.

Moreover, let us renounce the Western secular trends, and the cult of materialism. Also should we put an end to the attempts in which we seek to reconcile the religious minorities living in our midst, whose demands we have always been hastening to satisfy, until they were accorded a semi-trusteeship to which we have to conform.

Nevertheless, the issue, respecting the majority of Muslim youth who had completed the primary courses in foreign schools which lack any curricula for religious education, is nothing but a work of rescue, the outcome of which would hardly be satisfactory, owing to the difficulty of making any appreciable change in a young man's outlook, conformably to the Arabic proverb which says: "'Amr has grown up".

Thus, the youth who had developed his ideas, and built up his own personality is no longer manageable, even if the directions were exerted by his own family. Scarcely would he be convinced; and any conversation with him would be without avail.

Hence, we should have recourse to other means which prove to be more effectual.

The practical plan which is expected to realize positive results in directing our youth towards Islam, is to start from the years of primary education, going gradually from the simple to the complex, from inculcation and suggestion to instruction, and the solving of problems.

These steps are to be accelerated in subsequent stages until the youth imbibe guidance and the true knowledge of their Faith. Thus, would they be rendered immune against adverse intellectual trends arising from here and there.

I should like to relate, in this connexion, for mere consideration, that I had once been in Spain. My visit to the town of Granada happened to be on Monday which is the weekly holiday of the Spanish newspapers. There was only one which was issued on that day, and called "The Monday Paper", a copy of which I got to have a look at the news.

But there did. I find a small supplement for children, containing a lengthy article covering almost the whole of the front-page, and entitled.

"Muhammad, The False Prophet".

The article was written in a very simple style, but fall a mockery and contempt. The main theme was based on the writer's assertion that the Quran contains distorted quotations drawn from the Old and New Testaments, because Muhammad, its author—an alleged by the writer—had been illiterate, and that he gathered what he had heard from the Jews who had, then, been residing in the Arabian peninsula, and from the monks whom he happened to meet, during his journeys to Syria.

Such is how Christians initiate their offspring, during their tender age, into the articles of the Christian Faith. This is to say: Catholic Spain still pursues in Granada its fanatically religious campaign against Islam, even in children's newspapers, many centuries after it had driven away its adherents from their last stronghold (in the Iberian peninsula).

Thus veraciously said the Prophet (P.B.U.H.), "Every infant is born according to the fitrah, the pattern (or constitution whereon God hath constituted mankind), then his parents make him a Jew or a Christian or a Magian".

If what has, hitherto, been mentioned is only related to those in charge of working out educational programmes, it must not be understood that they are the only people answerable for the wrong tendencies of the youth, and the waning of their religious beliefs. Public authorities have full share of responsibility in this respect.

Were they to fail in the performance of their duty, the whole efforts of educationists would be without avail. In olden times, it was said: "God refraineth (man from wrong—doing) through governmental action, much more than through (the sole guidance of) the Quran".

Reference has already been made to the influence exerted in the connexion by the religious minorities in certain Muslim countries. I should like to dwell further upon this point, considered to be the source of the grave reverses that had befallen the World of Islam. This is due to the fact that these religious minorities—though accorded all the rights with which no other religious minority is privileged in any non-Muslim country—could never be satisfied unless they control the government machinery and take part in the formulation of the constitutional laws, so as to acquire full sway over the countries to which they belong.

We even find in the constitutions of certain Muslim countries that the article specifying that the religion of the State is Islam had been crossed out for the sake of reconciling the dominating religious minority. This feature which shows the majority's subservience to the minority has no parallel in any other (non Muslim) country.

No mention, in this connexion, is made here about the important Muslim minorities in India, China, and the Soviet Union. But suffice it to refer to the Catholic minority in the United Kingdom (of Great Britain and Northern Ireland) which amounts to several millions.

Yet no one among these did ever aspire to dominate the Protestant majority, in a way identical with that prevailing in the Muslim countries. For instance, never has the British Catholic minority opposed the oath of allegiance to the Anglican Church a British Sovereign is required to take on his or her accession to the throne. The same holds true, respecting the religious minorities of Germany, Switzerland, and other European countries.

Our statesmen have gone to such great lengths in reconciling the religious minorities as to cede the majority's right in the defence and preservation of its Faith. Nay, they had, even, cancelled some of that Faith's ordinances.

Conformably to the principle requiring laws to be formulated in accordance with the article of the constitution, the abrogation of the article, specifying that the religion of the State is Islam, entailed the relinquishment of drawing civil and penal laws from the ordinances of Muslim Jurisprudence.

Thus had been offset the principles of Islamic law; and Muslims came to be ruled by the foreign codes which had been introduced into their countries; a state of affairs considered to be the worst sort of oppression. It is as if France were to be governed by Italian laws or vice versa; despite the great similarities between these two (Latin) countries.

This innovation had, even, been introduced, through imitation, into Muslim countries with no religious minorities. So, therein, had the restraints of the Shari'at been abolished. Disregard of the Islamic ordinances had, thus, become a feature, identical with what is obtaining in countries containing religious minorities where it is hardly possible to distinguish between Muslim and non-Muslims.

No doubt these novel institutions exercise a baneful influence on youth's morality, and that of society at large. Speedy disruption is the fate of the countries that had been subjected to foreign rule. Indeed the decline and collapse that had befallen Islamic society within forty years, shortly after the first World War, had, hitherto, had nọ parallel. Nobody did ever expect such degeneration in Muslim countries which was entirely due to foreign domination throughout that period.

Family bonds which had been held in great sanctity were ruptured. Chaste women have gone out in the streets making a wanton display of their charms and beauty; thereby challenging the teachings of the Quran which prohibit such a show to strangers (other than their close relations).

Trading in alcoholic drinks and addiction to them have become too common (to attract and notice). Probibited brothers, public dancing halls, and gambling-houses, having been made open, and licenced by Muslim Government. In this way, Muslim society which had long been a model of holding fast to virtue, and keeping away from immorality, has turned, within a short while, into a den of vice and depravity.

This is evidently due to the fact that the laws which are, at present, in operation, no longer consider these acts as punishable, nor do they contain any deprecatory remarks about them; thought they are held to be enormities, according to Islamic law.

Hardly would it be possible to introduce any reform and to lead our youth to the right path, save by going back to our exalted Shari'at from which we can draw right decisions, and prescrible effective cures to our society. Such task would never be too arduous to accomplish, where we to resolve unanimously upon coping with these issues, and to take the initiative in leadership from these minorities which only desire our ruin, and would never be satisfied unless we follow their creed.

This is one point; but still there is another which is no less important, though nobody is to be held answerable for it. It dates from the rule of despotic regimes, when we, all had arisen, claiming to be accorded freedom of thought, freedom of speech, etc., which we deemed as the sole means of salvation.

Yet, in accordance with our want, we have outstripped all bounds, as regards these freedoms, especially in matters, closely related to our Faith, morals, and spiritual principles. Although it is alleged that law has imposed certain limits upon these public liberties (that is to say they should not be inconsistent with public public order and public morality), they are, in fact, untrammelled by all the established social restraints that had, hitherto, been in force.

According to the provisions of the law, freedom of religion and freedom of thought are guaranteed to all individuals. The former sort of liberty signifies the citizen's right to believe in any creed or doctrine without being interfered with by public authorities.

But there is here a clash with the recognized law of Islam,

respecting the Muslim who abjures his religion. Though the Shari'at has accorded non-Muslim who are subject to Islamic rule, the free exercise (whether public or private) of their creeds, it has categorically prohibited the apostasy of the Muslim, and decreed a severe punishment, in case such a crime be committed.

Them how do we tolerate no limits to that sort of freedom, and encourage deviators and *waverers*to toy with religion which we have to defend and safeguard against profanation of sacrilege?

Moreover this freedom affords the widest scope for the efforts made by the Christian missionaries who captivate the common people by various mean such as medical services acts of charity etc. They may deceive the youth through offering general courses of study, teaching foreign languages and travelling abroad.

Thus, the one who is a believer at morning time might turn into an unbeliever in the evening, as had been said by the Prophet (P.B.U.H) in a well authenticated tradition.

In this way inroads are made in Muslim territories, and the campaigners are left unhindered because they pursue their activities within the limits specified by the law of the State.

No mention is here made about the political consequences resulting from the aggravation of the missionary movement as is especially witnessed in certain African States.

As to the second sort of freedom entitling individuals to express their opinions and feelings without being interfered with by public authorities, it comprises freedom.of speech writing publication, and other means of communication. No doubt it caused considerable evils to Muslim society, because it allowed anyone to say whatever he likes.

Thus, the press publishers articles by writers who deprecate Islamic customs and morals. Such writers have gone to the extent of criticising beliefs and sacred traditions in the name of the above-mentioned freedom. Equally are issued books disparaging Islam its history and leading personalities without ever being censored. Nay, some of these books had been prescribed in educational programmes.

A number of such books written by an Egyptian Christian had been chosen as readers for secondary schools in a certain Muslim country.. In justifying that choice, it was claimed that the author is a leading thinker and an advocate of free thought, and as such is he considered in Egypt.

Yet, it is to be remarked that whenever the author, in question, wrote an article deprecating religion and sacred traditions, he used to write another quite contrary to the former so as to be published in the Christian review entitled al-Manarakal-Masihiyyah" the Christian LIghthouse which is issued by the Coptic Church in Egypt.

Nobody did ever unmask such double-faced mode of action to let people know the real worth and hypocrisy of that author who is considered by fools as a leading thinker and an advocate of free thought.

What has been said about the press and literature is equally true, as regards the movies broadcasting the television where are shamelessly shown to the public scenes of nudity courtship and effeminancy the evil effects of which on the youth and the adolescents nobody can afford to ignore.

All these and much more have been committed (with impunity) in the name of what is termed as freedom of opinion which is fully guaranteed by law. How then can we aspire to maintain the significance and worth of religion and to cultivate to our youth some sort of religiousness and devotion to their Faith, especially in this atmosphere in which religious beliefs and virtues and discarded and renounced?

In objecting to our statements someone might ask: "So long as you are finding fault with the law of public liberties would you want it to be repeated so that we might go back to the despotic rule of the old regimes?"

It is only in fact that I seek the preservation of the Community's Faith, the rectification of youth's errors, the building up a Muslim society, that is distinguished for the full sway of virtue and adherence to the rule of enjoining what is right, and forbidding what is wrong; since conformity to such a rule has rendered Muslims the best Community that has ever been raised up for mankind.

In this way, would be realized the Message Islam had commanded us to convey, as stated by God, Glory be to Him in His Saying: "Thus have We made of you a justly balanced Community that ye might be witnesses over the nations, and the Apostle a witness over yourselves (II, 143).

Such are the moral censors watching over the human conscience, and the spiritual guardians who guide mankind to the right path, so as to safeguard the supreme values and ideals against depravation and debasement.

If the law of public liberties or any other law were to be consistent with these noble aims, how excellent that would be! Otherwise, these laws have to be repealed without being affected with any sense of regret.

It is to be remarked that the abrogation of such laws had been made more often than not by countries which claim to be popular and progressive. Yet, the considerations for the sake of which laws had been repealed were never of greater weight nor higher merit than the aims which we have already mentioned.

Such considerations were merely based on the desire to suppress anything proving to be prejudicial to the policies of these countries, or to foil the attempts of some of their influential peoples to wield despotic authority. "But, verily, remembrance of God is more important. And God knoweth what ye do". (XXIX, 45).

(Revised and edited)

9

Belief Among Youth

D. IBRAHIM AL-LABBAN

Youth is one of the successive stages of a person's life. He passes from childhood to youth; and from there to manhood, middle age, and old age. If we examine this long journey, we find that youth is the stage most abundant in physical, mental and spiritual experiences which have been the interest and concern of psychologists, biologists, as well as men of religion. The child leads a quiet life of calm stability and obedience. He accepts matters as they stand, and submits to the authority of parents and teachers, from whom he receives his ideas, knowledge, and religious education without much argument. At the stage of manhood, the person gradually moves to a stage of relative stability. His views, ideas, and habits gradually take a certain pattern; which he usually retains throughout the long journey of his life. Midway along this long road is youth which begins with adolescence, adulthood, them maturity. To the careful examiner, it seems to be a stage rich in physical, psychological and religious experiences. It is during this stage, that a person's religious and non-religious fate is determined.

The Religious Problem of Youth

We cannot understand the religious difficulties experienced by youth during this stage, without a general consideration of the radical change; which the person undergoes during this stage. We sill concern ourselves here with two important matters: the first being the careful scientific approach to the situation. Fortunately psychology, like other sciences of life, has adequately studied this stage of life. The findings of these studies have shed clear light on the mental changes, and developments which youth undergo during this stage, thus enabling educators, physicians, and men of religion to solve many *educational*, religious and medical problems. Our second guiding principal in this study will not be to prope into its various aspects, overlooking our definite aim—the religious aspect alone.

What does science—and psychology in particular—say about the subject?

Youth is ushered in with an overwhelming eruption of all the components of human nature. Body, mind and emotion abruptly rise from their long *dormant* state in childhood to affect rapid leaps in all directions. The quite, calm and tender child, obedient to his parents and teachers soon disappears giving way to a tall, wiry, sharp-eyed intelligent, hot-blooded youth rebelling against every authority and control, event that of parents and school. We had been ignorant of these phenomena until psychologists studied them, thereby uneveiling their nature causative factors and future. We will here refer briefly to the main aspects of this change unless they are closely related to the religious side.

Among the first thing noted by psychologists in their study of the changes that occur during youth were the many rapid almost abrupt physical changes, the first of which is the sudden increase in height. The short plump child rapidly shoots up into man's height, and hair grows on various parts of his body. His new moustache and hot-blood, mark the beginning of the journey.

The sex instinct makes its first move in a chain of physical and psychological phenomena, controlling a considerable part of the thoughts, feeling and emotions. Our main concern here is the psychological changes, the mental and spiritual changes in particular. In general, we can state that an equally violent psychological change occurs, unleaching the child's various talents and abilities, and in a short time the youth attains the high standard usually characteristic of youth.

In youth, emotions shed their previous slackness and assume

a kind of new activity characterized with acuteness and violence, covering a wide range. In the family circle, the youth's emotions change, turning from the parents to a person from the same sex, and shortly to one of the opposite sex, in preparation for forming a new family. The emotional phenomenon which is hailed by both educators and men of religion is thc development of ethical and moral sentiments. At this stage, the youth admires all kinds of heroism-bravery, courage, loyalty and sacrifice for religion and country. This admiration marks the beginning in the development of noble ethics, derived from one's readings about great men and heroes, who influence him psychologically and morally, inspring him to acquire their virtues and ethical values.

Power of imagination develops, enabling youth to appreciate and enjoy arts and visualize great men, and leading historical figures mentioned in literature books. This enchances his appreciation and admiration of their virtues, thus constituting a new factor, which alongside with emotions, plays an active part in the development of the fine morals and ethics, which play a vital role in the life of every individual.

These important facts have helped educationalists find the method that should be adopted in moral education. More important to the youth's life in general and his religious life in particular, is the development of his intelligence; for it is an accepted fact that during this state, intelligence develops considerably to prepare the youth for the study of various theoretical sciences such as mathematics. This change is accompanied by another very important psychological fact—the appearance of a critical spirit, and a tendency towards independence thinking. The youth sheds the garb of obediences, submissiveness, and blind imitation which is considered one of the main characteristics of childhood. This change takes the form of rebellion against parental and school control; and often against the traditions and beliefs of society.

Careful scientific research has indicated that from the religious aspect, this stage is characterized by two important things:

1. *The spirit of piety :* real piousness emanating from the depths of the soul appears not in the submissive imitative age of childhood, but in youth age of mental independence and freedom.
2. *Scepticism:* since the earliest times, educators have been alarmed by the scepticis characteristic of this age—scepticism towards all traditions, even religion itself.

Religiousness in Youth

Findings of the researches conducted by Starbeck, Coe, James, and Hall in this field agree on a basic fact—that youth more than any other stage, is the stage during which the genuine religious feeling appears. Studies based on statistics generally agree that religion is implanted in the human soul in the early years of life. This may, undeniably, occur during the second childhood or in manhood, but a powerful religious felling emanating from the depth of the human soul usually occurs in youth. This phenomenon has led some psychologists to assume the existence in human nature of an instinct which they termed "the religion instinct", concluding that it appeared during adolescence.

It is certain beyond doubt that this phenomenon occurs under the impact of various factors; for education, environment, and physical and mental development have undeniable effects on this phenomenon. Religious awakening is not the product of human instinct alone, but is a response to external factors and influences.

The gravity of this phenomenon—as far as the religious aspects is concerned—leads us to review the decisive scientific evidences which prove that religion develops within the individual during adolescence.

The first evidence was proved by religious psychology, which discovered that the phenomenon of turning to religion occurred most often between the ages of 10 and 25, that is the stage of youth. This supports the above mentioned statement that adolescence marks the appearance and sound strong beginning of religion. Starbuck states that if religious transformation does not occur before the age of twenty, it seldom does later. Coe, concludes after a study of 1784 cases that the usual age at which the phenomenon of real religious transformation occurs is sixteen. Stanley Hall studies over 4000 cases, stating that transformation occured mostly at the age of sixteen. He quotes observations of men of religion concerned with the propagation of religion, which support the same fact.

All this proves the validity of the previous statement that youth is the period during which the phenomenon of religious transformation mostly and powerfully occurs. General conclusions of psychological studies in this field agree in indicating that the period between 10 and 20 years of age is the time during which religious awakening occurs. Cases where this phenomenon was detected before or after this period are relatively few. This, in turn, proves that adolescence is the stage at which active religious feeling awakes, often leading to the religious transformation referred to. But things do not end here, for the youth at this stage of life, is also subject to religious scepticism, one of the most serious phenomena from the religious aspect which it is imperative to study.

Religious Scepticism

Religious scepticism in youth is among the general characteristic features of the period starting at 16 years of age. It is common for youth to pass through this religious experience, particularly if they are keen in intelligence. The causes of this phenomenon are not difficult to detect, as psychologists have studied it, and were able to determine the active factors behind it. In this paper, we will only underline the most important factor:

1. Work Bases of Religious Education

The first cause of this scepticism is brought about by religious educators who present religion to children in a native crude inadequate from that cannot cope with mental development and growth. They should keep in mind that those children will inevitably move to a next phase in which their in which their mental faculties develop and the critical spirit becomes stronger. They would then re-examine and criticise what they had previously learned of religion.

Obviously the resulting scepticism will correspond in violence and strength to the degree of inadequacy with which religious teachings and creeds had been presented. Should these educators have kept in mind to present religion to the child from the very beginning in a form satisfactory to the mind and heart at all ages, they would have spared many of their students the mental and spiritual agonies of doubt and disbelief.

2. Impact of Mental Training

Modern education imposes on the contemporary educator the task of developing scientific thinking. Educators have lately sought to devise teaching methods which envisage careful training liberal scientific thinking in various curricular subjects. The teacher's function has consequently changed. His task is no longer that of the presentation and explanation of facts, but his duties are restricted to setting the stage and motivating students to independent individualistic thought. Such methods naturally prepare the student's mind to free liberal thinking and careful scientific criticism. This new educational trend in teaching natural and other sciences has changed student's attitude towards the religious teachings which religious educational books offer them. At present they study religion with minds trained in criticism, analysis, examination, and logical and rational education. If alien ideas which do not agree with sound logical rationalization—such as "Al Israeliyyat", and remnants of fake ancient philosophies—had crept into the religion taught to them in the early years of schooling, such ideas will only result in scepticism and disbelief in the mentally-mature critical youth. The cause of all this would be the improper subject-matter where religion is mixed with other concepts.

Effect of the Study of Sciences

Among the active factors in arousing religious scepticism within students, is the study of natural sciences in secondary schools, according to modern scientific methods. This concerns mainly the general effect of using modern research methods in the study of natural sciences, and mathematics and of scientific conclusions, and funding concerning the universe, and of the unshakable confidence in their truth.

The precision and clarity of scientific research inspire the student's full confidence in it and in its conclusions. Such confidence threatens anything contrary or contradictory to these young minds, some modern scientific theories obviously seem contrary or contradictory to the phenomena described in religious books. I will not go into more *details* on the matter, but suffice it to mention the basic features of this delicate situation beginning with some scientific experiments made on this subject.

Professor Everill made an experimental study on the extent and main causes of religious scepticism among youth. His book *"The Adolescent"* on the psychological condition of youth from all aspects includes parts of this study. In this study he depended partly on reports submitted to him by a number of students on their religious faity. Many reports revealed the causes behind these doubts, and the subjects around which they are centred. I will not deal extensively with this study and its results, as the phenomenon itself is not unknown and has been the subject of many studies, thus its basic facts have become known and common. I will, therefore, refer to it only as would suffice to reveal to the reader the gravity of the case of evidenced in the young people's reports on their religious doubts.

In one report, the student says that when he went to the college he chose, plunged into the social life, young people usually led and took part in various religious debates, he could no longer believe that the Holy Book could be taken without interpretation. He them described the change in his image of God—drawing a distorted, disfigured image in no way similar to that denoted by religions in general.

Another student relates that in the secondary school he was overcome with doubts about the existence of God, wondering where. He was if actually existed, why the good *suffers* and what use is prayer, etc.

A nineteen-year old girl states that after studying natural sciences, she began to have doubts about many of the religious facts she had learnt. Her study of the theory of evolution affected her deeply. She could not help comparing between this theory and the religious concept she had been taught on Creation. She mentions how she told her parents that if the theory of evolution and development were true, then God was not the Creator people thought He was.

A prominent writer told me the same thing about his son, when I met him in Alexandria one afternoon last summer. The boy began to compare the process of creation as indicated in the Qur'an with the version depicted by natural sciences and was finally covercome with doubts and worries.

There are, in short, differences between what natural sciences say, and the language in which Heavenly Books present the evolution and development of major natural phenomena. These differences often shake the firm religious faith which the innocent youth had enjoyed, because of the latter's inability to combine the two divergent sides.

The Critical Religious Situation of Youth

Youth, according to psychology, has violent emotions and keen intelligence and often experiences many religious doubts which in some cases reach an extent where belief and faith in morality and ethics collapse. In this state youth is surrounded by a vicious circle of propaganda which only worsens the situation.

Attempts at corruption are usually characterized by careful selection of ends and means, and perseverance in pursuing these means. Long years are spent in these attempts, without being dissuaded by boredom, weariness or financial drawbacks. The objectives of these attempts very considerably. Some groups which are preoccupied with misleading youth are satisfied with nothing short of the total disruption of religious bonds and impregnating young minds with new alien ideas. Other groups are content with the mere dissemination of doubt and the shattering of creed. They are not reluctant to let youth stumble in the darkness of doubt without hope of salvation. Another group seeks to implant in the minds of youth and people in general an attitude of indifference towards religion and living according to the dictates of whims and desires.

It may be useful to deal briefly with some of these groups, starting with the atheist existentialists. Atheist existentialists are a newly-formed but active group, whose regular activities have spread in many countries even in the Middle East itself. This group based itself on the common experience of doubt among adolescents and adults. Its carefully and cleverly-drawn plan of action is attempting to spread scepticism on the widest possible scale, and then pretending to sympathize with those who fall in the dark abyss of doubt, and consequently surrender to this group. The latter lead the victims to adopt a dangerous mode of life, based on the absence of indications of good and evil and man's right, therefore, to choose the mode of life he desires.

While philosophers spread their philosophy by presenting its principles and general bases in the conventional logical style familiar to philosophy books, existentialists reject this method completely. They are aware of one's natural love for stories, and know that youth enjoy interesting descriptions by prominent story-writers and novelists and therefore sought to write captivating stories and used them as a means of presenting their call and introducing their views, appealing to the vivid imagination and warm feelings of youth to win them over.

Existentialist leaders produce a gushing stream of stories to propagndize their doctrine. These stories, which are being translated into Arabic and read by young people everywhere, seek to spread scepticism first, and then lead youth to accept existentialism.

There are those who try to exploit the scepticism of youth in the Islamic world to spread other religions. Like existentionalists, they have finally despaired of the scientific approach and decided to use art. The cinema has been one of the prominent branches of art which they have employed. A few years ago this group produced in one year ten of the greatest and most influential films which they distributed in all parts of the world in the hope that these films would yield the desired results in terms of religious propaganda.

Advocates of depravity do not call for a certain religion or philosophical idea, nor do they resort to scientific or artistic propaganda; but depend on the temptation of pleasures which divert people from religious and moral virtues. They believe that this alone is sufficient to enfeeble religious feelings and gradually turn away from religion.

This brief analysis of the means of tempting youth and the factors leading to their deviation is not restricted to one country or another, for these universal trends may have their roots in one country but always seek to spread to all countries of the world.

Means of Salvation

When religious education in schools of all religious countries came to suffer lack of care and attention for insurmountable difficulties, religious men in the west were alarmed. They tried to remedy the situation and save people in general and young ones in particular from these elements that threatened their religion—the most important of which was the internal element of doubt and the external element of propaganda. So what were the means they resorted to and used in this rescuing operation?

Young Men's Christian Associations

Among the foremost which Western nations resorted to, was the establishment of what they called "Young Men's Christian Associations". This is an original system devised to serve religious education in an attractive way suitable to the mind and likes of youth. But despite their development and advanced systems, these associations could not fulfill the desired objective in the manner hoped for, and this led to the Sundry idea. We will cast a general glance on its history, development, and the phases it went through until it proved its efficiency and became a model to be copied. It was weak as it appeared in a Western Kingdom and developed until it finally took its present form.

Sunday Schools

The first amendment of the basic law in that kingdom was the separation of church from state. This led to the cancellation of religious education from public schools which alarmed the people and made them worry about how to give their children and youth a real religious education. The Sunday school was the answer, for it was set up for this purpose and these schools increased between 1814-1824. The burden of spreading these schools at the beginning was shouldered by Protestant churches individually, then collectively. Their primary task was the religious education of children, while youth and men were not a main concern. At the beginning, these schools were rather elementary, with no definite curricula, no set levels of education or training of teachers. Nevertheless, they had considerable effects:

1. They made Sunday a delightful day for students. For many students, Sunday had been a day of laziness, leisure and roaming in the streets subjected to temptations. These schools provided them with a pleasant environment particularly that they were entrusted with its partial management. They gave students a chance to meet and become acquainted on the one hand, and learn to appreciate religion and worship on the other.
2. It brought the group spirit into religious life, strengthening relations and developing the love for cooperation in good-doing and religious action.

The Second Stage

The second stage covers the period from 1824-1872, and is characterized with organization and development. There was a great concern during this period with giving children and youth the proper religious education. The most prominent feature of this period was regional organization. The whole country was divided into nine main sections, each of which was under the control of a supervisor general to whom every worker in the section was directly subordinate. The resulted in efficient work and rapid production.

National meetings were held annually to examine problems,

propose solutions and submit reports on the condition of Sunday schools, their activities, obstacles they face, and their expected success.

The important contribution which was uniquely characteristic of this period was the emphasis laid on publishing as complementary to the work done by the Sunday school. Unified lessons for Sunday schools were prepared, printed and distributed. The scope was then widened and special books were written to help Sunday school teachers in their task. Booklets explaining and interpreting biblical themes were written, as well as small pamphlets for students and laymen explaining various religious questions. Efforts then turned to publishing cheap edition of the Bible and religious books to make them available to the widest circle of people possible. Libraries were formed in the Sunday schools themselves, containing many books of student level. All this was done under the directions of the general supervisory authority of these schools.

The Third Stage (1872-1903)

The new era was unshered in with the spread of the movement to the whole Western world. The idea of universalizing the movement was met with general consent, and in the annual general meeting the idea was adopted and the Sunday school movement became an international movement.

Attention was focussed on the basic educational principles and it was decided to adopt them successively. The first principle to be implemented was the division of Sunday schools to age groups-schools for children, for young men and for older groups. This naturally led to the preparation of books and curricula for these levels. Then the question of training Sunday schools teachers and providing them with material and technique came into focus. Special classes were organized for this purpose and many of them later developed into colleges. This marked the appearance of educational institutes for Sunday School teachers in many ways modelled after institutes for general education.

The Fourth Stage

Sunday schools entered their fourth stage about 1953, when the Religious Education Association was formed. It was formed of a fine group of leading men of religion, educators, university professors, deans and rectors, sociologists, psychologists and social workers.

The task of this big association was to introduce unity and the spirit of cooperation among the many authorities working in the field of religious education, at the head of which are Sunday schools and Young Men's Christian Associations. The most significant educational event was that the general annual meeting decided to devise a system for Sunday schools exactly corresponding to general schools, beginning with kindergartens. We can state here that the aim sought by the movement sixty five years ago was gradually realized. With the introduction of this unity, those separate schools followed the same lines, used the most modern educational techniques and got the best teachers. They became greatly concerned with the preparation of teachers. The result was that religious education which did not have a proper place in general schools in the West was fully appreciated by the people. This saved it from weakening and collapsing. Not only were there schools for religious education established, but there was also a special educational system comprising all the components of the general education system-schools for the various levels, educational institutes and special books and curricula on the most modern and soundest bases. It is better than the system of general education in that it is international not national. This reference to this system is motivated by my belief that these examples have a miraculous effect in arousing active interest on the one hand, delineating plans of action on the other.

Improving the Situation at Home

It is no secret that Western methods of attempting to solve human problems are copied in the East in its attempts to overcome the same obstacle. It was therefore not unexpected that in considering the obstacles impeding religious education Eastern minds would turn to methods devised by the West to solve the same problem. Christian minorities in the East were the first to take this essential step to save religious education. The first modern system they copied was that of Young Men and Young Women's Christian Associations which spread in Eastern kingdoms where Christian minorities lived. Wherever, they were established, these associations tried to provided Christian youth with the opportunity to increase its religious information and strengthen its spiritual and mental relations with its religion and creed. They were built on the same base as those of the West. Seeing the effect of these associations in raising the standard of religious culture among Christian youth, Muslems adopted the idea and Young Men's Muslim Associations were formed everywhere and achieved unexpectedly remarkable success.

But it is regrettable that these associations did not have the same bases or systems adopted by Young Men's Christian Associations. I myself undertook a serious study of the matter. In 1946, I made a careful comparison between the two systems to find a marked difference in many respects. As a result, Young Men's Associations failed to fulfill in a satisfactory manner, the religious purpose for which they were formed. Moreover, they became rigid in certain aspects or developed along secondary lines which did not serve their primary objective.

Christian minorities took the second expected step. They established Sunday schools after those of the West and for the same purpose. They have drawn for them the curricula and methods which should be used in conveying the material to students, taking into account all considerations of religious education. Although still at their start, they are rapidly advancing in great strides every year.

I believe that it is time to adopt this system too, for current religious conditions make imperative for Moslem youth at present cannot be said to be needless of the cultural and religious assistance offered by these schools.

Friday Schools

Friday schools have now become an imperative necessity to deal with the religious condition of youth and base their behaviour and life on sound religious basis. We formed Young Men's Muslim Associations for this purpose, but neither in the East nor West did they realize all the hopes and desired aims. Establishment of Sunday schools in the West was the natural reaction to this partial failure. We are facing the same results in Young Men's Christian Associations, so is it not natural in such a case to think of filling this gap by establishing Friday schools.

I do not wish to go on proving the essentiality of this religious institution, for I believe that reason as well as current conditions serve to convince us not of its necessity along, but of the importance of taking the initiative to realize this significant project on the widest possible scale.

It should be stated that it is our duty to study the bases of the project in East and West as guide lines for us in order to avoid unnecessary setbacks. Our enthusiasm should not let us—at this stage—insist on establishing these schools on the highest standard. This may not be possible now, but it does not prevent us from starting one a humble modern scale to be developed later in the light of other countries previous experience.

I should like here to refer to some practical points which facilitate the task, such as determining the authority to be entrusted with the task. It is clear that it is religious work and should therefore be entrusted to religious bodies, such as Al-Azhar and the Ministry of Wakfs in Egypt. As for the premises needed for the work, it seems to be advisable to depend, in the beginning at least, on the premises of Young Men's Moslem Associations, their branches and religious primary and secondary schools.

I will not conclude this point without reiterating the necessity of establishing a general Islamic Publishing Organization to be entrusted with the publication of books for Moslems in general and young persons in particular, including books used in Friday Schools.

This Publishing department should give great attention to determine the points where people imagine a disparity between science and religion. It should then publish essays, books and pamphlets for various ages with the purpose of solving this apparent difference and proving the validity of Islam's philosophical and scientific statements; and an appropriate selection of books and essays should be taught to Friday school students.

Religion in Friday Schools

I have mentioned above that one of the causes of religious scepticism in youth is the presentation of religion during childhood in an inadequate form or one influenced by foreign superstitions mixed with Islamic teachings. It is, therefore, essential in Friday schools to present religion in its pure unvarnished form. Islamic renovators in the late 19th and early 20th century laid down the basic principles of Islam in its true form and eliminated and misrepresentation or any foreign element; and in drawing curricula for religious education in Friday schools we should benefit from the results of this renovation movement.

Renovation neither implied creation nor introduced any novelty, for the principles and concepts of Islam are uniform in all ages. It was a rediscovery or reassertion of many Islamic principles overlooked or underestimated by previous ages. This was motivated by the challenge of Western civilization in the late 19th and early 20th century. The West boasted its intellectual life, its natural sciences as well as democracy then socialism. This constituted a heavy burden on the traditional pride and dignity of Islamic nations, for it entailed an attack on the social, political and economic aspects of Islamic law. Leading Islamic thinkers and scholars cleared their eyes and reviewed Islamic law to determine the scope and extent of its reference to human life in terms of social, political and economic systems and to compare the Islamic system found therein with those introduced by the West.

It will not go into more details, for the Islamic renovation movement is well-known and its results in the political, social and economic fields have become familiar to the educated everywhere. But it is not untrue to state that its benefit in practical Islamic life is very weak and limited. It has not found its place in school curricula or programme of action or execution. Such results and conclusions should occupy the proper place in the religious revival movement which should be the aim sought by Friday schools. I do not deny that these findings have been put in a concise brief form lacking in accuracy and detail; but is there any reason for not reconsidering them with the purpose of examining, verifying, edition and presenting them to the masses of our people whether young or old to serve as a beacon in their intellectual and practical life.

We must now face the Western challenge in the economic field. Islam has not ignored the organization of material life in its general and specific aspects. It has based it on the loftiest and soundest principles and prohibited its rejection and contempt which are preached by many oriental religions. It than laid down the sound principles which help us succeed in the economic field. The first principle is the condemnation of abstention from work and production in the name of resignation. Islam is a religion which calls for and respects work and abhors unemployment as is indicated in several statements. It has opened the doors wide for every attempt at the industrial civilization needed by mankind.

Islam has condemned the life of depravity and need as a general mode of living, and has permitted the enjoyment of good things and beautiful attire, thus encouraging the consumption of the output of the production movement it advocated and encouraged. The distribution system laid down by Islam constituted a major revolution which shook the the roots of social injustice prevailing everywhere. This revolution came at the beginning as a general spirit condemning the evil feeling characteristic of capitalists ownership and the attitude of the rich who care not about the poor and needy around them, as is clearly indicated in the Qur'an. It described them as being great lovers of money and actual eaters of inherited wealth, who abuse the orphan and do not exercise charity. It their hunger for money they forget everything else until they come to their end and the world is relieved for their evils and injustices inflicted and heaped on the weakers classes of society. This is accompanied by a call to spend openly and in secret any time of day or night as is clearly indicated at the end of the chapter on "The Cow" (Surat Al-Baqara). For the first time in history, the optional sunna of charity became an imperative duty the distribution of which became a state duty in the interest of the poor and needy members of society. The system of distribution in Islam is based on the principle of social justice but zakat (almsgiving) despite its significance and importance, does not represent Islamic social justice as a whole, for renovators succeeded in recent years in finding the missing link.

Ibn Hazm-eminent Islamic socialist-sensed the spirit behind this wise legislation—the spirit of kidness and mercy towards the poor and needy and seeking their good and happiness. Upon considering the matter, he concluded that the 'zakat' (alms) may not suffice to suffice to achieve this aim. Thereupon, he reviewed the history of Islamic legislation and found that a number of great Muslim thinkers headed by Ali Ibn Abi Taleb, stated that Muslims have a duty other that zakat, that the duty of the rich includes sufficient food and essential clothes for the poor. He also considered the spirit of the quotations and verses on Islamic fraternity and found that they called for the same objective. They emphasized fraternity as a fundamental bond between Muslims. Meaningless is the barren fraternity which does not drive one to offer assistance to his poor helpless brother. The spirit of human sympathy and kindness which flowed from the Qur'an since the beginning and aroused Abi Zarr's great enthusiasm for the poor and needy, inspired Ibn Hazm to lay down the principle of Islamic social justice in one of its most forceful forms, stipulating that:

1. Muslem rulers should provide sufficient food for every poor person throughout the year, and two costumes per year—one for summer and the other for winter—as well as lodgings which shelter him from intruding eyes.
2. It zakat is not sufficient to serve the purpose, he may

> take another sum from Muslims funds to be added to the zakat in order to achieve this living standard for every poor man in the country.

We can thus see that the idea of socialism appeared in a vague indefinite form in Abi Zaar, then assumed some of its basic features through practical thinking and developed all its components in the mind of Ibn Hazm who is rightly called the great socialist of Islam. It is needless to state that this Islamic socialism should be a basic part of Friday school curricula.

We now come to the Islamic political system which should be emphasized in the minds of Muslim youth alongside with above mentioned economic system. We need not dwell on it at length here, for its general picture has become familiar to all. Youth should know that Islam and the history of Islam in the early period defined the general lines of the Islamic political system, which are purely democratic lines, as revealed by Muslem renovators. The political regime is linked with the citizen's duty of defending his country. Curricula of modern Islamic schools should make students realize this duty and give them a complete and correct picture. They should receive practical training to exercise this duty in preparation for an enthusiastic fulfilment of it in future.

Friday schools should, likewise, give their students a comprehensive idea of Islam, including the social aspect as well as ethics, morality and creed. They should give due concern to religious doubts particularly those prevalent among youth. These doubts should be examined, their sources and week points studied and then clearly and explicitly discussed at Sunday school, to reveal their feebleness and save youth from their evil and harm. Such discussions and debates should be conducted in a way that ensures their full benefit and avoids any expected or unforeseen harm that may be done in such circumstances. The first rule in not to discuss any of these doubts or assumption unless it has actually occurred to a group of mind and the discussion should be conducted by men well versed in these matters and who have arrived at the second view in keeping with the spirit of religion. We should not forget to put in the young hands pamphlets and booklets dealing with these problems in all honesty and faith which are written and published for this purpose.

Friday Schools and Islamic Social Service

Social service is a fundamental part of the Islamic religion. Yet it does not enjoy the appropriate position in the life of contemporary Muslims Public institutions for social service are few and small if compared to corresponding ones in other nations. It is even more regrettable that the love of public service and the honest will to exercise it, is very weak and almost fails to appear except on a very limited scale. Most people are dominated by egoism and selfishness—a psychological defect that harms the orphan, poor, needy and widow. Negligence in the payment of zakat—a common thing is recent vears—has deprived the poor and needy from one of the sources of livelihood set forth by Islam.

This bring us to another task of the Friday School. It should eliminate selfishness and egoism from the hearts of youth and implant in them the love of good and the strong firm desire to offer assistance—in terms of effort and money—to the needy, and give them regular training in the exercise of these social services in all their kinds. Such training should be based on religion and the spirit of Islam.

I need not mention that Islam has called attention since the very beginning to the injustice experienced by the poor and orphans in society. It rebuked the rich for ignoring the poor and needy and called for almsgiving on the widest scale and by all means and forms and for all kinds of social services.

Most significant it that fact that things were not limited to the call, but exceeded it to actual action. Many correct hadiths refer to the work done by the Prophet in this field. When an exhausted poor group of people came to him, he would preach generous giving and alms would be given and *accumulated* in heaps in the mosque court. As he distributed these alms, his features wore a contented expression. He often rose to preach, voicing a general call for charity and almsgiving without excepting anyone not even women who gave their ornaments in charity. He called for the exertion of efforts in public services even cleaning streets.

In short, Islam calls for voluntary services—with efforts and money and combines urging and guidance with actual training on the work itself. These are principles that should be introduced in Friday schools—so that students would realize the place of social service in religion and receive practical training in the field. Training should preferably take into consideration certain principles. The assistance offered should be on a wide scale, so that students would offer money, clothing, books, and toys to be distributed among needy families and children. Appropriate seasons should be chosen for this work—most significant of which is the month of Ramadan, the two feast, the 10th day of Moharram. Before Ramadan, students should be urged to donate money and clothes, so that distribution would start with the beginning of Ramadan, and it is preferable that students exercise the distribution operation themselves. Similarly before the feasts, Friday school students should be called upon to donate and they, or the school, would distribute the donations among the needy members of the school environment. It is advisable that Friday school girl student be trained in sewing and similar skills to the benefit of poor girls.

It is no less important to utilize the enthusiasm and eagerness of youth, particularly during summer, in cleaning streets and building public services, provided that such operations be organized and under careful supervision that ensures their success.

To put in briefly, Friday schools should be a centre for developing the spirit of benevolence and love to serve the students. They should provide ample grounds for exercising various kinds of social services in the spirit of Islam and in obedience to its commandments and directives.

Islam has introduced a social revolution which should be felt in young hearts and constitute a part of their faith, and it is the task of Friday schools to shoulder this serious educational burden. The social change ushered in by Islam comprises self-denial and altruism, which it regards as a part of the private life of every individual if he wishes to lead a proper Islamic life. This concern with others is manifested in many ways with one factor in common-spending effort and money to help and serve the needy and handicapped.

In short, Islam condemns ego-centricity and commands every individual to be concerned, in his private life, other and that this be in the form of continued assistance. It is therefore the duty of Friday schools to emphasize this as a general characteristic feature of the Muslim spirit.

The Motive Behind Social Services

Friday schools should provide students with the Islamic motive. It should be made clear to their minds that social service occupies a significant place among the obligations on Muslims in all corners of the earth. They should be taught verses and quotations on social service so that their services would be motivated by the spirit and wise guidance of religion.

The basic fact here is that zakat (almsgiving) is not the only Islamic obligation, for God Almighty demanded Muslims to observe charity and urged them to spend money for all good deeds and actions, promising them multiple reward. I will not attempt to cite all the verses on this point, which are numerous and in various parts of the Qur'an, but will quote some verses at the end of the chapter on the Cow (Surat Al-Baqara).

On urging Muslims to offer money and assistance, God Almighty says: "O ye who believe! Spend of that wherewith We have provided you are a day come when there will be no trafficking, friendship, nor intercession. The disbelievers are the wrong doers."

On warning against the devil's dissuation: "O ye who believe: Spend of the good things which ye have earned, and of that which we bring forth from the earth for you, and seek not the bad (with intent) to spend thereof (in charity) when ye would not take it for yourselves save with disdain and know that Allah is Absolute. Whatsoever good thing ye spend, it will be repaid to you in full and ye will not be wronged. The devil promiseth you destitution and enjoineth on you. But Allah promiseth you forgiveness from Himself with bounty. Allah is All-Knowing. Those who spend their wealth for the cause of Allah and commit no wrong or do harm; their reward is with their Lord and no fear shall come upon them, nor shall they grieve!"

He encourages benevolence and charity on a wide scale "Those who spend their wealth by night and day, privately and openly, verily their reward is with their Lord and no fear shall come upon them, nor shall they grieve".

The Almighty explains the extent of the reward awaiting charitable good-doers: "Those who spend their wealth in Allah's way are like a grain which growth seven ears, in every ear a hundred grains. Allah giveth whom He wills. Allah is All-Embracing, All-Knowing".

It is needless to point out that if well-understood and properly presented, such verses would reveal to Muslems the significance of contributing to social service in Islamic teachings. It behoves our sons to study them since their early childhood to guide them in their lives. Quotations from the Prophet's sayings (hadith) are too numerous to be cited in this paper. A selection of these saying should be given to Friday school students together with Qur'anic verses on charity, so that the Qur'an and Sunna would motivate students to do the desired social services.

Al-Ghazali—God rest his soul—clearly realized the significance of spending on good deeds and charitable acts in Islamic teachings. In the book "Al-Arba'in" he said, "Know ye that spending on charitable deeds is one of the pillars of religion. The secret behind this obligation besides the interest of the country and people—is that money is loved by all creatures and they are commanded to love God—so dear things are spent for the sake of the one most dearly beloved.

It is noteworthy to call attention to the significance in Islamic teachings of spending money for the sake of good deeds in general; which as El-Ghazali stated—constitutes one of the pillars of Islam. The second point which should not escape us is that Al Ghazali realized the modern meaning of this spending—serving the interest of country and people—which constitutes the social function of charitable spending.

Al—Ghazali went on to divide the people into three classes, the weakest of which is the third class of those who limit themselves to the payment of zakat. He called upon Muslims to exceed this limit, "Strive the transcend the third degree...Strive to donate more than is dictated by duty."

Perhaps the most powerful renovation by Al-Ghazali was that he considered social service or Islamic charity as not restricted to the spending of money, but comprise various forms of work. He said, "If you own nothing charity is not all limited to money; but every good word, act or help in need, visit to the sick, or mourning a dead. If one should give something of whatever he can in terms of influence, power, or words to appease the heart of Muslim.... all this is charity".Al-Ghazali widens the scope of charitable deeds to include assistance in need, which is modern social service in its widest scale.

These ar all principles which should be conveyed to the minds of Friday school students, for they give them the Islamic motive and religious scope for various kinds of social service.

We should not forget to make use of the long summer vacation in organizing Friday school students and directing them towards social services which include individuals, groups, towns and villages throughout the country.

(Revised and edited)

10

The Qur'an on Islamic Education

SHEIKH NADIM AL-GHISR

(Abstract: As a prelude leading to the study of the Qur'an as guidance for education, I shall outline briefly some modern thinking on education as a process; and then deal with the subject matter).

I the Man intended to be Educated

Man is made up of bones, flesh, blood and nerves. His body is furnished with various systems such as the respiratory, the alimentary and the reproductive systems. These are necessary for the preservation of human life and the species. Above all comes the nervous system which controls all the other systems either voluntarily or involuntarily. Allah has provided man with a spirit, reason and instincts (Blessed be Allah, the noblest Creator).

What concerns us here is the nervous system together with the reason and the instincts. As for the spirit we believe in its existence but fail to comprehend its reality.

Accordingly, we shall content ourselves with the study of these three elements, referring to scientific facts and conclusions reached by psychologists and comparing them with those propounded by the most Omniscient and Wise.

II Modern Theories of Psychology and Pedagogy

1. *Nervous system*

It is no exaggeration to say that of all the organs of the human body the nervous system is the most marvellous and complex, being the seat of the spirit, reason and instincts. Two of its features are most important in the field of education :

First, the unconscious mind which proves a powerful motive force in overt behaviour and controls our actions and wills without our noticing it.

Second, the nerves which are so sensitive and elastic as to be easily affected by repetition, which forms habits. The repetition of an action makes it easy to perform it and increases the tendency to practise it until it becomes a habit, which forms behaviour.

2. *The effect of habits :*

Habits have a great effect on the physical, moral, and behavioural aspects of private and social life. Most virtues are the outcome of fixed habits. It has been established that 99 per cent of man's actions are merely mechanical habits. Hence the saying that habit is second nature.

3. *Riddance of evil habits*

According to psychologists one can get rid of a bad habit only when one abandons it irrevocably. A relapse into an old habit will destroy the effect of previous efforts to get rid of it and a new attempt has to be made all over again. This may be likened to a reel which slips out of the hand and must be rewound once more. The same example is given by the Qur'an in the verse : "Be not like a woman who unravels to bits the thread which she has firmly spun." (16 : 82)

4. *Instincts*

According to modern theory, as generally accepted, instincts are innate. Allah has endowed man with many such instincts so that he may live and preserve his life and his offspring on earth. The most important instincts concerned with the field of education are :

1. The food instinct; 2. the instinct of hoarding and acquisition; 3. the pugnacity instinct; 4. the instinct of fear and escape; 5. sexual instinct ; 6. maternal and paternal instinct; 7. the instinct of

ostentation, self-assertion and love of praise; 8. the instinct of curiosity ; 9. the instinct of imitation; 10. the instinct of sociability.

5. It is a psychological fact that instincts cannot be crushed because they are necessary for the preservation of life. It is wrong to repress them, for this would only serve to drive them down into the sphere of the unconscious where they give rise to serious psychological complexes. But instincts may, or rather must, be controlled modified and sublimated through proper methods of education.

6. When unchecked the instincts may develop into pernicious passions and carnal desires. The check lies in the reason which distinguishes between right and wrong. But reason is not always sufficient to control instincts, being unable to distinguish between right and wrong in all cases except after long experience. Hence the need for guiding the reason in this respect. This guidance can only be given by Divine Revelation.

7. Sublimation is one of the chief methods of curbing ungovernable instincts and directing their energies. To sublimate an instinct is to direct its energy from a baser aim to a higher and nobler one. The ugnacity instinct, for instance, may be sublimated into defence of one's country and honour and of the weak and the oppressed; the instinct of ostentation into generosity and liberality; the instinct of luxury and extravagance into charity for the cause of Allah.

8. One of the facts established by modern psychology is that man is most anxious about everything relating to his personal interest. Man is not actuated in most cases by the dictates of reason and logic. These have to be supported by persuasive methods affecting his own interests, including the interest of his children and property.

9. Among the facts of psychology in the domain of education is the fact that fear is the chief deterrent to evil actions.

10. Prompted by the ostentation instinct, man loves praise and

respect and hates condemnation and contempt. This tendency is one of the chief persuasive methods used by the Qur'an to urge man to do good and divert him from the path of evil.

11. An idea suggested by a tutor or reformer would be more readily accepted and adopted if supported and respected by society.

12. The influence of a teacher or a preacher upon his learners or hearers varies according to the concord between his teaching and practice, seeing that example is better than precept and actions speak louder than sermons.

13. *Repetition and emphasis* also help to fix ideas in the mind. Pedagogues tell us that the same lesson should be reiterated in a different accent and illustrated in a variety of ways, so that boys may pay attention without losing interest. Stories and parables render a great aid in this respect.

14. *Monotony and Variety :*

But repetition should not verge on monotony which gives rise to boredom and consequently distracts the attention of boys, nay, it may cause them to feel drowsy. In contrast to this, variety attracts and excites their attention. This method is also adopted by the Qur'an.

15. *Interest*

Psychologists also tell us that lessons should be short and interesting. The average child cannot concentrate his attention on abstract subjects for a long time. His attention should, therefore, be stimulated by interesting things such as stories. This course is also adopted by the Qur'an in relating true stories of prophets.

16. Among human inclinations arising from the instinct of ostentation is the fact that man is apt to attribute to others many of his own defects and vices in order to relieve his sense of guilt and the contempt of society. This is also taken into account by the Qur'an.

17. A man steeped in vice is prone to lure his companions into

the abysmal depth of his moral degradation, with a view to relieving his pricks of conscience and the contempt of society. This is a course usually adopted by misers who encourage avarice in others as well as by infidels who tempt the faithful to abjure their religion.

18. It is a well-established fact that sound sleep is the most effective remedy for fatigue, being most beneficial during night.

19. It is an established fact that energy begins just before dawn and reaches its climax at 10 a.m., then slackens until it becomes lowest at 2 p.m. when it begins to rise gradually up to 9 p.m., after which hour it decreases rapidly down to dawn and so on. Night, therefore, is the most suitable time for rest.

III. Instincts, Dispositions and Propensities in the Qur'an

The instincts, dispositions and propensities discovered by psychologists in the nineteenth century were mentioned, expressly or implicitly, by the Qur'an in the seventh century.

1. In the following verses there is a reference to the instinct of hoarding and acquisition ingrained in man :

a. "Man is ever niggardly" (17:100).
b. "He loves riches with all his heart." (100:8).
c. "You love riches with all your heart." (89:20).
d. "Man is prone to avarice." (4:128).

2. In verses quoted below there is a reference to the instinct of fear and human weakness, the instinct of niggardliness, impatience and the unruliness of instincts beyond the control of reason :

a. "Man was created weak." (4:28).
b. "Truly man was created very impatient, fretful when evil touches him, and niggardly when good reaches him." (70:19,20,21).
c. "Truly man is ever impatient." (17:11).
d. "Man is a creature of haste." (21:37).
e. "Nay, but you love the fleeting life." (75:20).

3. "The human soul is certainly prone to evil." (12:53).

Here we find a reference to the inordinate nature of instincts.

4. "We said: 'Get ye down, all (ye people) with enmity between yourselves.'" (2:36).

This verse refers to the instinct of pugnacity and the struggle for existence.

5. "But man is, in most things contentious." (18:54).

6. In the following verses there is a reference to the instinct of ostentation, arrogance and boastfulness.

a. "Allah loveth not any arrogant boaster." (31:18).
b. "Nay, but man doth transgress all bounds, in that he looketh upon himself as self-sufficient." (96:6'7).
c. "Think not that those who exult in what they have brought about, and love to be praised for what they have not done, that they can escape the penalty." (3:188).

7. In the following five verses there is a reference to the instincts of fear, ostentation and man's failure to exercise control over his instincts :

a. "Verily man is given to injustice and ingratitude." (14:34).
b. "Truly man is most ungrateful." (17:67).
c. "Man does not weary of asking for good (things), but if ill touches him, he gives up all hope and is lost in despair." (41:45).
d. "If we give man a taste of our mercy, and then withhold it from him, he yields to despair and becomes ungrateful. But if we give him a taste of Our favours after adversity hath touched him, he is sure to say 'Gone are my sorrows from me' and grows jubilant and boastful." (11:9,10).

e. "There are among men some who serve Allah on the very fringe of the true faith. When an ordeal befalls them they turn upon their heels.

8. Here are two verses referring to the maternal and paternal instinct.

a. "It is he who created you from a single person, and made his mate of like nature, in order that he might dwell with her in love. When they are united, she bears a light burden and carries it about. When she grows heavy, they both pray to Allah their Lord, saying, 'If thou givest us a goodly child, we vow we shall ever be grateful.' " (7:189).
b. "Let those who are solicitous about the welfare of their young children after their own death take care not to wrong orphans. Let them fear Allah and speak for justice." (4:9).

9. The following verses imply the belief in God is ingrained even in the minds of confirmed atheists, manifesting itself in times of danger :

a. "When some trouble toucheth man, he crieth unto his Lord, turning to him in repentance." (39:8).
b. "When a wave covers them like a canopy (of clouds), they call to Allah, offering Him sincere devotion." (31:32).

10. "O mankind! We created you from a single pair of a male and a female, and made you into nations and tribes, that you may know each other." (49:13).

In this verse there is a reference to the instinct of sociability.

IV. Inculcation of Virtues

The virtues inculcated by the Qur'an are too numerous to be counted. Considering that this paper is meant for non-Muslims who should have a clear notion of Qur'anic ethics, reference will be made only to such moral quanlites as are set forth by the Qur'an in explicit terms.

1. *Sublime Character :*

The Qur'an praised the holy Prophet Muhammad as having a sublime character, for thus saith Allah : "Verily thou art of a sublime character." The other prophets, though all of them are infallible, are credited with a special trait of human character. Some are praised as clement and patient, others as righteous and truthful, others agian as grateful and kind to their parents. The term "sublime" with which the character of the holy Prophet is credited indicates that in his personality are combined all virtues such as patience, courage, fulfilment of promises and covenants, honesty, justice, magnanimity, kindness to kindred, support of the weak, hospitality to guests and succour to the needy. It was the Qur'an which preached this nobility of character, ask is clear from the following verses :

2. *Truthfulness*

"Believers, fear Allah and be with those who are true in word and deed." (9:119).

"Believers, fear Allah, and speak the truth. (33:78).

3. *Establishment of Testimony :*

"And keep your testimony upright for Allah." (65:2).

"Who is more unjust than those who conceal the testimony they have from Allah?" (2:140).

"Conceal not evidence; for whoever conceals it, his heart is trained with sin." (2:283).

"The witness should not refuse when they are called on for evidence." (2:282).

4. *Honesty*

"Believers! Betray not the trust of Allah and the Apostle, nor misappropriate knowingly things entrusted to you." (Sura 8:27).

"Those who faithfully observe their trusts and their covenants." (Sura 24:8).

5. *Fulfulment of Engagements and Treaties even with Enemies :*

"And fulfil every engagement, for every engagement will be enquired into (on the day of Reckoning)" (Sura 17:34).

"Fulfil the covenant of Allah, when you have entered into it...." (Sura 16:91).

"Those who fulfil the covenant of Allah and fail not in their plighted word." (Sura 13:20).

"But if they seek your aid in religion, it is your duty to help them, except against a people with whom you have a treaty of mutual alliance." (Sura 8:72).

"But the treaties are not dissolved with those pagans with whom you have entered into alliance and who have not subsequently failed you in aught, nor aided anyone against you. So fulfil your engagements with them to the end of their term : for Allah loveth the righteous." (Sura 9:4).

6. *Giving Just Measure and Weight*

"Give measure and weight with full justice" (Sura 6:152).

"Give just measure and weight, nor withhold from people the things that are their due." (Sura 7:85).

"So establish weight with justice and fall not short in the balance." (Sura 56:9).

"Wœ to those that deal in fraud, those who, when others measure for them, exact in full, but when they measure or weigh for others, defraud them!" (Sura 83:1,2,3).

7. *Justice :*

"Allah enjoins justice." (Sura 16:9).

"When you speak, speak justly, even if a near relative is concerned." (Sura 6:152).

"Believers, fulfil your duties to Allah and bear true witness. Let not your hatred for other men turn you away from justice. Be just : that is next to piety." (Sura 5:8).

8. *Patience:*

The holy Qur'an has laid stress on patience in about 70 verses. Here are a few of them :

"Believers, persevere in patience and constancy; vie in such perseverance." (Sura 3:200).

"Allah is with those who patiently persevere." (Sura 2:153).

"And bear with patient constancy whatever betide you, for this is firmness of purpose in the conduct of affairs." (Sura 31:17).

"And exhort each other to patience." (Sura 130:3).

"But give glad tidings to those who patiently persevere, who say, when afflicted with calamity : To Allah we belong and to him we shall return.'" (Sura 2:155).

"I swear by the declining day that perdition shall be the lot of man, except for those who have faith and do good works and exhort each other to justics and fortitude." (Sura 103).

9. *Forgiveness*

"So overlook any human faults with gracious forgiveness." (Sura 15 : 85)

"The recompense for any injury is an injury equal thereto (in degree); but if a person forgives and makes reconciliation, his reward is due from Allah." (Sura 42:40).

"Let them forgive and overlook. Do you not wish that Allah should forgive you? (Sura 24:22).

10. *Modesty and Gentleness :*

"And lower thy wing to the believers who follow thee." (Sura 26 : 215).

"Wert thou severe or harsh-hearted, they would have broken away from about thee." (Sura 3:159).

11. *Doing good*

"But do good, for allah loveth those who do good. (Sura 2:195).

"For the mercy of Allah is near to those who do good." (Sura 7:26).

12. *Self-sacrifice*

"The give others perference over themselves, even though poverty were their own lot. Those that preserve themselves from the covertousness of their own souls shall surely prosper." (Sura 56:9).

13. *Mercy :*

In more than 200 verses of the Qur'an Allah credited himself with the attribute of mercy. Further, each chapter of the Holy Book opens with the *Bismala,* which includes the two divine names of Most Gracious and Most Merciful. Mercy is recommended in many verses of the Qur'an, of which only a few may be mentioned:

"Then will he be of those who believe, and enjoin patience, and deeds of kindness and companion." (Sura 90:17).

"We sent after them Jesus, the son of Mary, and bestowed on him the Gospel; and we ordained in the hearts of those who followed him compassion and mercy." (Sura 57:27).

"And He has put love and mercy between your hearts." (Sura 30:21).

"Therefore, treat not the orphans with harshness." (Sura 93:9).

14. *Kindness to Parents:*

Filial piety is enjoined in many verses of the holy Qur'an. This enjoinment is linked up with the command to worship the One True God, as is evidenced by the following verse:

"The Lord has decreed that you worship none but Him, and that you be kind to parents. Whether one or both of them attain old age in thine life, say not to them a word of contempt, nor repel them, but address them in terms of honour. And, out of kindness, lower to them the wing of humility, and say: 'My Lord! bestow on them Thy mercy even as they cherished me in childhood.' (Sura 17:23,24).

"We have enjoined on man kindness to parents." (Sura 29:8).

"And We have enjoined on man to be good to his parents; in travail upon travail did his mother bear him, and in years twain was his weaning: (hear the command), 'Show gratitude to Me and to thy parents.' To Me is thy final Goal."

"But if they strive to make thee join in worship with Me things of which thou hast no knowledge, obey them not; yet bear company in this life with justice and consideration...." (Sura S1:14,15).

15. *Kindness to Neighbours :*

"And do good-to parents, kinsfolk, orphans, those in need, neighbours who are near, neighbours who are strangers, the companion by your side, the wayfarer (ye meet),... (Sura 4:36).

Kindness to neighbours and kinsfolk may help in solving the problem of social security which is engaging the attention of social reformers at the present time. If every rich man begins by paying the poor-rate to his neighbours and relations in his own locality the number of the needy and destitute will become less in the country and thus the aims of social security will be achieved.

16. *Kindness to Kith and Kin:*

"Allah commands justice, the doing of good and liberality to kith and kin...." (Sura 16:90)

"Let not those among you who are endowed with grace and amplitude of means resolve by oath against helping their kinsmen, those in want,...."

"But it is righteousness—to believe in Allah, and the Last Day, and the Book, and the Messengers, to spend of your substance, out of love for Him, for your kin, for orphans, for the wayfarer, for those who ask, and for the ransom of slaves..." (2:177).

17. *Kindness to Non-Muslims :*

"Allah does not forbid you to be kind and equitable to those who have neither made war on your religion, nor driven you from your houses. Allah loves the equitable." (60:8).

18. *Concession and Charity:*

"If a debtor is in difficulty, grant him time till it is easy for him to repay. But if you remit it by way of charity, that is best for you...." (2:280).

19. *Defence of the Weak:*

"And how should you not fight for the cause of Allah, and for the helpless old men, women, and children...." (4:75).

20. *Rendering aid to Women:*

"And when he (Moses) arrived at the watering place in Madyan, he found there a group of men watering their flocks, and besides them he found two women who were keeping back their flocks. He said, 'What is the matter with you?' They said: `We cannot water our flocks until the shepherds take back their flocks; and our father is a very old man.' 'O my Lord! Truly am I in desperate need of any good you send me!" (28:23,24).

21. *Kindness to orphans :*

"They ask what they should spend in charity. Say: 'whatever you bestow in charity must go to your parents and kindred, to the orphans and to the poor man and to the wayfarer...'" (2:215).

"And they feed, for the love of Allah, the indigent, the orphan and the captive...." (76:8)

"Yet he would not scale the Height. Would that you knew what the Height is! It is the freeing of a bondsman; the feeding, in a day of privation, of an orphan with claims of relationship, or a needy man in distress." (90:11,16).

Nay, nay! But you honour not the orphans! Nor do you encourage one another to feed the poor! (89:17,18)

22. *Kindness to the wayfarer:*

The foregoing verses and the verse of alms (9:60) mentioning specifically the right classes of people having a claim to alms.

23. *Kindness to the Captive:*

This is one of the highest moral qualities preached by the Qur'an. Speaking of the virtues of the righteous, the Qur'an says: "They feed, for love of Allah, the indigent, the orphan, and the captive, saying, 'We feed you for the sake of Allah alone: no reward do we desire from you, nor thanks.' The verse refers to the old state of things when captives were often starved, slain and flayed and their flesh was given as food to wild animals.

24. *Generosity, Liberality and Munificence:*

The Qur'an does not preach charity in terms of which the pagan Arab were proud. On the other hand, it includes numerous verses which enjoin charity for the sake of Allah. The reason for the omission of these terms in the Qur'an seems to be that the Arabs practised generosity and liberality for the sake of ostentation, grudging the poor the favour of liberal charity. This defeated the noble aim of charity, namely, to foster love and sympathy among the members of society; it diverted charity into the base aim of ostentation and self-glorification which gives rise to envy and disputes between the rich and the poor. The Qur'an aimed at sublimating this tendency into a nobler aim. It enjoined charity for the sole aim of seeking Allah's pleasure, and not in return for someone else's favour, or in expectation of any recompense; for thus saith Allah: "A warn you, then, of the blazing fire, in which none shall burn save the hardened sinner, who denies the truth and gives no heed. But the good man who purifies himself by almsgiving shall keep away from it: and so shall he that does good works for the sake of the Most High only, seeking no recompense. Such men shall be content." (92:14:21).

25. *Hospitality*

This is referred to in the verse :

"Have you heard the story of Abraham's honoured guests? They went in to him and said: 'Peace!' 'Peace!' he answered, and seeing that they were strangers, betook himself to his family and returned with a fatted calf. He set it before them saying: 'Will you not eat?.'...(Sura 51:24:27).

In this verse and another verse of Sura 11 (Houd) which says: "and hastened to entertain them with a roasted calf" (there is reference to the duty of extending hospitality to guests, even if they are strangers.

26. *The Covering of Adornments and Finery:*

"Enjoin believing men to lower their gaze and restrain their carnal desires. This will make their lives purer. Allah is well acquainted with all their actions. And enjoin believing women to lower their gaze and to preserve their chastity; to cover their adornments except such as normally displayed, to draw their veils over their bosoms and not to reveal their finery and let them not strike their feet in order to draw attention to their.

27. *Asking permission before entering chambers:*

The Qur'an lays stress on rules of decorum within the family circle. It enjoins servants and children to ask permission before they enter the chambers of their masters and parents; for thus saith Allah: "Believers, let those whom your right hands possess and the children among you who have not come of age, ask your permission when they come in to see you on three occasions: before morning prayer, the while you doff your clothes in the heat of noon and after the late night prayer. These are three times of undress...." (24:58).

28. *Asking permission before entering others' houses:*

"Believers, do not enter the dwellings of other men until you have asked their owners' permission and wished them peace..." (24:27).

"Nor walk on the earth with insolence: for you cannot rend the earth asunder, nor reach the mountains in height." (17:37).

29. *Low voice in conversation:*

"Be modest in thy bearing and subdue thy voice. Surely the harshest of voices is the braying of the ass." (31:18, 19).

V. Denigration of Vices

Anyone who counts the vices forbidden by the Qur'an would think they exceed the virtues preached by it. This illusion will soon vanish if we remember that the enjoinment of a virtue implies the prohibition of its antithesis and *vice versa*. In fact the numerous subdivisions of the same vice are implied in the roots of major virtues. For instance, the prohibition of falsehood, hypocrisy, lie, perjury, is implied in the enjoinment of truthfulness, just as the prohibition of injustice, libel, backbitting, calumny and dishonesty is implied in the enjoinment of justice. But the Qur'an did not charge people with the task of drawing their own conclusions. It called vices by their names, inasmuch as there are certain ethical points which might present some difficulty to the elite, much less the layman who is more in need of guidance than the scholar or the philosopher. Some may also be so tempted by their weakness, or ignorance, or rather the desire to excuse themselves as to claim that certain vices are not prohibited by the Holy Book. Many ignorant people say that wine is not prohibited in express terms except for the verse which enjoins that it should be avoided. Should they reflect a little, they would find that the same verse described wine as an abomination, a term usually applied by the Qur'an to unbelief and polytheism, which are much worse than wine. It was for this reason that the Qur'an called every vice by its name in order to shut the door of false pretexts in the face of the ignorant and the sinners.

1. *Faleshood :*

"They swear to falsehood knowingly. Allah has prepared for them a severe penalty: evil indeed are their deeds." (58:14).

"And the witnesses will say, "These are the ones who lied against their Lord!' Behold! the curse of Allah is on those who do wrong!" (11:18)

2. *False accusation:*

"Who does more wrong than he who invents a lie against Allah." (6:21).

"The forger must suffer frustration." (20:61).

"And those who traduce believing men and women undeservedly, shall bear the guilt of slander and a glaring sin." (33:58).

3. *Hypocrisy and ostentation:*

"Woe to those who pray but are heedless in the prayer; who make a show of piety....." (107:4,5,6).

"Believers, do not mar your almsgiving with taunts and mischief-making, like those who spend their wealth for the sake of ostentation and believe neither in Allah nor in the Last Day." (2:264).

"And who spend their wealth for the sake of ostentation, believing neither in Allah nor in the Last Day." (4:38).

"The hypocrites will be in the lowest depths of the Fire." (4:145).

"The hypocrites are rebellious and perverse." (9:67).

"When they rise to pray, they stand up sluggishly: they pray for the sake of ostentation..." (4:142).

4. *Defamation of chaste women:*

"Those who slander chaste women, indiscreet but believing, are cursed in this life and in the Hereafter: for them is a grievous penalty." (24:23).

"Those that defame honourable women and cannot produce four witnesses shall be given eighty lashes. No testimony of theirs shall be admissible ever after, for such men are wicked transgressors." (24:4).

5. *Spreading slanders:*

"Those who delight in spreading slanders against the faithful shall be sternly punished in this world and in the next. Allah knows them all, but you do not." (24:19).

6. *Public scandal of evil:*

"Allah loveth not that evil should be noised abroad in public speech, except where injustice hath been done." (4:140).

7. *Backbiting:*

"Nor speak ill of each other behind their backs. Would any of you like to eat the flesh of his dead brother? Nay, you would abhor it...." (49:12).

8. *Scandal-mongering, defamation, offensive nicknames, mutual ridicule:*

"Woe to all scandal-mongers and backbiters." (104:1).

"As for those that taunt the believers who give freely and scoff at those who give according to their means, Allah will scoff at them. Theirs shall be a woeful punishment." (9:79).

"Believers, let no man mock another man, who may perhaps be better than himself. Let no woman mock another woman, who may perhaps be better than herself. Do not defame one another, nor call one another by nicknames. It is an evil thing to be called by a bad name after embracing the true faith.... (49:11).

9. *Bearing false witness :*

"And shun the word that is false." (22:30).

"Those who do not bear false witness and who avoid futilities in a dignified way."

10. *Discrepancy between words and deeds:*

"Grievously odious is it in the sight of Allah that you say that which you do not." (61:3).

11. *Calumny:*

"Heed not the type of despicable man,—ready with oaths, a slanderer, going about with calumnies." (68:10,11).

"Say 'I seek refuge in the Lord of men, the King of men, the God of men, from the mischief of the slinking prompter who whispers in the hearts of men: from jinn and men."

"Believers, if a wicked man comes to you with any news, ascertain the truth, lest you harm people unwittingly, and afterwards become full of repentance for what you have done." (49:6).

12. *Spying:*

"And spy not on each other." (49:12).

13. *Arrogance and haughtiness:*

"Is there not in Hell an abode for the haughty?" (39:60).

"Thus doth Allah seal up the hearts of arrogant and obstinate transgressors." (40:35).

"Those who behave arrogantly on the earth in defiance of right—them will I turn away from my signs." (7:146).

"And frustration was the lot of every powerful obstinate transgressor." (14:15).

14. *Wrong-doing and trespasses (excesses of every kind):*

"As for the wrong-doers, He has prepared for them a grievous penalty." (76:37).

"Allah...He forbids all shameful deeds and injustice and rebellion...." (16:90).

"Say: the things that my Lord has indeed forbidden are: shameful deeds, whether open or secret, sins and trespasses against truth or reason....." (7:33).

"The blame is only against those who oppress men with

wrong-doing and insolently transgress beyond bounds through the land, defying right and justice: for such there will be a penalty grievous." (42:42).

15. *Miserliness and avarice:*

"But he who is a greedy miser and thinks himself self-sufficient and repudiates the good—We will indeed make smooth for him the path to misery; nor will his wealth profit him when he falls headlong into the Pit." (92:8,9,10).

"Let not those who covetously withhold of the gifts which Allah has given them of His grace, think that it is good for them: nay, it will be the worse for them: soon shall the things which they covetously withheld be tied to their necks and their collar on the Day of Judgment." (3:180).

"Allah does not love arrogant and boastful men, who are themselves niggardly and enjoin others to be niggardly also; who conceal the riches which Allah of His bounty has bestowed upon them, for We have prepared a shameful punishment for the unbelievers." (4:37).

"Men's souls are swayed by greed." (4:128).

"And those saved from the covetousness of their own souls,—they are the ones that achieve prosperity." (59:9).

"Proclaim a woeful punishment to those that hoard up gold and silver and do not spend it in Allah's cause. The day will surely come when their treasures shall be heated in the fire of Hell, and their foreheads, sides, and backs branded with them. Their tormentors will say to them: 'These are the riches which you hoarded. Taste then the punishment which is your due." (9:34,5).

"Truly man was created very impatient, fretful when evil touches him, and niggardly when good reaches him." (70:19,20,21).

"Throw into Hell every contumacious rejecter (of God)." (50:24).

16. *Extravagance, wastefulness, stinginess:*

"But waste not by excess: for Allah loveth not the wasters." (6:141).

"Squander not your wealth in the manner of a spendthrift. Verily spendthrifts are brothers of the Evil Ones." (17:26,27).

"Those who, when they spend, are neither extravagant nor niggardly, but hold a just balance between those extremes." (25:67).

17. Greediness and gluttony:

"Eat and drink, but waste not by excess, for Allah loveth not the wasters." (7:31).

Here the word "waste" is used not in the sense of squandering wealth but of eating too much as is seen from the verse:

"Say: Who has forbidden the beautiful gifts of Allah, which He has produced for His servants, and the things, clean and pure, which He has provided for sustenance?" (7:32).

18. *Luxury :*

"When We resolve to annihilate a people, We first warn those of them that live in luxury. If they persist in sin, We rightly pass Our judgment and utterly destroy them." (17:16).

"We have sent no apostle to any nation whose message was not denied by those of them that lived in comfort." (34:34).

19. *Treachery and dishonesty :*

"Allah loveth not one given to perfidy and crime." (4:137).

"Allah loveth not the treacherous." (8:58).

"Allah loveth not any that is a traitor to faith, or shows ingratitude." (22:38).

"Believers, betray not the trust of Allah and the Apostle, nor misappropriate knowingly things entrusted to you." (8:27).

20. *False oaths:*

"And take not your oaths to practise deception between yourselves, with the result that someone's foot may slip after it way firmly planted...." (16:04).

"And they swear to falsehood knowingly." (58:14).

"Heed not the type of despicable man,—ready with oaths." (68:10).

"Those that sell the covenant of Allah and their own oaths for a paltry price shall have no share in the world to come. Allah will neither speak to them, nor look to them, nor purify them on the Day of Resurrection. Theirs shall be a woeful punishment." (3:77).

21. *Perjury and the concealment of evidence :*

"Shun the abomination of idols and avoid all falsehoods." (22:30).

"Those who witness no falsehood and avoid futilities in a dignified way." (25:72).

"Conceal not evidence, for whoever conceals it, his heart is tainted with sin...." (2:283).

"We should hide not the evidence before Allah, for we should then be wrong-doers." (5:109).

"Who is more unjust than those who conceal the testimony they have from Allah?" (2:140).

"And establish the evidence as before Allah." (65:2).

22. *Conjecture and suspicion :*

"Conjecture avails nothing against truth." (49:12).

"Believers, avoid suspicion as much as possible, for suspicion, in some cases, is a sin." (49:12).

"Do not follow what you do not know. Man's eyes, ears, and

heart—each of his senses shall be closely questioned." (17:36).

23. *Circulation of false rumours:*

"If the hypocrites and those who have tainted hearts and those who circulate false rumours in Medina do not desist, We shall stir you up against them and their days in the city will be numbered." (33:60).

24. *Envy :*

"Say: I seek refuge with the Lord of Daybreak from the mischief of His creation; from the mischief of the darkness as it oversoreads; from the mischief of conjuring witches; from the mischief of the envier, when he envies." (113).

25. *Reminders of charity :*

"Believers, cancel not your charity by reminders of your generosity or by injury...." (2:264).

The above are the majority of vices referred to in the Qur'an. As for the major sins, namely, unbelief, polytheism, murder, theft and fornication, the prohibition is well-known in all religions. That is why I have deemed it unnecessary to mention the verses prohibiting them, and confined myself to stating the details of virtues and vices which the Qur'an alone revealed and prohibited.

VI. General Principles of Islamic Education and Persuasive Methods Prescribed by the Qur'an

We next state a few of the general principles, mental, psychological and social, prescribed by the Qur'an as a basis for Islamic education.

1.*Allah imposes no burden on man that he cannot bear :*

"Allah does not charge a soul with anything beyond its capacity." (2:286).

"Fear Allah as much as you can." (64:16).

"Allah does not charge a man with more than He has given him." (65:7).

"Allah has given no man two hearts in his breast." (33:4).

2. *Avoidance of destruction :*

"Do not cast yourselves into destruction with your own hands." (2:195).

3. *Mistake and intention :*

"But there is no blame on you if you make a mistake therein, what counts is the intention of your hearts." (33:5).

4. *Necessity :*

"But if one is forced by necessity, without wilful disobedience, nor transgressing due limits—then he incurs no sin." (2:173).

"But even so, if a person is forced by necessity, without wilful disobedience, nor transgressing due limits—thy Lord is Oft-forgiving, Most Merciful." (6:145).

5. *Concession :*

"If shall be no offence for the blind, the lame, and the sick to eat at your tables...." (24:61).

6. *Facilities :*

"Allah intends every facility for you; He does not want to put you to difficulties...." (2:185).

7. *Danger of Tumult and Oppression :*

"And guard yourselves against tumult or oppression which affects not in particular only those of you who do wrong...." (8:25).

"Tumult and oppression are worse than slaughter." (2:217).

8. *Danger of Disputes :*

"And fall into no disputes, lest you should lose courage and your resolve weakens." (8:46).

9. *Fancy and Truth :*

"Truly, fancy can be of no avail against truth." (10:36).

10. *Falsehood is weak :*

"Falsehood shall never triumph." (17:81).

11. *Wisdom of the Law of Equality :*

"Men of understanding! In the law of equal retribution there is a safeguard for your lives that you may restrain yourselves." (2:178).

12. *The Result of Luxury :*

"When We resolve to annihilate a people, We first warn those of them that live in luxury. If they persist in sin, We rightly pass our judgment and utterly destroy them." (17:16).

"And how many populations We destroyed, which exulted in their life of ease and plenty." (28:58).

13. *Good things are allowable :*

"Say: Who has forbidden you to wear the decent clothes or to eat the good things which Allah has bestowed upon His servants..." (7:32).

14. *Divine Balance :*

"Had Allah not checked one set of people by the might of another, the earth would have been utterly corrupted." (2:251).

15. *Freedom and Compulsion :*

"Let there be no compulsion in religion." (2:256).

"Will you compel mankind against their will to believe?" (10:199).

"Have we not shown him the two paths" of virtue and vice. (90:10).

"We have shown him the right paths: whether he be grateful or ungrateful rests on his will." (76:3).

"By the soul and Him that moulded it and inspired it with knowledge of sin and piety...." (91:7,8).

"Say: This is the truth from your Lord. Let him who will, believe, and him who will, reject it. (18:29).

16. *Personal Responsibility :*

"Each individual is responsible for his deeds." (52:21).

"And if any one earns sin, he earns it against himself." (4:111).

"No soul shall bear another's burden." (35:18).

"Each man shall be judged by his own labours." (53:40).

"Whoever works evil, will be requited accordingly." (4:125).

"Verily, never will Allah change the condition of a people until they change it themselves." (13:11).

"Because Allah will never change the grace which He has bestowed on a people until they change what is in their own souls." (8:53).

VII. Particular Principles of Islamic Education

Now that we have mentioned the general principles of education, we shall proceed to point out the particular ones.

1. *Teaching people in their own language :*

"We have sent it down as an Arabic Qur'an, in order that you may understand." (12:2).

"A book, whereof the verses are explained in detail—a Qur'an in Arabic for people who understand." (41:3).

"We sent not an apostle save with the language of his own people...." (14:4).

2. *Attention and Listening :*

"When the Qur'an is read, listen to it with attention." (7:204).

"Verily, in this is a message for any that has a heart and

understanding or who gives ear and earnestly witnesses the truth." (50:37).

"Those who listen surely accept the truth." (6:36).

3. *Meditation :*

"Will they not ponder on the Qur'an? Are there locks upon their hearts?" (47:24).

"A book which We have sent down unto you, full of blessings that they may meditate on its signs and that men of understanding may receive admonition." (38:29).

4. *Appealing to Reason and Understanding :*

The verses in which the Qur'an calls upon us to appeal to reason are too numerous to mention. Following are a few of the most eloquent verses in this respect :

"For the worst of beasts in the sight of Allah are the deaf and the dumb and those who understand not." (8:22).

"He will visit His scourge upon those who will not understand." (2:171).

"Deaf, dumb and blind, they will not understand." (2:171).

5. *Following Fancy and Conjecture :*

The Holy Book condemns conjecture and fancy in many verses. Suffice it to mention the following :

"Fancy can be of no avail against truth...." (10:36).

"They follow nothing but conjecture, and conjecture avails nothing against Truth" (53:28).

6. *Following the Example of Ancestors :*

The Holy Qur'an prohibited adherence to ancestral traditions and superstitions of yore, as is seen from the following verses :

"When it is said to them: 'Follow what Allah has revealed,

they say" 'Nay! we shall follow the ways of our fathers.' What! even though their fathers were void of wisdom and guidance?" (2:170).

"They say: 'Enough for us the ways we found our fathers followings." What! even though their fathers were void of knowledge and guidance?" (5:107).

7. *Disputing without Knowledge :*

"But why do you dispute in matters of which you have no knowledge?" (3:66).

"Do not follow what you do not know. Man's eves, ears and heart—each of his senses shall be closely questioned." (17:36).

"You uttered with your mouths things of which you had no knowledge; you thought it to be a light matter, while it was most serious in the sight of Allah." (24:15).

"And yet among men there are such as dispute about Allah, without knowledge...." (22:3).

8. *Reasoning in the most courteous manner :*

"Call men to the path of your Lord with wisdom and kindly exhortation. Reason with them in the most courteous manner." (16:125).

"Dispute not with the followers of the Scriptures except in the most courteous manner." (29:46).

9. *Repelling Evil with Good :*

"Repel evil with that which is best." (23:96).

"Requite evil with good, and who is your enemy that will become, as it were, your intimate friend. But none will be granted such goodness save those who exercise patience and self-restraint and are greatly favoured by Allah." (41:35).

10. *Divine Vigilance :*

"It was We Who created man, and We know the promptings

of his soul, for We are nearer to him than his jugular vein." (50:16).

"There is no secret in heaven or earth but is recorded in that glorious book." (27:75).

"Allah knows what you conceal and what you reveal." (16:19).

"Nothing whatever is hidden from Allah, whether on earth or in Heaven." (4:38).

"Allah knows the furtive look and the secret thought." (40:19).

"They may hide their crimes from men, but they cannot hide them from Allah, seeing that He is in their midst when they plot by night, in words that He cannot approve, and Allah compasses round all that they do." (4:108).

"Whatever deed you may be doing, We are witness thereof." (10:61).

11. *Enjoining what is right and forbidding what is wrong :*

"You are the best of the peoples, evolved for mankind, enjoining what is right, forbidding what is wrong." (3:110).

"Let there arise out of you a band of people inviting to all that is good, enjoining what is right, and forbidding what is wrong. They are the ones to attain felicity." (4:104).

"The believers, men and women, are protectors one of another: they enjoin what is just, and forbid what is evil." (9:71).

"The hypocrites, men and women, hold together. They enjoin evil and forbid what is just." (9:67).

12. *Mutual teaching of Truth :*

"I swear by Time (through the ages) that man is in loss except such as have faith and do righteous deeds, and join together in the mutual teaching of Truth, and of patience and constancy." (103).

13. *Enjoining patience and compassionate kindness :*

"Then will he be of those who believe, and enjoin patience (constancy and self-restraint), and enjoin deeds of kindness and compassion." (90:17).

14. *Courteous Speech :*

"Tell my servants to be courteous in their speech." (17:53)

15. *A Goodly World :*

"A goodly word is like a goodly tree whose root is firmly fixed and its branches reach the sky; it yields its fruits at all times by the leave of its Lord." (14:24).

"Thus doth Allah (by parables) skim the Truth from Vanity. The scum is cast away, but that which is of use to mankind remains." (13:17).

16. *Secrecy for good ends :*

"In most of their secret talks there is no good, but if one exhorts to a deed of charity or justice or conciliation between men, secrecy is permissible. To him who does this, seeking the good pleasure of Allah, we shall soon give a reward of the highest value." (4:114).

"Believers, when you hold secret counsel, do it not for iniquity, and hostility." (58:9).

17. *Do not despair of God's Mercy :*

"Your Lord has inscribed for Himself the rule of Mercy. Verily, if any of you did evil in ignorance, and thereafter repented and amended his conduct, Lo! He is Oft-forgiving, Most Merciful. (6:54).

"Say : O my servants who have transgressed against their souls! Despair not of the Mercy of Allah, for He forgives all sins." (39:53).

"If any one does evil or wrongs his own soul but afterwards seeks Alllah's forgiveness, he will find Allah Oft-forgiving, Most merciful." (4:110).

"Those who do wrong but repent thereafter and truly believe—verily thy Lord is thereafter Oft-forgiving, Most Merciful." (7:153).

"Truly, no one despairs of Allah's soothing Mercy, except those who have no faith." (12:87).

"And who despairs of the mercy of his Lord but such as go astray.?" (15:56).

VIII. Self-Discipline

For promoting self-control the Qur'an has established many measures and principles, viz., pilgrimage, fasting, atonement, observance of religious duties, fulfilment of promises and convenants, repentance, perseverance in giving up bad habits and resistance of temptation.

The Qur'anic principle in combating vice is that prevention is better than cure. It is well-known that man cannot easily resist temptation. Hence the Qur'an has made it incumbent on the Muslim to lower his gaze and on the woman not to show her adornments and finery save to her husband. It has also enjoined asking permission before entering chambers at the times of undress whether by day or by night. It also prohibited wine entirely.

The Qur'an has also paid great attention to physical training and has planned many measures for perfecting it.

1. *Purification :*

Cleanliness is incumbent on Muslims all day long from dawn till bed-time, since it is an essential condition for the validity of the five daily prayers.

2. *Ablution (Wodu):*

Ablution is required for saying the five prayers. It consists of washing the hands, the mouth. The nose, the face, the arms, the head, the ears and the feet after a certain manner. It invigorates the body and strengthens it.

3. *Washing (Ghusl):*

Ghusl is bathing the body with pure water after sexual intercourse, menstruation, and child-birth. It purifies the body and renders it active.

4. *Prayer :*

Prayer constitutes also a very useful bodily exercise for all the organs of the body.

5. *Fasting :*

Fasting which is enjoined for one month during the whole year and as a means of atonement is very beneficial to the body. It accustoms man to bear hunger and thirst and to restrain his organs from satisfying their lusts, specially in cases of emergency such as travel, siege and war. Moreover, the assigning of a lunar month for fasting is meant to accustom man to physical endurance in all the seasons of the year.

6. *Pilgrimage :*

Pilgrimage teaches both men and women how to brave the hardships of travel. It also teaches people to abandon luxury and finery and to rough it. The fact that pilgrimage is also incumbent on women proves that Islam aims to make the Muslim women a strong patient creature able to endure the hardships of travel.

7. *Temperance:*

The Qur'an urges moderation in everything, especially in food and drink, and warns against gluttony which leads to many diseases, especially the weakness of the liver.

8. *Sleep by night :*

By urging man to go to bed at night and work to earn his living by day, the Qur'ạn has shown us its deep understanding of human nature. Modern science has confirmed the advantage of this practice. This fact is quite evident in many a divine verse :

"It is He Who hath ordained the night to cover you as a garment; and sleep to give you rest; and hath ordained the day for waking." (25:47).

"And of His signs is your sleeping by night." (30:23).

"And He hath ordained the night for rest." (6:96).

"Do they not see that We have ordained the night that they may rest therein." (27:86).

IX. Social Training

It is self evident that society consists of individuals; if these individuals are good, the whole community will be good. Our purpose here is not to deal at length with the details of social training, as this would require deep researches in sociology, economics and politics, the sciences which deal with our social life.

I shall confine myself to three commandments within the framework of Islamic social training. Here they are in brief:

1. Enjoining what is right and forbidding what is wrong.
2. Mutual teaching of Truth and Mercy.
3. Co-operation for good ends.
4. Reconciliation of hearts.
5. Prevention of sedition.
6. Resistance to excess and luxury.

What concerns us most as regards social training are the last three commandments.

1. *Reconciliation of hearts :*

The Qur'an saith : "Alms are to be distributed only unto the poor and the needy, and those who are employed in collecting and distributing them, and unto those whose hearts have been reconciled, and for the redemption of captives, and unto those who are in debt and insolvent, and for the advancement of God's religion, and unto the wayfarer. This is an ordinance from God : and God is Knowing and Wise." (9:60).

Where is the portion assigned to the reconciliation of hearts to go now that Islam has been firmly established ? I am of the opinion that this portion should be allotted to two purposes: the first is the reconciliation of those Muslims who out of poverty and infirmity side with the enemies of Islam and work as mercenaries for them, and the second is the preaching of the Islamic call. This can be achieved by training preachers and teaching them foreign languages, by translating and publishing books, and establishing cultural and religious centres in foreign countries. Some maintain that the money required for preaching the call should be taken from the portion assigned to the advancement of Allah's religion. But although this is admissible, my view is that it is preferable to take this money from the portion assigned to reconciliation of hearts and to spend the portion assigned to the support of Allah's religion on defence and the establishment of hospitals and schools.

2. *Prevention of Sedition :*
The Holy Qur'an saith :

"Beware a sedition, it will not affect those who are ungodly, among you particularly, but all of you in general." (8:25).

Sedition does not mean merely dividing people into hostile groups, but it also means all that leads to the weakening of Muslims and the invasion of their land by enemies. It has catastrophic results not only for those who take part in it, but for all people in general. Therefore, those who incite it should be several punished.

3. *Resistance to Intemperance in Luxury:*
The Holy Qur'an saith :

"When We resolve to annihilate a people, We first warn those of them that live in luxury. If they persist in sin, We rightly pass our judgment and utterly destroy them." (17:16).

The fact embodied in this divine verse has been treated in detail by Ibn Khaldoon in the introduction of his historical treatise. Luxury makes people money-hunters whether by honourable or dishonourable means such as theft, treachery and bribery. This will lead to the entire collapse of the nation internally and externally. We should stick to what the Qur'an has guided us, as it directs us to the right path.

"Verily this Qur'an directeth unto the way which is most right." (17:9).

"Now have We proposed unto mankind, in this Qur'an, every kind of parable, that they may be warned." (39:27).

"Do they not therefore attentively meditate on the Qur'an? Are there locks upon their hearts?" (27:24).

Public opinion as a means of Islamic training is of great significance in the view of Islam. The Qur'an has urged us in many verses to propagate the right and forbid the evil, and has imposed this duty on every Muslim, whether male or female. This duty has to be carried out within everyone's power as can be clearly deduced from the tradition of the Prophet—may Allah bless and give him peace :

"Whosoever sees an evil has to forbid it by force, if it is not in his power to do so, by publicly condemning it, or if he could not do either, by disapproving it in his heart." This type of persuasion is dependent upon the instinct of ostentation, love of praise and fear of scorn and condemnation. The wisdom of the Qur'an underlying this principle and the sublimation of instincts are quite in line with the latest theories adopted by psychologists and pedagogues.

There are some people to whom all the previous persuasive methods are of no avail. Fortunately they are a minority. Then there is another method which is more powerful, namely, persuasion through authority. This method consists in punishments prescribed by the Qur'an for some crimes, these punishments being usually carried out by the rulers.

Thus we have clearly seen that the Qur'an has not confined its admonitory and persuasive methods to a single type or to two types but enjoins resort to all the methods that may produce the desired effect on the individual concerned. Neither is resort to reason, nor resort to conscience, nor to threat or promise, nor fear of public opinion or of god's punishment sufficient by itself. Appealing to reason may prove useful only with wise and learned people, and appealing to conscience may be futile in the case of unscrupulous criminals. Intimidation without the other methods would be of no use for those who doubt resurrection or those who love this fleeting world, nor public opinion be of any use in the case of many of those who are steeped in vice. Persuasion through public opinion may be ineffective when vice prevails to such a degree that there is no feeling of shame. We pray to the Almighty that we may not be cursed like those to whom the following verse refers are cursed : "Those among the Children of Israel who believed not, were cursed by the tongue of David, and of Jesus, the son of Mary. This befell them because they were rebellious and transgressed: they forbade not one another the wickedness they committed; and woe unto them for what they committed." (5:78, 79). But all these methods combined may prove effective measures for reforming the majority of people and this is the wise method adopted by the Qur'an.

(Revised and edited; originally published in *Islamic Culture*, Jan. 1968)

11

The Islamic Pulpit as a Medium in the Iranian Constitutional Revolution

ASGHAR FATHI

(Abstract: Examines the Islamic pulpit as a medium of public communication in terms of the social organization which sustains, controls, and integrates it within the community. The period under study is the 1905-1911, which is called the period of constitutional revolution).

The pulpit is ordinarily seen as an adjunct to the congregational Friday prayer in the mosque from which sermons are delivered and religious instructions given by the preachers. Seldom is the pulpit seen (much less examined) as a medium of public communication similar to the mass media of today. To appreciate this role of the Islamic pulpit in the life of the Muslim community it is necessary to look at the social organization responsible for such phenomena as the recruitment and patronage of the preachers, their audience, the content of their homilies, the nature of the formal and informal control of such contents and their effects, and the relationship of all these to the social and political issues of the day.

To accomplish this task, this paper focuses on the 1905-1911 constitutional revolution in Iran when the society was undergoing a major transformation and social issues were of interest to many citizens. Further, to provide specific issues and vivid illustrations for our discussion, this paper concentrates on one well -known preacher of that period, although references to other, lesser-known preachers are also included.

Religious Organization in Twelver Shi'ah Iran

To appreciate the social base of preachers in Iranian society at the turn of the century, one must understand the religious organization of the Twelver Shi'ahs, the main branch of Islam in Iran, at the time.

There was no formal hierarchical organization among the Twelver Shi'ahs. Prominent religious leaders gained their status through their intellectual ability and reputation among their peers. When a *Mujtahid* or prominent religious leader died, there was no immediate successor. It took some time before one of the competing candidates was gradually accepted in his place. Indeed, the organization was characterized by a high degree of flexibility, and those on the lower levels of the system enjoyed a great deal of autonomy. Local religious leader were seldom accountable to higher authorities, and to become a religious leader one needed simply to be accepted by other religious leaders and by the people.

At the turn of the century, the prominent Shi'ah religious leaders were either residents of the shrine cities of Najaf, Karbala and Samara, in Iraq, where some of the Shi'ah Imams (the descendants of the Prophet) are buried, or they lived in Iran.

Some of those living in Iran shunned worldly luxuries, lived a simple life, and kept aloof from government and its officials, whom they considered irreligious oppressors. These religious leaders, who ordinarily took care of marriage, divorce, inheritance and other daily affairs, enjoyed a high degree of respect among the rank and file.

Among the Shi'as religious leaders who resided in Iran there were some who became judges and accepted other appointments from the government. This group tended to intermingle with government officials and led a comfortable and sometimes even a luxurious life. Because of their worldly orientation and association with the officials, these religious leaders did not command as much respect among the masses.

There was a third group in religious garb in Iran whose influence and respect originated from another source. These were the men of the pulpit. Since the celebration of the martyrdom of Imam Husayn, the grandson of the Prophet Muhammad, had become an essential part of the Shi'ah faith, the public recitation of his story (and those of other saints) from the pulpit during the holy months of Muharram and Safar, or on any other occasion, was considered a very important foundation of the faith.

The Rawdah Gathering

Held in a mosque, a private residence, or almost any place, the celebration of the martyrdom of Imam Husayn was also an important social occasion. The elaboration of the dramatic points of this emotionally charged religious story and the melodic recitation of poetry in praise of the Shi'ah saints by a skilful from the pulpit in a place often lavishly decorated with religious symbols attracted many people, especially from the lower class, to these gatherings, called *rawdah.*

Attending a *rawdah* was not only a meritorious act in the eyes of Allah, but also an occasion for diversion, meeting friends, and keeping up with the news. Usually before or after the recitation of the saints' stories, a preacher told edifying and sometimes amusing anecdotes and discussed current events. The *rawdah* was often concluded with prayers for the followers of the faith, a prominent figure, and its sponsor.

The shah, princes and high government officials, prominent religious leaders, and other wealthy and influential members of the community all arranged *rewdah* meetings to demonstrate their piety. Most neighbourhoods also organized *rawdahs* through their community associations.

Although feeding was not necessarily a part of the *rawdah*, many prominent people fed their guests, especially the poor. Thus, during the months of Muharram and Safar, many poor people from neighbouring districts poured into the cities to enjoy such hospitality.

Rawdahs were usually attended by men, but there were special *rawdahs* held for women alone. At large *rawdah* gatherings where the audience was mixed, men and women were seated separately and there was usually a partition between the two groups.

Wa'is and Dhakir Preachers

Yahya Dawlat-Abadi, a constitutional leader of the time,writes that the *wa'izin* were foremost in prestige and rank among the preachers at the turn of the century. These were men with good religious training who, in addition to recitations of the saints stories, also gave religious instructions and discussed moral and social issues from the pulpit. Then came those preacher-reciters who were at least literate. After them in rank came *dhakirs* or *rawdah-khwans,* recites who usually had a melodic voice and confined themselves to the recitation only.

When a *wa'iz* progressed and became established and famous, he attracted attention from influential persons, both lay and religious. This was so because these preachers had influence among the masses. They could very easily stir public opinion.

Because of the loose organizational structure of the Shi'ah religious establishment, preachers, like other religious leaders, appear to be autonomous. Ultimately, however, they were under the control of the prominent local religious leaders who recommended them to the *rawdah-* sponsors, and protected them when they were in trouble because of their pronouncements from the pulpit. In addition to payment for their services by the *rawdah-* sponsors, financial assistance was sometimes made available to the preachers from pious foundations under the control of the prominent religious leaders.

Many preachers were actually mouthpieces of the prominent religious leaders. Sometimes they were even encouraged to attack their patron's rivals, lay or religious, from the pulpit. Considering the fact that some of the prominent religious leaders were dependent on the government for such jobs as judgeships or trusteeships of wealthy pious foundations, it is not difficult to see how the government found access to the pulpit as a medium of public communication. Of course, there were also some well-known preachers who, in addition to their contacts with the religious establishments, were actively sought by the court and the grand vazir in the capital or the prince- governors in the provinces.

The Constitutional Revolution of 1905-1911

Islam is a political systems as well as a religion. For instance, in the Ottoman Empire(c. 1299-1919) the sultan was considered both a successor to the Prophet Muhammad and the head of State. In Iran, however, where Twelver Shi'ism was the main religion since 1502, a split had developed between the religious leaders and the State, and a rule legitimized through religion was denied the Iranian monarchs.

The tension between the Shi'ah religious leaders and the State was an important factor in the development of the constitutional movement, begun in 1905 by two religious leaders in collaboration with some Western -oriented intellectuals. There is little doubt that the verbal attacks on the despotic court from the pulpit were instrumental in the unfolding of the events which led to the granting of the constitution by Muzaffar al -Din Shah in August, 1906.

At the death of the shah in January 1907, his son was crowned Muhammad 'Ali Shah'. The new Shah began by ignoring the parliament, and mutual suspicion and dissension culminated in an attack on the parliament by the Shah's troops in June 1908. For ten months after the destruction of the parliament, the constitutionalists in the north-western city of Tabriz kept up the struggle against the royalists. Again, the role of the preachers of Tabriz in this struggle is evident. Finally, in July 1909, the constitutionalist armies from the south and north captured the capital and forced Muhammad 'Ali Shah' to abdicate in favour of his twelve-year-old son Ahmad Shah.

A full account of the 1905-1911 constitutional movement in Iran is not intended here. We are interested in the role that the preachers played during this period, and more specifically in the activities of the most influential among then Seyyed Jamal Wa'iz Isfahani.

Seyyed Jamal Wa'iz Isfahani

Seyyed Jamal (1862-1908) was born in a family of religious scholars in Hamadan. He lost his father in early childhood, and his mother moved to Tehran to live with her sister's family. In Tehran Seyyed Jamal did manual work in his uncle's workshop. At the age of 14 he started school, and because of his academic success, he went to Isfahan at the age of 21 to continue his higher education. Four years later he married.

In Isfahan, Seyyed Jamal and a few of his educated and progressive-minded liberal friends formed a secret society where they discussed politics and social issues. Seyyed Jamal and another member of the group, Malik al-Mutakallimin, were preachers, and the close collaboration between them continued even when both later became well-known constitutionalist preachers in Tehran.

The goal of the secret society was to awaken the people and arouse them against the despotic system which ruled them. Thus, Seyyed Jamal and Malik preferred to discuss progressive ideas from the pulpit instead of conducting routine religious rituals and inducing their audience to weep for martyred saints. The members of the secret society also wrote articles which were published abroad anonymously.

The new style of homilies and the indirect criticism of temporal as well as religious authorities by Seyyed Jamal and Malik was not well received by either group. Consequently both men were accused of heresy and thereafter found it difficult to preach during the months of Muharram and Safar (the months of religious mourning among the Shi'ahs).

One of the goals of the secret society was to encourage the establishment of native industries in place of the traditional crafts, which had been ruined by competition from goods imported from Europe. At one point a group of businessmen from Isfahan established a modern textile factory. This prompted both Seyyed Jamal and Malik to encourage their audience to use locally manufactured textiles instead of imported goods. Again, when Seyyed Jamal was banned from the pulpit in Isfahan during the holy months, She was sent to Shiraz, a city in the south, by some textile manufacturers from Isfahan. There he addressed the people with his eloquent homilies and encouraged the consumption of textiles made in Iran. While in Shiraz he also wrote a book on the subject.

The prince-governor of Shiraz, appreciating the eloquence of Seyyed Jamal and especially his popularity among the masses, took the preacher under his wing and recommended him to the local religious authorities. However, one of the local grandees, with deep roots and much influence in the region, was a strong antagonist of the governor and did not like Seyyed Jamal's homilies in which the preacher criticized him and his family and praised the governor. When Seyyed Jamal discovered that this person intended to harm him, he left Shiraz and did not return.

Incidentally several years before this event, the prince -governor of Isfhan had also helped Seyyed Jamal, hoping to take advantage of his eloquence and popularity. However, the favour did not last long. Seyyed Jamal and a few other members of the secret society wrote a book entitled *A True Dream* in which they described some scenes from the Day of Judgement when *Allah* cross—examines the prince -governor and the most influential religious leader of Isfahan extensively, and condemns them to eternal hellfire because of their greed, injustice, and other unforgiveable sins. The book, published surreptitiously in Russia by a progressive member of the Iranian embassy, was widely circulated among the literate elite, both conservative and liberal.

After his unsuccessful experience in Shiraz, Seyyed Jamal went to Tabriz during the holy months of the year, when he could not preach in Isfahan. Meanwhile, his wife in Isfahan heard that the prince governor had some evidence connecting her husband to the publication of *A True Dream*. She altered Seyyed Jamal of the danger awaiting him in Isfahan. Consequently he decided to stay in

Tehran, and his family later joined him there.

In Tehran, Seyyed Jamal was unknown and penniless. Fortunately for him, the summer in that year was unbearably hot, and the preacher of one of the central mosques decided to leave the city for a vacation. In order to keep his regular audience during his absence, he introduced to them a fellow Isfahani acquaintance, Seyyed Jamal.

Jamal's eloquence and entertaining style attracted more people to the mosque. *Imam-i Jum,'ah,* the religious authority in charge of the administration of the mosque, was very pleased and decided to keep Seyyed Jamal.

Soon the popularity of Seyyed Jamal made him famous in the capital and he was in great demand. Even the household members of the Shah begged His Majesty to grant permission for the preacher to give weekly homilies in the seraglio. Thus, while Muzaffar al-Din Shah was alive, Seyyed Jamal preached regularly at the court.

However, his popularity did not deter Seyyed Jamal from propagating his progressive, liberal, and patriotic views. For instance, he was once invited to preach to a large gathering of the book-sellers and publishers of Tehran. After the customary preliminaries Seyyed Jamal openly scolded his audience for importing paper instead of manufacturing it at home. He especially made an issue of printing the holy Qur'an on paper made by unbelieving foreigners.

Seyyed Jamal's unusual and novel ideas aroused many traditional religious leaders against him. On one occasion, because his sermon about the pilgrimage to Mecca did not meet with their approval, a group of religious students, who were in those days the informal army of the established religious leaders, positioned themselves amongst the audience, and in the middle of Seyyed Jamal's address raised their voices in protest and hurled insult at him. Fortunately, a group of *looties* (young men who were usually members of the local athletic clubs and very much devoted to their own neighbourhood) took the preacher's side, put the students to flight, and escorted Seyyed Jamal safely to his house.

On another occasion a group of thugs was hired to attack Seyyed Jamal. His followers discovered the plot and prevented him from attending the mosque that day. But another preacher who had replaced Seyyed Jamal was mistaken for him and attacked as he left the mosque.

Seyyed Jamal's popularity was such that on some days he preached more than once and in defferent mosques. The audience usually filled the mosque courtyard, doorways, and even adjacent rooftops. It is reported that some unemployed people came to the mosque several hours before the sermon and occupied the preferred location, and sold their seats to enthusiastic members of the audience shortly before the began. Again, the demand for Seyyed Jamal's preaching was so great that durirng the constitutional revolution some of the constitutionalists decided to print his homilies in newspaper form, so that those who could not attend his sermons, especially those in other parts of the country, would have access to his sermons.

Seyyed Jamal and the Constitutional Revolution

It was during the constitutional revolution that Seyyed Jamal reached the height of his popularity. He was in the midst of events right from the beginning. When the abusive governor of Tehran clashed with the business community in December 1905, a crowd, led by the prominent religious leaders, gathered in a central mosque to protest. Seyyed Jamal was asked by the religious leaders to ascend the pulpit and speak out on behalf of the oppressed businessmen. But those among the religious leaders who were on the government's side and were looking for an opportunity to disrupt the assembly, protested some of Seyyed Jamal's remarks as insulting to the Shah and then, according to a previous arrangement, signalled their followers to disrupt the assembly.

Following the incident, the anti- government religious leaders took refuge in a shrine near the capital to continue their protest. But

Seyyed Jamal, fearful for his own safety, hid in friend's houses. Meanwhile, the crowd followed their religious leaders to the shrine, and the request of the grand vazir for their return to the capital was ignored. To prevent more trouble the Shah finally granted their request and promised changes in the government. He sent royal carriages for the return of the religious leaders.

A few months later the grand vazir, recognizing Seyyed Jamal as an effective spokesman of the opposition, asked the new governor of Tehran to exile him to a faraway eastern city. The constitutionalist religious leaders intervened and the grand vazir relented, provided that Seyyed Jamal would stay out of Tehran during the month of Muharram, when religious sentiments were at their height. Seyyed Jamal, on the advice of the constitutionalist religious leaders, accepted the condition and left the city. However, the members of the Shah's household were unhappy about the banishment of their favorite preacher, and begged the Shah for Seyyed's return to Tehran. Two weeks after his departure, by order of the Shah, Seyyed Jamal returned to Tehran.

On another occasion, the grand vazir, who was very well aware of the influential role of the preachers in arousing the public, decided to arrest Shaykh Muhammad Wa'is, another popular preacher, early in the summer of 1906. While a contigent of soldiers surrounded the preacher in the street, passers -by and the student of a nearby religious school came to his defence. The ensuing skirmish resulted in the death of a student. The preacher and the crowd took the bloody body to a mosque and the constitutionalists religious leaders joined them. The soldiers surrounded the mosque. There were more clashes and more "martyrs."

As the crowd in the mosque grew, the grand vazir blocked traffic to the mosque (including food and water) in order to force the crowd to disperse. Finally , the constitutionalist religious leaders, who had given up hope for the fulfillment of the Shah's promise of reform in the system (including the dismissal of the grand vazir), decided to migrate *en masse* to the shrine city of Qum, about 100 miles south of the capital.

The departure of the prominent religious leaders from the capital upset the population, and many took refuge in the British Legation in protest. Finally, the Shah replaced the grand vazir and on August 5, 1906, he signed a decree granting the Constution.

The ailing Muzaffaral -Dom Shah died a few months later, and at the coronation of his son, Muhammad 'Ali Shah, Seyyed Jamal gave the official sermon. But this attention and other favour from the new shah did not change Seyyed Jamal's attitude.For instance, at the memorial service for the assassin of Atabak, the prime minister who was suspected by the constitutionalists of scheming to do away with the parliament, Seyyed Jamal gave a very moving speech praising the assassin as a martyr and condemning the murdered prime minister and, by implication, the Shah.

As already mentioned, Seyyed Jamal and his old friend from Isfahan, Malik al-Mutakallimin, both worked very closely with the constitutionalists, and their homilies were invaluable to the cause. After the bombardment of the parliament building by Muhammad 'Ali' Shah in July 1908, many constitutionalist leaders were arrested. Malik was among them, and a few days later he was put to death. Seyyed Jamal managed to hide and flee from Tehran, but he was later captured and executed in the city of Brugerd.

The Islamic Pulpit as a Medium, of Public Communication

The objective of this paper is to examine the Islamic pulpit (among the Iranian Twelver Shi'ahs) as a medium of public communication in a pre -industrial society. In previous sections we have observed the operation of the Islamic pulpit in a historical context, that is, the Iranian constitutional revolution. It is the purpose of this section to focus more directly on the social organization of the Islamic pulpit in terms of recruitment and control of the preachers, the composition of their audience, the content of their homilies and the effects of these homilies.

A. The recruitment and control of the preachers , as already reported, were dependent on the patronage of prominent and influential members of society. It is true that practically anybody dressed as a religious leader could ascend the pulpit in a mosque. But to continue and succeed, he needed at least the tacit support of a prominent religious personality in the town.

We have already noted that through controlling the appointment of the prominent religious leaders to the directorship of certain mosques(*imam-i Jum'ah)* or pious foundations (mutawalli) the government had indirect control over the pulpit whose preachers were under its appointees. Moreover, some religious leaders were not averse accepting gifts and favours from the government in return for supporting its policies. In extraordinary situations the officials banished the out spoken preachers.

However, generally speaking, government control over the pulpit was not only indirect but also limited. This was the case because there were many religious leaders who were not under its influence. first, there were some who were the directors of mosques and pious foundations which were not under government control. There were other religious leaders who were financially independent because they came from wealthy families. There were still others whose prestige depended on their learning and piety. These were men whose independence brought them the admiration and support of the public.

Regarding the direct control over the content of the homilies, there are reports of explicit instructions to the preachers on specific issues or occasions. Some prominent religious leaders in the shrine cities of Iraq, for example , used to send telegrammes asking for certain messages to be relayed or certain issues to be discussed from the pulpit. There are also reports of some preachers who, on the instructions of their patrons, discussed, attacked, or defended certain issues or persons. But, in general, control over the content of the homilies was not direct. Most preachers knew the stance of their supporters and did not need direct and daily instruction.

A new method of control of the pulpit developed during the constitutional revolution. Before the bombardment of the parliament in June 1908, a secret committee composed of two prominent preachers, two newspaper editors and other constitutionalists met every morning before sunrise to discuss current events and monitor the behaviour of the anti- constitutionalists in order to develop strategies for dealing with them from the pulpit and by the newspaper editorials.

B. The audience of the pulpit varied in size and composition -from a small group of ten to twenty persons of the same sex in a *rawdah-* gathering at a private residence to several thousand people of diverse backgrounds in the cathedral mosque (*masjid-i jami)* in major cities for the celebration of religious holidays (the martyrdom of Imam Husayn or a n event related to another saint). There were also prime times for exposure to the pulpit. During the months of Muharram and Safar, during the fasting month of Ramadan when pious Muslims flocked to the mosque in the afternoon, and, of course, on special religious holidays, the pulpit was very popular.

The reputation of the religious leader who conducted the prayer of the assembly also was a factor in attracting people to the mosque and the subsequent homily from the pulpit (whether he himself delivered it or not). But it was the popularity of the preacher himself that counted most. There are reports that on the occasion of Seyyed Jamal's orations, many fewer people attended the prayer before his homily than listened to his sermon.

As member of the secret police who regularly followed Seyyed Jamal to report on his preachings once reported that before the arrival of the preacher, he noticed several groups of men sitting here and there in the courtyard of the mosque, with their backs toward Mecca discussing politics, while only a few persons were praying. By this statement he meant to suggest that most of the members of Seyyed Jamal's audience were not pious Muslims, but rabblerousing irreligious constitutionalists. There are also other pieces of evidence indicating that at least a portion of the audience during Seyyed Jamal's popular orations was politically motivated.

Another secret police officer on the trail of Seyyed Jamal

reports that one day he saw such a crowd in the mosque and the surrounding area that traffic had come to a halt, and the mosque's doors had been closed. Again, on one occasion Seyyed Jamal himself told his audience. "you are about four or five thousand people here of every kind". Sometimes he also admonished to women in his audience for crying too much and for not understanding the significance of his message. In a picture reproduced in a book by a European who attended one of Seyyed Jamal's orations (inconspicuously, of course, by climbing to the roof of a nearby shop), the courtyard of the mosque and adjoining rooftops are shown to be full of men (and some veiled women) with almost no room for standing, while Seyyed Jamal was sitting on a high pulpit in the middle of the crowd.

C. Regarding the content of pronouncements from the pulpit, besides the well-known poems and the saint's stories, religious and moral issues and significant events were also discussed.

Although we do not generally have direct access to the specific content of the homilies of bygone years, there is an exception in the case of Seyyed Jamal. As reported earlier, some constitutionalists thought it useful to take down some of his orations on the spot and reproduce them in the form of a regular newspaper. There are thirty six issues of this paper (called *al-Jamal),* published between 1907-1908, now available.

I will use this newspaper as a sample of Seyyed Jamal's orations during the constitutional revolution. My content analysis of these recorded homilies is of an informal nature.

From a cursory examination of the contents of *al-Jamal* it is very clear that Seyyed Jamal was a committed constitutionalists with rational orientation toward life and was, for a man of his time, quite knowledgeable about Western civilization.

Regarding the political information that Seyyed Jamal intended to impart to his audience, we see that, within a religious frame of reference, he tells his audience about the oppression of the despotic system of government. In very simple language he tells them about their "right" as human beings and citizens. He also discusses freedom of assembly, speech, and voting.

Seyyed Jamal also informs his audience about the technological, scientific, and social achievements of the West, such as paper manufacturing, wireless telegraphy, modern medicine, the European taxation system, and superior educational institutions.

Syeed Jamal staunchly supports the Qur'an and the Shi'ah faith. But he also advocates constitutional monarchy, the establishment of modern industry, the consumption of goods manufactured in Iran, the establishment of modern schools, and the hiring of foreign educators, technicians and other specialists from neutral countries. He is in favour of elevating the status of women through education, and supports the protection of minority groups (he specifically mentions Jews as an example).

Interpersed throughout Seyyed Jamal's homilies are criticisms of various sorts. He attacks injustice by and corruption among government officials, religious leaders, tribal chiefs, and landlords. He deplores Iran's dependence on foreigners. He attacks illiteracy, fatalism, poverty, idleness, and conflicts among Muslims. He is unhappy about polygyny, temporary marriage, and misuse of pious foundations by the greedy and ignorant religious leaders.

Turning to the influence of the communications from the pulpit, events before the constitutional revolution had already demonstrated its extent and potency. For instance, the famous ban on the use of tobacco in 1891 by Hasan Shirazi, a very prominent Shi'ah religious leader living in Iraq, was heralded from pulpits all over Iran in protest against the concession granted by Nasir al- Din Shah for the sale of tobacco to an "infidel" British subject. In a matter of day "almost everybody" stopped smoking, and the Shah had to cancel the concession to prevent an open rebellion.

Many government officials also were well aware of the influence of the pulpit. We have already reported the insistence of the grand vazir on sending the constitutional preacher, Seyyed Jamal, out of Tehran during the month of Muharram when religious sentiments ran high. Further, the attention that Seyyed Jamal received from the crown prince and the prince- governors of Isfahan and Shiraz, who showered him with gifts (and titles), and their eagerness to attract him to their side clearly demonstrated their awareness of the impact of the preacher's words on the minds of the populace.

After the bombardment of the parliament by Muhammad'Ali Shah, and while the city of Tabriz was under siege by royal troops for ten months, the daily orations of preachers in the city mosques played an important role in agitating the masses and encouraging the people to take up arms. Throughout the siege, in collaboration with constitutionalists who organized the resistance, these preachers, by their pronouncements from the pulpit, guided the public and sometimes even restrained the masses when the situation required calm and patience.

Turning to specific examples of the immediate effect of the preacher on his audience, on one occasion during the constitutional revolution the homily of Shaykh Muhammad Wa'iz against the foreign domination excited his audience to the point that they left the mosque for a site where construction for a Russian bank was in progress on an abandoned Muslim cemetery and demolished it.

In another case, when Seyyed Jamal criticized the government for borrowing money from abroad and explained to his audience the advantages of a national bank, some veiled women in his audience removed their earrings and bracelets and placed them on the step of his pulpit as their personal contribution to the formation of the national bank. On the same or another occasion a woman in the audience stood up, pledged a large sum of money, and declared that she knew of other women who would support the cause. In a society where women were veiled and no stranger was supposed to hear their voices, such a gesture in public was very unusual indeed, and had a dramatic impact on both the audience and the preacher.

Conclusion

This paper has examined the social organization of the Islamic pulpit as a medium of public communication during the constitutional revolution in Iran. Our cursory examination of this historical event clearly reveals the established place of the Islamic pulpit in the social fabric and its role in the development of socio-political events. It is our contention,therefore, that a systematic examination of the media of public communication from a cross-cultural historical perspective deserves more attention from the social sciences and probably would enhance our understanding of the modern mass media.

REFERENCES

1. A Fathi, "Role of traditional leaders in modernization of Iran," Int. J. Middle East Stud., 11, 1980, pp. 87-98.
2. A Kasravi, The history of the constitutional meovement in Iran, (in Persian), Tehran, 1965.
3. Nazim al-Islam Kirmani, The history of the Iranians' awakening (in Persian), Tehran, 1967.

(Revised and edited; originally published in *Islamic Culture,* October 1987).

12

The Myth of Race

ABDEL AL-AZIZ KAMEL

(Abstract: 'race' implies group with similarities in sematic characteristics which are perpetuated according to the laws of biological inheritance, allowing for a margin of individual variation. Here race is limited to color of people as a significant factor).

The classification of human groups are defined by a single or many characteristics, the most prominent being colour of the skin and eye, the shape of the skull and nose and the height of the body. At the very most it would be possible to define a pure race in terms of the incidence of one selected sematic characteristic but never in terms of all or even of the majority of hereditary traits.

Some scholars try to divide mankind on the basis of 'pure blood.' this notion of 'pure blood' or 'one blood' is a meaningless criterion because the elements of heredity have no link whatsoever with blood. Heredity is not a fluid transmitted through the blood although this classification remains standard in some societies that describe themselves as scientifically advanced. In the United States of America those individuals are considered 'Negroes' or 'Indians' who have one sixteenth part of Indian Blood or Black blood that is when one of their sixteen direct ancestors was a Negro or Indian.

In accordance to this criterion a Negro will not be considered a 'biological being,' in fact he would be a member in a group or a particular social economical and cultural society. These Negroes, according to the above oriterion do not differ biologically from their white counterpart. They have fair skins, blue eyes and blonde hair.

The situation, according to individual who has a very small amount of Negro blood running in his veins where as it would be just, if we, conforming to the same logic, defined an individual white, if he had some 'white blood' running in his veins. That is if there be white or black in the blood.

The Scientific View

In 1950 Unesco published a scientific document on the question of Racial Discrimination. This document was signed by a nucleus of well-known authropologists. They concluded their study by presenting their decisions. One of their main decisions was that all human beings descend from one origin and that there is no link between the races of people and their civilisations. For his reason we cannot call the Americans, French, Germans, a 'Race' nor can we use that term on Muslims, Christians or Jews. Nor can we call the people who speak the English language a "race."

There are, however, ways of dividing the various races. Anthropologists divide the human race into three large groups ; Mongoloids, Negroids and Caucasoids. Division cannot be affected by any single sematic character like that of colour. This feature alone cannot distinguish any group of people from other. It is also not possible to use any single characteristic to explain the complex of superiority or inferiority that is generally enforced upon communities. Most of the sematic characteristics found in the individual of a single race — are comparatively greater than those found in two races that make a large community. The majority of anthropologists do not consider mental characteristics when dividing races. There is an ample evidence to show that if two groups of people live in a single social and cultural environment — from their infancy — the difference in their outlook would be insignificant. Psychologists who had earlier spread the view that there exist mental differences in various communities have now accepted the above view.

The conclusive scientific data that have been collected by these renowned authorities, say : "The principal factor in the main difference is not heredity but cultural experiences which have been lived by a certain community. There is a evidence of a pure race nor is there any biologically confirmed testimony against miscegenation, and mixed marriages. There is also no evidence that such mixed marriages are influenced by social element.

Later in September 1967, UNESCO reiterated its call to humanity and issued a second document saying :

"Every human being is born free and equal in dignity and rights." This democratic principle which we are conveying to the world is exposed to danger in areas where human populations differ in cultural, social, economical and political fields and areas where there are obstacles in acknowledging equality and dignity to each human being. Racialism appears as ghost of some particular king and continues wrecking humanity. Racialism is an obstacle in the way of progress of those who come under its fire, an evil for those who want to implement it, a factor for discrimination between the nations, an element provoking world tension and a danger to world peace. Racialism completely distorts and misrepresents immediate information about human life. It is therefore clear that the problems created by racialism have social roots more than physical factors.

The most important technical means to uproot Racialism is to work towards balancing the social situation which creates isolation, and to stop those who creating this segregation from fulfilling their ideas. We must also combat the very iniquities of this error.

The most important technical means that should be employed to fight racialism is to work towards balancing the social situation which creates isolation.

The above statement was issued by a committee sponsored by UNESCO which held its meeting in Paris and was attended by eighteen physicists and specialists on human rights. They represented sixteen countries.

Earlier a number of unbiased scholars had persued some of the doubtful scientific facts which had arisen out of colour prejudice. By means of laboratory experiences they tried to prove the inferiority of the black people. Their objective research led them to discover the fallacy of this theory.

Rose describes a special study undertaken by Robert Been in the beginning of the 20th century. He tried to show that the skull and brains of the Negro were smaller than his counterparts among the white. He also showed how Robert Bin had reviewed many of the samples that were studied and proved the grievous mistakes of both the criteria and the results that had come to light.

Objectively speaking many segments of humanity in Asia and Africa have made considerable progress after they were able to liberate themselves from the shackles of Imperialism. This is a living evidence that shatters the entire myth of mental superiority possessed by certain races. This, as mentioned earlier, does not negate the atmospherical influences that have their effect upon the activities of mankind nor does it negate the influence of social and historical factors. What it does basically discard is the concept that groups of people are by nature, distinct from one another.

What it the Cause of Discrimination

If Racial Discrimination is a scientific myth and is minus any meaning then why has it ever occurred? Why has this problem taken such aggravating proportions in certain segments of humanity. Why have certain groups of people made racial differences in the basis of their legislation and social activities. By so doing they are directly refuting scientifically proved facts and results. Its colour, in its biological sense, natural or acquired?

The dictates of science and realities prove that the question of colour is acquired and is embedded in man from the early stages of infancy. This is so because children always love to imitate elders and among the things child acquires unconsciously his attitude towards colour.

This attitude in white man has its social, political and economic motivations which only become an international problem after European navigators had discovered geographical territories which attracted the people of Europe to travel across seas. With the progress of capitalism the spirit of profiteering became a distinct feature of the West. The discovery of new lands in America provided vast fields for their pursuits. On the other hand they lacked the necessary man power for production. The white emigrants began to annihilate the Red Indians who possessed an old civilization which they were reluctant to abandon in the face to this new formidable threat. The whites gained a strong footing and systematically began to annihilate the Red Indians by isolating in slum areas. Simultaneously they began to bring the Negroes from Africa to work on the farms of their new world.

European philosophers and some religious authorities tried to justify the ill-treatment met by the Negroes. They tried to suppress voices of some humanitarians who protested against this evil. Long, in his 'History of Jamaica' in 1774 wrote the following words about the Negroes :

> "We can say with confidence that they are fundamentally unsuitable for civilisation whereas it is possible to teach monkeys to eat, drink, rest and dress like men. We can see their mental ability which is retarded by nature. It appears of all the races discovered so far, that they are the last to possess the faculty of thinking and initiative, unless they are helped by some miraculous intervention."

While at this point we may recall the incidence mentioned by Kent Little in a book published by an international organisation wherein he describes the planned effort to destroy the characteristics of an entire community in a bid to reduce them to more items of merchandise. The incidence of a ship named 'Zong' illustrates the success of this effort. A hundred and thirty Africans were thrown into the sea under the pretext of water shortage on the ship. The case was dragged to the court not as a criminal case of murder but as a loss of merchandise. This was done to establish whether the "items" were really thrown into the sea thereby obliging the Insurance Company to pay the cost or was it an act to deceive the company.

This European conception, as mentioned by Montesque in his book "The Spirit of the Law' 1848 reaches the most ignoble proportions in disgracing human dignity. Defending the rights of his people to shed the blood of the black Africans and their enslavement he says :

> "If I were to elucidate our rights to enslave the Negroes I would say ; "The European nations after eliminating the Red Indians of America began to enslave the people of Africa. They did this to make them work in their lands and fields. The Negroes are people who are ivory black from the tip of their heads to the bottom of their feet. Their noses are so flat that it is impossible to even pity them. It is my belief that the Almighty Lord, Whose power is great, is much wiser than placing a spirit, in a pitch black body! Let alone a virtuous spirit!"

I have mentioned as examples, these references despite their inexorable contents and merciless thought on human dignity to illustrate the efforts of European philosophers to justify their racial superiority over the coloured races in general and the black races in particular. I have done so to confirm the fact that racial discrimination is basically, founded upon social, economical and political principles. It is also a fact that the western world does not lack an objective knowledge of this reality. That is time of writing this article, I have before me a pamphlet with the heading 'Objective Justice.' UNESCO has began publishing these pamphlets against "Racial Discrimination in South Africa" and "Racial Segregation and Imperialism in 1969." Its second issue published in June 1970 was exclusively devoted to South Africa.

These documents and those of their kind condemn Racial Discrimination scientifically and 'officially' in he world's greatest assembly. With all that the gap still remains wide and prejudice still incredibly strong. Humanity is still trying to traverse across the borders of theory to reach the borders of practice through enlightenment and silence, and thereby cutting across the confines of Racialism. These pamphlets which are published in New York may very well find the most disgusting scenes of Racial Discrimination in that very city. This is apparent when we compare the slums of Harlem where the Negroes live with the suburbs of the whites, where power and authority dominate.

After this scientific journey which exposes the bitter and merciless sufferings of human conscience, let us return to our majestic Book, the Holy Quran, from where we can draw inspiration, guidance and light.

Conjunction Between Science and Islam

Since science has eventually declared equality among peoples, and has destroyed the baseless arguments of western scholars who tried to justify Racial Discrimination, and pursued their efforts, and finally crushed the principles upon which they were to establish discrimination, this long and strenuous scientific journey has eventually corresponded with the teachings of Islam that have been revealed by God and which have been lived by the Muslims from their first society. They lived in a spirit of brotherhood that never knew any discrimination.

"He it is Who supporteth thee
With His Help
And with believers
And (as for the believers) hath
Attuned their hearts
If thou hadst spent all that is in the earth
Thou couldest not have attuned
Lo, He is mighty Wise."

Surah Al-Anfaal.
62-63

They followed the dictates of the Almighty who addressed the entire humanity reminding them of the One Creator and One father, saying :

"O mankind!
Be careful of your duty
To your Lord,
Who created you from a single soul
And from it created its mate
And from them spread
Multitude of men and women.
Be careful of your duty
Toward Allah
In Whom you claim (your rights) of one another
And towards the wombs (that bore you)
Lo! Allah hath been
A Wather over yiu" z

Islam, Responsibility and the Unity of Mankind

The great danger in the question of Racial Discrimination is that it imposes upon man something for which he is not responsible; a responsibility of which he is not the author. Why am I of this colour or that hue?

In tackling the problem of human equality Islam does not begin with the colour of the skin. It approaches the problem from the very roots of creation and existence. The Almighty addresses man, every man, in the following words :

"Whosoever goes right
It is only for (the good of) his own soul
And whosoever erreth
Erreth to hurt itself.
No Laden soul can bear another load
We never punish

Until we have sent a messenger."

"A muslim believes in the One and Only True God:

Allah (Himself) is witness
That there is no God save him
And the angels and men of learning
(Too are witnesses)
Maintaining His creation in Justice
There is no God save Him
The Almighty, the Wise."

From this monotheistic belief in the One True God issues the conclusive unity of the entire human race; a unity wherein man does not carry anybody's responsibility but his own, and is on equal basis with his fellow human beings for all times and in all places.

This leads us to the Islamic concept of creation and its responsibilities upon mankind.

The story creation, as portrayed in the Quran, has too unambiguous. stages :

The first stage is the creation of Adam from clay after which Allah blew a spirit in it and it became a perfect man.

"And He taught Adam all the names
Then showed them to the Angels
Saying "Inform Me of the names of those
If ye are Truthful!"
They said, "Be glorified!
We have no knowledge save
That which Thou hast taught us
Lo ! Thou, only Thou
Art Knower, The Wise."

"He said : O Adam!
Inform them of their names
And when he had informed them of their names
He said : Did I not tell you
That I know the secret
Of the Heavens and the earth?
And I know
That which ye disclose
And that which ye hide"

The question of prostration is connected with this stage when the Lord says :

"And when We said
Unto the Angels
Prostrate yourselves before Adam
They fell prostrate
All save Iblis
He demurred through pride
And so became a disbeliever."

Adam's first experience during this stage was successful. He was taught all the names which he learnt and comprehended. He gave evidence of his comprehensive knowledge. Thereafter came the stage of living in Paradise by abiding to the commands of the Almighty and abstaining from what He has forbidden.

The Second Stage

In this trial there exists very distinct something which deserves some pause over its broad outlines :

1. The command of Allah has various aspects which draw attention. The Almighty says :

"We said, "O Adam ! dwell thou

And thy wife in the Garden
And eat of the bountiful things therein
As (Where and When) ye will.
But approach not this tree.
Lest you become transgressors."

Various descriptions are given in the Quran about the living of Adam and his wife :

"There is therein (enough provision)
For thee not to go hungry
Nor go naked
Nor to suffer from thirst
Nor from the sun's heat".

There is a positive command giving them the freedom to eat whatever they liked and from wherever they wished in Paradise. At the same time there is a command not to eat from a particular tree.

2. Connected with these two commands there is a warning from the Devil.

The positive and negative command, and warning were not directed to Adam only but to both Adam and his wife. This is explicitly clear from the following verse. Together with the previous verse of Chapter II verse 35, we may read the following verse :

"O Adam! dwell there
And thy wife in the Garden
And eat from where you like
But approach not this tree.
Lest you become transgressors.
Then Satan whispered to them
That he might manifest unto them
That which was hidden from them
Of their shame. And he said,

"Your Lord only forbade you this tree
Lest you should become Angels
Or become of the immortals."
And he swore to them
(saying Lo I am a sincere
Adviser unto you"

"Then We said: "O Adam !
Verily this is an enemy
To thee and thy wife :
So let him not get you.
Both out of the Garden.
So that thou art landed.
In misery."

The Divine Command, is therefore, addressed to Adam and his wife simultaneously. Both are to follow the command, and both are to stand responsible should any one of them break the law.

3. The strong incentive that led them to eat of the forbidden tree and which enabled the Devil to influence them with - was ambition. It is with this characteristic that man transgresses the Laws of God. Adam and his wife were swept by an ambition to become Angels or become immortals.

The situation in which they found themselves was a conflict between a clear command of God and the pangs of human ambition with which man transgresses that very command. God had bestowed upon them the spiritual gift of knowledge and the materialistic gift of paradise. With all this the human mind gazed at something beyond the nature of man.

To this day this problem continues to have a very deep influence in the lives of human beings. Mankind still staggers at this point of submission or transgression in a bid to rise higher than mankind can. In so doing, it shows total disregard for existing mankind. Now isn't this the very essence of racial Discrimination? The refusal of man to acknowledge the essence of man in himself or in others and he himself tries to become something else. If he fails he tries to reduce others to a lower level so that they could continue being lower than himself. In our world he tries to sow the seeds of discrimination by all the means at his disposal—but in vain.

It is in this conjunction that we see that wisdom of the Quran in its far-sighted usage of the expression :

"Thus did he lead them with guile"

It was this guile and human pride with which Adam and his wife tried to ascend to the most elevated station in life which turned out to be a slide to the lowest and basest position.

Our Relation with the Problem

We pursue the story of Adam and his wife and so we read the story of repentance coming from our earliest forefathers :

"They said "Our Lord !
We have wronged our own souls
If Thou forgive us not
And bestow not upon us Thy Mercy.
We shall certainly be the losers."

This was the first school for humanity; a school wherein mankind has the first experience of success and failure. Here we read of God's Mercy at prayer. It envelops them and saves them from the hardships of the experience. This is mentioned in the following words :

"And Adam disobeyed his Lord
So he went astray
Then his Lord chose him
(For his Grade) : He turned
To him and gave him guidance."

The first story draws to an end; a story of success, error, repentance and the acceptance of repentance.

This is followed by the third stage of man's journey in life. It is the story of his vicegerent on earth. Despite the error that was committed and will continue to be committed as a result of the process of experiences in man's long journey through the passage of time—and the process of his submission and transgression of the Laws of God, man was made Lord's vicegerent on earth.

The story of man's existence on earth, as portrayed by the Quran, is not a story of retaliation or punishment. No human being bears the iniquities of Adam, just as Adam bears no responsibility for the temptation of his spouse. On the same basis every human being in this life - opens a clean sheet both with his creator and his society. This clean sheet from the Islamic point of view is absolutely new and bears no ignominies of sin and consequently requires no sacrifice.

Our first father and his wife have a story of their own with God. It is different from my story with The Almighty, save in one respect. And that is how much have I benefited from the two experiences they went through. These two experiences represent the continuous struggle in the human mind between submission and transgression — between justice and injustice :

> "They said, Our Lord !
> We have wronged our own souls."

Personal Responsibility of the Individual

There are numerous verses in the Quran that go to confirm the responsibilities of the individual and go to show—irrespective of their being in contemporary or in successive generations, that all man kind is equal. Before the Almighty and society in all matters concerning responsibility they are equal; they are one. We may read the following verses wherein God invites mankind to righteousness:

(1) "Did you (O Muhammad) see him

Who turned away.
And gave a little—then was grudging
Hath he knowledge of the Unseen so that he sees?
Or had he not bad news of what is in the book of Moses
And Abraham who paid his debt :
That no laden one shall bear another's load
And that man has only that for which he makes effort.
And that his effort will be seen
And afterward he will be repaid for it
with fullest payment
And that Your Lord, He is the gool."

(2) "And every man's fate
We have fastened on his own neck
On the Day of Judgement
We shall bring out
For him a scroll
Which he will see spread open.
Read your book
It is enough for you to be your own judge."

Man and The Kingdom of Nature

Throughout his life, In his strenous endeavour to reach God, man, together with his surroundings live with nature and humanity. This relationship is termed by the Quran as "Souls and Worlds". Now what are the broad outlines defined in this relationship?

(1) The very nature of man's task on this earth is to play the role of God's vicegerent for whom God has made the earth subservient :

"He has spread out the earth
For (His) creatures."

Addressing us the Lord says :

"It is God Who has created
The heavens and the earth
And sends down rain
From the skies and with it
Brings food to feed you.
It is He Who has made the ships subject to you
That you may sail through the seas.
By His command,
He has made the rivers subject to you
And He has made subject to you
The sun and the moon
Both diligently pursuing their courses
He has made subject to you
The night and the day
And He gave you
But if you count the bounty of God,
Never will you be able.
To number them
Verily, man is a wrong doer
And ungrateful."

As for man himself — Islam — views him to be a part of the substance of this earth.

"And Allah has produced
You from the earth
Growing (gradually)."

Man is not foreign to the earth nor is he thrown on to it. He is neither punished in it because of it. Man's relation to the earth is based on mercy and righteousness. It is not based on the foundations of arrogance, enmity, and corruption.

It is on the above basis that the prophet P.B.U.H. and his companions and those who came after them, offered them advice. They instructed their armies to behave like the earth and its bounties. They were ordered not to mow down fruit laden trees, not to destroy buildings, and not to set fire to date groves.

(3) This tenderness and grace are spread to all creatures on the earth; Islam forbids torture of animals and rewards those who show kindness to them. We have preserved a tradition of the Prophet P.B.U.H. which is reported by Imam Malik from Abu Hurairah. It reads :

> "While a man was walking in the street he felt the pangs of thirst. He found his way to a well and descended into it to drink from it. He them cam and while proceeding he was suddenly confronted by a panting dog. The dog was licking the earth. The man said (to himself) "Thirst has got this dog as it got me." Using his shoe as a container he went down into the well and brought some water in it. He held the shoe by his mouth so that he could climb out of the well. He offered the water to the thirsty dog and was grateful to God for opportunity. He then asked for forgiveness for his sins. The people who were around said :
>
> "O Messenger of Allah !
> Will we be rewarded for showing sympathy to animals?
> The Prophet replied :
> "There is reward in rendering service to every living creature."

The deep moral lesson that runs through this is that the animal is dumb and speechless. Not only is it unable to reach the water, it is also unable to ask for it. Man's service and kindness to such that are weaker and helpless — are in themselves a most telling evidence of his moral greatness. When man offers help to the stronger the element of fear may be at work, and in showing endearment to his equals it may be mere gesture of friendship. But in the above case it is the fruit of man's sterling quality.

This mercy is reflected in our Islamic history. Endowment trusts were created specifically for feeding and offering veterinary services to sick and stray animals and purchasing of grains for birds. To this day some of these practices are found. Pilgrims who go to perform their Haj feed the birds that surround the sacred precincts of Mecca and Medina.

The Quranic review of the kingdom of Nature is that it is the sign of God for those who comprehend, heed and reflect. Perchance by doing so they would show gratitude, and seek guidance. The Kingdom of Nature with all that is in it, is created for man to ponder. It stands as invitation to think and perform noble deeds. As for the varieties and differences that are found in size, colour and functions of these signs — it must be said that they all go to prove the power of God.

Mankind : One Great Family

From the Kingdom of Nature - Islam takes us to the Kingdom of man; from nature to human society. It illustrates the features of similarities and differences in human life and human society after discussing nature.

On the basis of monotheism which is the pivot of Islam and its essence, Islam calls for the unity of human life says :

> "O mankind! fear your Lord
> Who created you
> From a single person
> Created of like nature
> His mate and from them scattered
> Countless men and women
> Fear Allah through Whom
> You demand your mutual (rights)
> And (fear) the wombs (that bore you)
> For Allah watches over you."

God is One and the Soul of Man is One

From this single soul God created its mate, and from this couple issued all men and women. The command to fear God and the wombs is an evidence of the bond that binds all men together, irrespective of the lands and times that separate them and irrespective of the differences in their colours, languages, economic and social standards.

As human beings we have not witnessed the creation of our souls. We have neither seen how the heavens and the earths were created nor the human soul itself but in the variety of their colours and languages. Now what is the Islamic point of view on this variation?

The Islamic view on this subject does not overrun its stand on the question of colours and their differences in the Kingdom of Nature. The Quran discusses them together and does not treat them separately as specific studies. In the verses of Chapter we observe a presentation of God's power in Nature and man. The same fact is stressed in another verse :

"Won't you see that
Allah sends down rain
From the sky?
With it We then bring out produce
of various colours,
And in the mountains
Are tracts white and red
Of various shades of colour
And black intense in hue.

"And so amongst men
And crawling creatures and cattle
Are they of various colours.
These truly fear God,
among His servants

Who have knowledge :
Fro God is Exalted in Might
Oft-Forgiving."

These verse indicate the link that exist between the external phenomena of things and the necessity of scientific research in them. It also indicates the satisfaction of the Quran at any result obtained by unbiased and unprejudiced scientific research.

From the unity of the human origin and the varieties of languages and colours, Islam proceeds to discuss the distribution and life-study of tribes and peoples :

"O, Mankind !
We have created you of a male and female
And made you into peoples and tribes to get acquainted
Behold ! The most noble in the sight of God
Is the most—God-fearing.
Verily God
Is The Knower, The Wise"

Islam looks at mankind as an enormous garden wherein there are flowers of every colour. Each has its beauty but in no way superior to others. The Prophet (P.B.U.H.) indicated this fact when he said :

"In Empracing (Islam)
I preceded the Arabs
Salman preceded the Persians,
Suhaib preceded the Romans
And Bilaal the Abyssinians."

The Prophet : All One Brotherhood

It was no easy task for mankind to accept this magnanimous desire which was brought by Islam at a time when territorial, natural and colour prejudices had wrecked its unity. Islam's first preoccupation was to adjust the mental and conceptional framework of the intellectual world and then have them transferred directly to reality and the practical life of man. In implementing the Divine Commands immediately after their revelation, lies one of the most dynamic features of Islam. Islam is unique in creating a society while Divine Revelations were still being revealed and in fact the Messenger of God was able to established his leadership in the mosque and the lives of the people simultaneously.

To emphasize the meaning of brotherhood of man, Islam directs its attention to the deep historical passage of mankind. Stressing this point it invites us to have implicit faith in all the prophets and messengers of Allah:

> "We make no distinction
> Between any of His Messengers
> And they say: "We hear and obey!"
> (Grant us) Thy forgiveness, Our Lord!
> Unto Thee is the end of all jouneyes."

The unflinching struggles of the prophets throughout the centuries are portrayed by the Quran. This is followed by the following comment:

> "Verily this nation of yours
> Is one nation
> and I am your Lord
> So keep your duty unto Me.

In a vivid example, the Messenger, illustrates the nature of co-ordination and co-operation between him and the earlier prophets. He portrays the affinity that runs through their efforts and struggles. The example runs as follows :

> "My example and the example of the prophets who preceded me is like that of a builder. He builds a house magnificently but in one corner leaves a brick unassembled. The people begin circumambulating around the house. They are fascinated and in admiration say :

"How nice it would be if this brick is assembled in its place?"
Behold I am that last brick!
I am the seal of all the prophets!"

During the Nocturnal Journey in the night of "Meraj' the Messenger met with the prophets. He described their features. Some he mentioned as "tan" in colour while others he described as "fair" in complexion. In doing so he did not stress the point of colours as a distinction of superiority.

Mankind : Brothers in Faith

During the deep hours of the night the prophet went into lengthy sessions of prayers with The Almighty. The following prayer is an extract of one his late night prayers :

"O Lord! I bear witness that Thou art our Lord
There is no Lord but Thee,
And that all mankind
Are Brothers.

Addressing the entire human progency he went on to say :

"You are all from Adam.
And Adam was created from clay.
People should, once and for all, put a stop
To boasting of their ancestors.
Or else they would descend—
In the eyes of The Almighty
to a lower level than the scarabs."

These teachings were put into practice. They were implemented in every sphere of Islamic life. Islam is a universal religion and addresses itself to all mankind irrespective to territory, colour and rank :

(1) In religious affairs — whether pertaining to the performance

of the official prayers, the times of fasting or fulfilling the pilgrim rites, all are equal. There is no discrimination on the base of tribalism as was practised by the Quraish in pre-Islamic times—who enjoyed the exclusive right to skip performing the sacred rites at Arafat and limit themselves to the precincts of the Holy Mosque. This was their discriminatory character which was illuminated by the Almighty :

"Then hasten onward

From the place whence the multitude hasten onward."

(2) Man's progress and advancement in the Islamic Society were not based on colour. Two of the most significant basic responsibilities at the mosque of Medina were :

(i) Leading the official five daily prayers (Imamat)
(ii) The duty to call the believers to prayers (Azaam)

The first responsibility fell on the shoulders of the prophet. He came from the Hashimi branch of the famous Quraish tribe while the latter responsibility was entrusted to Bilal Bin Rabah who was in terms of race, an Abyssinian. He was priviliged to be the first human being to have ascended on the roof of the Holy Kaaba and perform the call. He was also priviliged to perform the call at the Aqsa Mosque in Jerusalem when the Muslims entered the city after its conquest at the hands of Omar Bin Khattab.

(3) Islam fostered fraternal and family ties between the believers. The Prophet said the following in this respect:

"If someone — whose moral and religious background is of satisfaction to you — approaches you (for marriage) then get him married.

Beware if you don't do this the earth would witness corruption and monstrous evils."

The history of Islam overwhelms with practical examples in this respect. The sister of Abdul Rahman Bin Auf (an Arab woman belonging to the Quraish tribe) married Bilal Bin Rabah, an Abyssinian who was the Mo'azzin of the Prophet. Hossain Bin Ali freed a bondmaid and then married her. When ostracized for this by Moawiya he wrote back saying :

> "Allah has raised the status of man through Islam. He has crushed the idea of baseness and low caste. There is no censure upon any Muslim but in acts of sins. Only deeds of the days of ignorance warrant admonition."

(4) Before the law all mankind is equal. Even in the appointment of a judge there are no preconditions of race colour. The essentials for such an appointment are knowledge-effeciency and unblemished moral stature.

During the time of the Prophet an incidence took place. A woman from the Bani Makhzoon tribe (high ranking Arab nobility) was found guilty of theft. Accordingly, legal punishment was to be executed. The remaining members of the Quraish tribe found this intolerable. They could not bear it, and unanimously agreed to intervene. They decided to call upon Usama Bin Zaid — to intercede on her behalf. The choice fell on him because of his status and the exalted position of Prophet Muhammad, the Messenger of Allah who adopted his father. When the Prophet was told about this he reacted with unflinching steadfastness saying:

"Do you intercede in the Laws of Allah?"

He rose and addressed the people immediately thereafter saying:

> "Verily the people before you perished.
> They perished because whenever a noble committed a crime of theft they overlooked it, and waved off the law.
> But when an ordinary helpless man committed a crime they executed the Law.

Behold in the name of Allah!
Even if Fatima, the daughter of Muhammad, was caught for theft I would cut here hands off."

(5) Islam recognizes the personal rights of every individual to choose his own career and thereby practise the profession he is best qualified for. He is free to do this providing he does not harm himself and does not infringe upon the rights of others. Islam—in response to the call of the Moazzin from within the mosque—invites man to travel throughout the earth and to search for his subsistence. The following are the Words of Allah reiterated by the Moazzin :

"And when the formal Prayer
Is finished, then you may disperse
Through the land,
And seek of the bounty of Allah
And celebrate the praises of Allah often.
Perchance you may prosper."

From the above it is obvious that man enters the house of Allah in a spiritual frame of mind but leaves the sacred precinct in search of God's bounty. Both acts are inspired by devotion to the Divine Command. During the pilgrimage season man is permitted to enter into commercial contracts.

(6) In Islam the active labourer is superior to the idle isolated worshipper. Especially when the latter relies on others for his maintenance in clothing and food. In a tradition reported by Ibn Abbass it is said :—

"Some people came to the Prophet and said :

"A certain person observes fast during the day and prays all night celebrating the name of Allah."
The prophet asked who feeds him? They replied :

"Each one of us co-operates in fulfilling his needs, so that he may be free to devote himself to worship."

The Prophet said : "Each one of you is a greater worshipper than he."

(7) Together with all this, Islam protects his productions and earnings and looks after his life and sustenance. If he is a transgressor Islam is quick in requiting him and if he is the oppressed Islam illuminates his difficulty or reinstates his rights.

Islam sets a vast net of securities for man's life and blood. In a tradition reported by Abdullah Bin Masood from the Prophet it reads:

"The first issue that would be judged on the Day of Judgement would be human bloodshed."

In another tradition reported by Hamza from the Prophet we observe the following:

"Who kills his slave we kill him
And who disfigures him by cutting his nose
We do likewise to him."

Sanayee comments on the above tradition saying :

"On the same basis one may deduce the case of a murderer who is not a master". He thereafter quotes the opinions of Muslim jurists on criminology and their schools of thought.

Models for Excellence

According to this prophetic guidance — the companions of the prophet and those who followed them in all sincerity — disciplined their lives — on the question of equality without reference to colour. In the Islamic History we are able to find numerous personalities that emerged as models for excellence. Colour has never been a binding factor in their advancement and progress.

(1) In the early Islamic society at Medina the personalities as Bilaal Bin Rabah, and Miqdad Bin Aswad and Kuubaib emerged.

(2) Muslim historians and geographers have never taken an antagonistic stand against any race due to their colour. They studied various races objectively. They mention their positive and negative virtues and in the like manner study their "sematic characteristics. Masudi, for instance, when discussing the "Zanj" (Negroid Origin) applauds their eloquence, their power of speech, and their innate fear of God's Reckoning. Discussing the Kings of China — he mentions their justice, and the precautionary steps they impose upon themselves in looking after the rights of foreign merchants who visits them land.

(3) In his "Introduction" when Ibn Khaldun makes a study of various human races, he makes an effort to correspond their characteristics and their natural surroundings. According to him, characteristics change with the change of natural conditions and environments.

(4) Candidly speaking throughout the long Islamic history there has been some aberration in the implementation of this most illuminating line of action laid out by Islam. one example which is frequently quoted is the "Zing Revolution". Tabari has mentioned this in the incidents that took place in the year 255 and thereafter. He also quoted the statement of the commander of the Revolution, Ali Bin Muhammad Bin Abdul Rahim, to his colleagues wherein he exhorted them to social justice.

Addressing the Muslim masses—on the occasion of the Eid El Fitr festival, in the same year he elaborated on their unfortunate plight in the past. He went on to say that Allah had now rescued them from their miseries and was elevating their status. He was making them masters of slaves, owners of properties and possessions and was facilitating them to ascend to higher positions.

It does not concern us in our study to pursue the details of this conflict. What concerns us is that it was based on social and economic grounds specifically directed to repulse these injustices. Although in doing so they went off the path and the historical judgement went against them, this social and economic conflict in the Islamic society was never based on racial discrimination or colour prejudice. This conflict based on various degrees of tribal differences—or deep rooted cultural and historical background—took various shapes. Sometimes in its sweep it relied on colour without colour itself being the basis of the conflict. In any social or economical conflict it is only natural that each contending party exploits every possible means at its disposal to reach its goal. Among these means the issue of colour was readily available.

The profound reality that emerges above all such incidents that took place in Islam—is the fact that the Islamic society was able to absorb the various segments of human elements which today constitute what is known as the Islamic society. Not only that, these differences have been represented to establish positive features in its great human existence; variety of colours and varieties in sematic characteristics. With all this, islam pursues its course in a rhythemically humanitarian way.. While societies that outline to boast of progress and advancement find themselves stumbling on the issue of racial discrimination, they continue dealing with the coloured and certain specific people as second grade citizens or worse. We shall refer to these contemporary problems later.

At this stage in our research — we shall return to the Glorious Quran which is our principal source. It is also the criterion of our views and trends of thinking. The Quran is the running stream in which we purify our mentalities and thereby ascend to a level above contradictions reaching the horizon where humanity emerges as a united form before its Creator.

The Quran and Colour

In treating this subject we shall pursue a purely ethnological method. This fully corresponds with the objective and historical implementative method which we have employed earlier, in the beginning of this study. How many times have the words "black" and "white" appeared in the Quran? What are the relations of their contents with their contexts? To what extent do they prove the Quranic viewpoint on the colour question in particular and the race question in general?

The letters "seen" "waw" and "daal" in Arabic belong to one origin meaning "opposite white in colour." From this origin other words are derived. Black in colour is well known. According to some any colour that is against white—whatever the shade be, falls within the scope of black. The word derived "Sawaad" means person, and a leader is called "sayyed" because the people flock to his person. The law remains the same for all words that are derived from this origin : Words from this origin have appeared in the Quran on ten occasions.

On three occasions it is used to signify overlordship :

(1) The first occasion when portraying Sayyidina Yahya :

(John The Baptist, the precursor of Jesus)

"The Angels called unto him while he was standing
In prayer in the chamber, (saying)
"Verily Allah gives you glad tidings of Yahya to confirm
A Word from Allah,
Lordly, chaste,
A prophet of the righteous."

(2) The second occasion is found in the story of Joseph describing the Aziz of Egypt

"So they raced with one another to the door.
And she tore his shirt from the back.
They both found her Lord at the door...."

(3) The third occasion is when Quran portrays a scene of the Judgement Day :

"And they say : Our Lord!
Verily we obeyed our Lords and great men
And they misled us
From the Way"

In the first instance it is used as an eulogy and praise, in the second it is applied to express a report without any praise or disgrace and in the third it is used to denote dishonour and ignominy. In all three cases they are evaluated by the actions of the people whose actions they express.

The word "black" has appeared in the Quran on five occasions. it signifies the modes and shapes of the face in various situations but not as a permanent characteristic of the face. Two occasions are mentioned in the third chapter — when describing the blackness of the faces of the disbelievers of the Judgement Day:-

"On the Day when
Some faces will be whitened
And some faces will be blackened
To those whose faces will be black (will be said)
"Did you reject faith
After accepting it?
Then taste the punishment
For rejecting faith"

The issue of their original colour is not the theme of the above verse. What is directed in the above verse is their relation with punishment. In another verse we read the following :

"On the Day of Judgement
You will see those who
Told lies against Allah
Their faces would be turned black...."

On two occasions it describes the conditions of a people whose faces go black when they get the sad tidings of a female birth :

"When one of them receives tidings
Of the birth of a female,
His face darkens and is worth with inward grief."

This is a type of discrimination practised by the pre-Islamic Society between the sexes which the Quran criticized. The blackness mentioned here resulted from the narrow mindedness that a man exhibits when he is bestowed with some said-tidings. This is exactly what we observe in the chapter of the "Ornaments"

"When one of them reviews tidings (of the birth of)
What he sets up
As a likeness to Beneficent One
His face darkness and is worth with inward grief."

There remain two other occasions. The first in which a chain of mountains is so beautifully portrayed :

"and in the mountains
Are tracts white and red
of various shades of colour
And black intense in hue."

This wonderful description of God's artistry shows His power of creation. The tenth occasion is when the Almighty describes the night—(and indicates the time of fasting).

"Eat and drink
Until the white thread of dawn
Appears distinct to you from its black thread."

In summarising this we may conclude that the Arabic word in which the letters "Seyn, Waw and Daal" form the origin stand to signify "Lordship" by way of praise, dishonour or impartial statement—as may be the social circumstances of the persons it goes to describe. It has also been used to describe the atmospheric change of the night and day and of various shades of colour. It also describes the scenes of the Day of Judgement that appear upon the faces of people—each according to its own experience. All this makes it abundantly clear that we cannot impose a definite fixation upon its use for praise or expressing dishonour. In fact we cannot even connect it with praise and ignominy. The colour black according to the Quran, has therefore, 120 exclusive states differing from any of the other colours in existence.

White

If we turn our attention to the Arabic word "white" the letters "baya, and dad" belong to one origin and from it nouns are derived. Other nouns similar to the derived ones are also formed from this origin. The basic meaning of the word signifies the "white" in colour. The derived word signifies something that carries a shade of its meaning for instance of fowl's egg. A noun that is similar to the derived one is like "Bidatul Hadid" meaning a steel helmet. In metaphorical and figurative language the word is used to show the symbol status of the governor. When we say "Baidatul Balad". Like an egg he too protects the city. It is also said "Baidatul-Islam wa-deen" meaning protector of Religion and Islam.

This word in its origin has appeared twelve times in the Quran.

In the story of (Yousuf) as it depicts the most extreme stage or sorrow experienced by Yaquoob (Jacobs) :

> "And his eyes became white with sorrow."

The Quran uses this word on two occasions in describing the faces of the believers in the Hereafter :

> "On the Day when
> Some faces will be (lit up with) white..."

This continues till we read :

"But those whose faces
Will be (lit with) white
They will be in Allah's mercy
For ever and ever."

We have already discussed this issue when deliberating on the subject of "black" white signifies the brightening up of the face due to joy and happiness.

The word "White" is also used in the Quran to describe the drink that is exclusive for the people of paradise :

"Round will be passed
To them a Cup
From a clear flowing fountain
Crystal white-delicious to the drinkers."

It is also used to describe the chaste women of Paradise

"As if they were hidden eggs"

The Arabs used the ostrich's egg to symbolize purity and extensively quoted it as a proverb. It is also used to describe the dawn.

"Eat and drink
Until the white thread of dawn
Appears to you distinct from its black thread"

It is used to describe the colour of the mountains

"And in the mountains
Are tracts white and red"

The miracle of Moose A.S. (Moses) hand is also described by white. All five verses are connected with white in no way that is derogatory to other colours. It is the same in the following verses:

The purposes for which white is employed in the Quran are various. It is used to depict great sorrow, worthy reward, Almighty God's power in creation, description of women, cups, and prophet's hand. In all these usages there is no evidence of the word being used in a derogatory sense. It is also a well known fact that too deep white is virtually a sickness.

In conclusion we may reiterate that the Quran does not designate either black or white for any praise or expression of dishonour. The Quran does not correspond or connect colour with the status of life. The Quran's greatest evidence of truth is Equality among mankind, and as far as progress and advancement are concerned the basic requirement is to follow the Will of Allah.

"Lo! The noblest of you
In the sight of Allah
Is the best in conduct."

Our Contemporary World

In my study I have tried to limit my discussion to the question of discrimination based on colour, which is one of the most dangerous problems of our contemporary world. Its flames have swept the U.S.A., Republic of S. Africa, the British colonies, Rhodesia and Vietnam.

Parallel to these ghostly scenes, our world is witnessing other examples of greater wickedness and ferocity. The most obvious types are those based on the conception of blood purity, which has been tried out in Nazi Germany and is being perpetrated presently by zionism in Israel.

Ziqnist Racial Discrimination

In addition to the vital link between Zionism—a foreign element in our heartland and international imperialism—the political picture of Zionist imperialism in Israel—is distinguished by certain principal characteristics. The most outstanding of which are racism and

Discrimination and its complementary features of violence and expansionist policies : Faez saegh states "Racism is not an acquired characteristic of the Zionist inhabitants of the state of Israel, (nor has it emerged by sheer chance). It is not a passing scene in the Israeli play. On the contrary it is a deep rooted permanent basic characteristic. It springs from the heart of the Zionist faith and is the principal incentive that has been responsible for the creation of Zionist Imperialism and the Zionist State. Zionism is therefore the belief in a national unity for all the Jews who can be identified in the light of a common genealogy.

The so called Jewish National Bond, is therefore, not based on religion or language but upon the foundations of faith in Zionism. This is clear because Zionists who believe in the Jewish faith or practise its teachings are relatively in the minority. And as for the Hebrew language it must be said that it was only revived after the birth of Zionism. Recent legislations and decisions of the courts in the Zionist state and the political disciplines of Zionism from its inception, all prove that genealogy—in its abstract biological reality—upon which is based the policy of absorption of other Jews—is the factor that makes a person a Jew. This is the view of the Zionists. Implicit faith in this racialistic belief results in three things which form the essence of the Zionist ideology :

1. Racial Segregation
2. Racial Discrimination
3. Racial Superiority

We may pursue this study in Dr. Faez Saegh's book and in the valuable research papers published by the Research Centre of the Palestine Liberation Organisation especially the "Memoirs of Hertzel."

When we refer to the Encyclopaedia Brittanica we find the definition of Zionism given as a Jewish National movement with the aim of creating and consolidating a National Jewish State in Palestine as a National Home for Jews. The Encyclopaedia Brittanica pursues the study further from both the old and new points of view confirming its connecting with Zionism — The Jews — and Palestine.

From this study we arrive at the fact that we are in a dire need for a clarification of all these conceptions in their relationship to Zionism so that the Academy of Islamic Research can have, at its disposal, a clear, definite and unambiguous opinion for exposition to world opinion.

With this it should also possess the records of the daily implementations of Zionist Racialism in the ever escalating conflict between them and the Arabs. in this respect the reports of the various committees commissioned by the United Nations to investigate the atrocities of Israel in occupied Arab lands and their condemnations of Israel's aggression must be at hand. We should also possess the facts of Israeli bombardment of civilians deep inland, and how the enemy indiscreetly attacks schools, factories and hospitals. The most recent example being the aggressive attack upon a steel factory in Abu Zaabal on the 12th of February, 1970.

Conclusion

I wish to offer a suggestion on research of its kind — that clarify and expound the Islamic stand on contemporary world problems. I suggest that the Academy of Islamic Research publish a series of studies, in which it limits itself in presenting original textual references, relating to each problem, so that these series could be helpful to scholars, and could in themselves be a mine of information, upon which further studies could be made. On racial discrimination all the Quranic Verses, Traditions of the Prophet, statements and opinions of the theologians and references from our Islamic history, could be gathered together and their source could be maintained.

The pursuance of this topic may side track us from the methodical frame, in which the study of "Islam and racial discrimination" should be undertaken. This is so because—despite its importance — it does not deal with comparative studies. I have however made an effort to find the objective dimensions of the studies in the light of Islamic guidance. In doing so I have relied basically upon the textual references from the Quran and have concentrated upon the study of statistics and its objective analysis.

What draw our mind to such an objective frame of study are the series of research papers undertaken by UNESCO on matters of racialism and Modern thought. It has obliged the Research Scholar of any particular religion to present the view point of his religion as a follower of the same faith.

13

Circumcision: The Clitoral Inferno

MUNAWAR A ANEES

(Abstract: It would be a folly to assume that Islamic moral order is contingent upon a pair of scissors that excises the clitoris of a young girl. The pre-Islamic pagan rituals of clitoridectomy and infibulations must come to a halt in Muslim countries).

In El-Salvador, it is still not old-fashioned for a mother to inscribe the sign of the cross with a razor blade on the clitoris of her young girl in order to "make her a better worker and keep her from getting ideas." The court physician at Byzantium. Aetius of Amida, is known to have recommended the use of excision in case of clitoral enlargement. Some private doctors and nursing homes on London's Harley Street admit that they perform female circumcision for immigrant women against fees as high as $1,700.

What is the motivation behind female genital and sexual mutilations across such a wide historical and geographical continuum that now affect anywhere from 30 to 80 million women all over the world. Invariably, there is an intricate web of religious, social, cultural and medical pretexts for these notorious practices. However, these traditions are not limited to one religion. According to Morgan and Steinem:

> They are practiced by some Islamic people, some Coptic Christians, members of various indigenous tribal religions, some Catholics and Protestants, and some Fellasha, an ancient Jewish sect living in the Ethiopian highland... The overt justifications for genital mutilation are as contradictory as

> theories about its origin. explanations include custom, religion, family honor, cleanliness, protection against spells, initiation, insurance of virginity at marriage, and prevention of female promiscuity by physically reducing or terrorizing women out of sexual desire.

These authors further argue that, regardless of the supposed justifications, the real reasons for these heinous customs must be explored within the social context

> ... control of women's bodies as the means of reproduction, and resulting fear of the independent power of women's sexuality—both motives enforced by socioeconomic rewards and punishments. If marriage is the primary means of economic survival for a woman, then whatever will make here marriageable becomes desirable. If a bride who lacks virginity literally risks death of renunciation on her wedding night, then a chastity belt forged of her own flesh is a gesture of parental concern.

Similarly, one cannot fail to observe a congruence of thought between these authors and Bouhdiba when the latter comments on the social context of female circumcision across Muslim cultures :

> The operation carried out on the genital organs cannot be considered in isolation from a set of social, sometimes a-religious, even frankly anti-Islamic practices. From the cradle to the grave, or rather, 'from the uterus to the cumulus', and at every moment of life, the Arab female personality is ruthlessly, systematically, irremediably denied. The 'drama' of Arab frigidity that has all too often been observed clinically is to be inferred from a sexual life, physiological and psychological that is a series of traumata that bring with them insurmountable fears and anxieties. Sometimes excised to begin with, but always brought up in the cult of necessary virginity, deflowered almost publicly on her wedding night, transformed into a child-producing machine, the Arab girl comes in the end to lose even what is biological in the act of loving. Having

> become resistant to orgasm, an Arab woman needs, if she is to be satisfied, a husband who is prepared to make ever increasing proof of his prowess and try to acquire marvels of virility by resorting to artificial means.

It is not easy to ascertain when clitoridectomy and other variations on the same theme originated in human society. However, ethnographic and anthropological data point to a mix of mythologies and religious beliefs. For instance, Meinardus has argued that a belief in the bisexuality of the soul, as held by many African tribes and the Egyptians, was a corollary of their belief in bisexuality of their deities. Numerous Heliopolitic, Memphitic and Thebaic Pantheon may be counted among such hermaphrodite gods. For example, the Heliopolitic Atum, who engenders Shu (the god of the air) and Tefnut (the god of moisture) through masturbation and then generates them through this expulsion, possesses discrete androgynous ingredients. Since certain gods are believed to be bisexual so it is maintained that every human being is bequeathed with both feminine and masculine souls. These beliefs extend to circumscribe the location of the respective souls. "Thus, the feminine 'soul' of the man...is located in the prepuce, whereas the masculine 'soul' of the woman is situated in the clitoris."

It would be erroneous to assume that the hermaphroditic attributes of divinity were simply the relics from ancient myths. One of the great Sufi masters. Shaykh Muhyi al-Din ibn 'Arabi (d. 637/1240), surmised that God is both feminine and masculine. He also believed that Eve and Adam "both partook of both sexes :

> From this knowledge [that is, intuitive knowledge which comes from God's light rather than discursive reason] we know that women are exact moieties of men. Do you not see that Eve was created from Adam? Thus she possesses [like that of Adam] two characteristics, being masculine in her origin and principle and feminine derivatively. Thus, her nature [like that of Adam] is ambiguous. All humanity is thus a melange of masculinity and femininity.

Were the bisexuality of deities of Eve and Adam to remain a metaphysical notion, it would, perhaps, create little or no stir. Nevertheless, the ancient belief in the divine hermaphroditism and its extrapolation to distinct human genital organs meant that the clitoris is the price for initiation into femininity and so is the prepuce for masculine induction. Hence the circumcision of both sexes.

According to Huber, an ancient Egyptian papyrus describes the operation of female circumcision in detail and a female mummy from 16th century B.C., shows signs of clitoridectomy. Similarly, there is further evidence that the practice was in vogue in ancient Egypt. Chabas has shown a scene of Pharaonic circumcision dating back to 1350 B.C. The female circumcision is known to have remained a pre-marital ritual in the 2nd century B.C. Egypt. Moreover, the Greek geographer, Strabo, who was visitor to the Upper Egypt during 24-25 B.C., found that female circumcision was a custom among the Jews.

In the words of Tannahill :

> Though circumcision may have been perfectly common place in Egypt — as it was later to be among the Maya, the Aztecs, the Incas, and in some parts of Polynesia — it was not practiced in Mesopotamia until the Hebrews made it an article of faith. Possibly they brought the idea back from Egypt at the time of the exodus. Israel's lawgivers, however, transferred it from adolescence to infancy, made it mandatory, and represented it as an eternal symbol of God's covenant with the Jewish people, thus turning a pagan rite into an index of grace.

Thus, the successive transition from primordial myth and folk lore towards organized religion ossified the circumcision into a sacrificial rite. Invariably, the Biblical verdict :

> And God said to to Abraham, 'As for you, you shall keep my covenant, you and your descendants after you throughout

their generations. This my convenant, which you shall keep, between me and you and your descendants after you : Every male among you shall be circumcised... So shall my convenant be in your flesh an everlasting covenant. Any uncircumcised male who is not circumcised in the flesh of his foreskin shall be cut off from his people : he has broken my covenant. (Genesis 17:9-14).

Circumcision in Judaism, therefore, became a surrogate for a more fanatical human sacrifice. On the other hand, Christianity rejected circumcision. With the exception of the Church of Ethiopia, all Christian factions renounced it for both sexes. Following the decree of St. Paul—"neither circumcision counts for anything, nor uncircumcision, but a new creation"—it adopted baptism instead. Mazaheri is of the opinion that :

> Christianity rejected this Semitic custom and replaced it by baptism, which is of Zoroastrian origin; but Islam believing that it is following in the supposed footsteps of the prophet Abraham, preserved the practice of circumcision for both sexes.

On the contrary, the Copts in Egypt believe that the practice of female circumcision spread among Christians on account of 'the victory of the circumcised,' i.e. Jews. In this regard, Burmester has provided the following narrative for the adoption of this practice by the Copts, as noted by Michael, 12th-century Metropolitan of Damietta :

> After Sarah had driven away Hagar from her house and her son Ishmael with her, as the Law affirms. Hagar withdrew to Yathrib of the country of the Higaz and to Faran. And Ishmael grew up, and God beautified him in the eyes of the women of the people of Yathrib, and they asked his mother to give him in marriage. And she said : 'We are a circumcised people, both the men and the women of us, and we do not marry, except with those like us. And when they (the women) had circumcised themselves. Ishmael married them, and God

> fulfilled his promise to him, and granted to him twelve princes. And circumcision spread in that country and in that which was neighbouring it, and it became firmly established among the Copts of Egypt... And when the Apostle mark evangelised them, he did not disapprove it for them, and they continued it.

Furthermore, it is known that a 16th-century religious testimony by the emperor Claudius, submitted to the Emissary of the Pope, made note of female circumcision. It is mentioned not as a religious rite, as with the Jews, but as a custom of the people. As a grotesque display of hypocrisy. Catholic missionaries did not interfere with the "local customs" and permitted a continuation of female circumcision. This was done with the approval from Rome. In other words, circumcision may be a ritual prohibition by the Church, nonetheless, if it comes in way of winning converts, then abandon it. Interestingly enough, Dr. R.T. Ravenholt, a Director of the United States Agency for International Development (US-AID) Population Bureau, did not also want to disrupt the tradition fo female circumcision "because it is aimed at reducing female sex desire [clitoridectomy/infibulation] undoubtedly has fertility control as part of its motivation."

At least four types of female circumcisions can be identified. According to Verzin, these types are :

1. *Circumcision proper.* The circumferential excision of the clitoral prepuce. In certain Muslim countries, it is generally known as *sunnah* circumcision.
2. *Excision :* Removal of the glans clitoridis or even the clitoris proper and may include part, or the whole, of the labia minora.
3. *Infibulation :* This is also known as Pharaonic circumcision. It leads to partial closure of the vaginal orifice following excision of a varying amount of vulval tissue. Under the most radical circumcision, all or part of the mons veneris, labia majora, labia minora and the clitoris are removed.

4. *Introcision :* This is the severest form of female genital mutilation. This is the cutting into the vagina or ripping the perineum by means of a sharp device. This type of female circumcision has been recorded among the tribes in Australia.

Verzin has also noted that members of a Christian sect in Russia Skoptsi (for Circumcisers) — employ circumcision in order to pledge for the state of the so-called "perpetual virginity." Their inspiration comes from St. Matthew (19:12) : "there be Eunuchs that have made themselves Eunuchs for the Kingdom of Heaven's sake."

The biomedical implications of female circumcision are numerous, complex, well-documented, and above all, dreadful. For instance, Daw has listed both immediate and chronic complications :

Immediate

Shock may be neurogenic, or may follow haemorrhage, haemorrhage, which may be fatal, may primary from the perineal branches of the external pudendal artery and the dorsal artery of the clitoris or secondary following infection of the wound; injury to adjacent structures, urethra, bladder, vagina, perineal and anal canal, may be sustained; infection, such as urethritis, cystitis and abscesses may occur; chronic pelvic infection may eventually follow; retention of urine may be caused reflexly immediately after operation.

Chronic

Infertility due to chronic pelvic sepsis and inability to have sexual intercourse; implantation dermoids; menorhagia as a result of chronic pelvic sepsis; dysmenorrhoea due either to chronic pelvic sepsis or to obstruction of the menstrual flow by a pinhole introitus; cryptomenorrhoea may lead to haematocolpos or haematometra; Keloid scar formation; vaginal calcuh may be rarely seen; delay in the onset of menarche.

Similar observations have been reported by Verzin.

The geographical incidence of female circumcision involving one or more of the aforementioned types has been described from a number of African, Asian and Latin American countries. There are field reports on the occurrence of female sexual and genital mutilations in countries as diverse and distant as Egypt and Brazil, Mali and Indonesia, or Peru and Malaysia.

In recent years, investigations by the World Health Organization into the spread of clitoridectomy and infibulation have raised the specter that these practices are indigenous to Muslim culture. Sheehan. confounding such assumptions, has observed that the fanfare surrounding these studies.

> .... has served to arouse controversy while at the same time allowing Westerners, including otherwise detached social scientists, to view such a practice as being rooted in ideologies totally foreign to those of the West.

The hyperbole over female circumcision by the militant feminist factions and other assorted groups (Orientalists included) may make it appear as though clitoridectomy is an exclusive function fo the so-called under-development, since it is more visible in some Latin American, African and Asian countries. Imbued with a sense of ethical superiority, they do not hesitate to camouflage their cultural arrogance when discussing these issues with reference to Muslim social milieu.

Conversely, investigative studies into the history of gynophobic Western biomedical practices reveal a horrid picture. For example, Sheehan has described one of the procedures for clitoridectomy as employed by Isaac Baker Brown (1812-1873), a Victorian surgeon, who enjoyed the confidence of numerous members of the royal family, including one of Queen Victoria's daughters:

> Two instruments were used; the pair of hooked forceps which Mr. Brown always uses in clitoridectomy, and a cautery iron such as he uses in dividing the pedicle in ovariotomy... The clitoris was seized by the forceps in the usual manner.

> The thin edge of the red-hot iron was then passed around its base until the organ was severed from its attachment, being partly cut or sawn, and partly torn away. After the clitoris was removed, the nymphae on each side were severed in a similar way by a sawing motion of the hot iron. After the clitoris and nymphae were got rid of, the operation was brought to a close by taking the back of the iron and sawing the surfaces of the labia and the other parts of the vulva which had escaped the cautery, and the instrument was rubbed down backwards and forwards till the parts were more effectually destroyed than when Mr. Brown uses the scissors to effect the same result.

Elected president of the Medical Society of London, Brown's basic argument was that masturbation was the cause of all illnesses he deemed specific to women : hysteria, insanity, catalepy and epilepsy. His recipe for cure : excision of the clitoris!

Sheehan has observed that clitoridectomy was propagated as a "harmless operative procedure" and was in tune with the Victorian biomedical theory of biological determinism. It was practised in England despite its doom as a remedy for the alleged feminine disorders. The medical profession, for a long time, did little to ameliorate health care for women in Victorian England. In her own words :

> The fact that the operation is described in literature published well after the 1860s lends support to the idea that clitoridectomy in and of itself remained an acceptable medical technique.... Some doctors claimed that promiscuous women could be known by the size and shape of their genitals, particularly the clitoris. Masturbation led to madness, some said even to death. The tremendous freedom with which such beliefs were applied to patients' lives and the basis they formed for operating procedures are incredible when one realizes that throughout most of menstruation remained largely misunderstood.

In America, the medical establishment not only held ideas similar to that of Victorian medicine-female genital mutilations as normative treatment for masturbation, nymphomania and hysteria—but introduced chemical clitoridectomy" Several textbooks by famous gynecologists recommended the technique. For instance, in 1859, one Charles Meigs prescribed the use of a silver nitrate solution on the clitoris of female children who indulged in masturbation. Echoing the Byzantian tradition, clitoral enlargement was considered as the cause of nervous disorders and, therefore, amputation of the clitoris was made a medical necessity. Moreover, until 1925, training in clitoral surgery and infibulation continued to be offered by a medical group known as the Official Surgery Society. These "official" excisions of the clitoris were carried out as late as 1940s. That the last (?) American clitoridectomy was performed in 1940s upon a five-year old girl to relieve her of emotional disorders may no longer be a valid statement in light of the fact that :

> John Money, professor of pediatrics at John Hopkins, and his colleagues have for many years treated young girls who are born with "ambiguous" genitalia — that is, enlarged clitorises and sometimes foreshortened or closed vaginas. Few people realize that this procedure has routinely involved removal of the entire clitoris and its nerve supply — in other words, total clitoridectomy — in addition to the usually described reconstruction of a vagina when that is necessary.

And, a bizarre twist to the hideous excisions comes through the so-called "Love Surgery" that penetrated some of the American medical practice during the 1970s. It was cunningly named as "clitoral relocation." Only less than a decade ago, James Burt, a gynecologist from Ohio was reportedly promoting the "Mark Two" surgery : for $ 1,500, there was a promise to reconstruct the vagina in order to "make the clitoris more accessible to direct penile stimulation."

For Western woman, the onus of owning a clitoris did not finish with clitoridectomy. For her, apart from the overtly masculine culture that takes pride in desecrating femininity, genital mutilation came under many and varied masks. Psychic clitoridectomy, as promulgated by Freud, is one of those :

> In the phallic phase of the girl, the clitoris is the dominant erotogenic zone. But it is not destined to remain so; with the change to femininity, the clitoris must give with the vagina its sensitivity, and, with it, its importance, either wholly or in part. This is one of the two tasks which have to be performed in the course of the woman's development; the more fortunate man has only to continue at the time of his sexual maturity what he has already practiced during the period of early sexual expansion.

Since the dawn of Freudian analysis of female psychosexual development, the question has been furiously debated between feminists and gynophobics whether sexual response in the human female is clitorally-evoked or vaginally-evoked. Of course, feminists have vehemently attacked Freud, and rightly so:

> In their jokes and in their pornography, in their theories and in their marriage manuals, men treat the clitoris as simply one more erogenous zone like the breasts, underarms, or ears, to be used to arouse a woman sexually so that she will permit intercourse. They may remember the clitoris in foreplay, but for real sex, back to the vagina!

Sherfey is, therefore, pertinent in saying that :

> To reduce clitoral erotism to the level of psychopathology because the clitoris is an innately masculine organ or the original libido is masculine in nature must now be considered a travesty of the facts.

In her highly controversial study, Sherfey has compared human female sexuality with that of other mammalian species in an evolutionary context. Discussing role of the clitoris, there is, invariably, a reference to female organismic achievement. Sherfey has argued that :

> With full sexual arousal, women are normally capable for many orgasms. As many as six or more can be achieved with intravaginal coition. During clitoral-area stimulation, when a woman can control her sexual tension and maintain prolonged simulation, she may attain up to fifty or more orgasms in an hour's time.

From these observations, that are, by and large, based upon studies by Masters and Johnson on the sexual behaviour of volunteer couples engaging in coition under laboratory conditions, she concludes that :

> Consequently, the more orgasms a woman has, the stronger they become; the more orgasms she has, the more she can have. To all intents and purposes, the human female is sexually insatiable in the presence of the highest degree of sexual satiation.

It is obvious that Sherfey is yet another Freudian wolf in disguise. This denunciation may not be unpretentious when we see Sherfey present herself as an architect of a theory on the genesis of human civilization, based entirely upon the premise of asphyxiation of feminine sexuality :

> The rise of modern civilization, while resulting from many causes, was contingent on the suppression of the inordinate cyclic sexual drive of women because : (a) the tremendously increased supply of hormones of early human females associated with the hypersexual drive and the prolonged pregnancies was an important force in the escape from the strict heat-cycle sexuality and the much more important escape from post-pregnancy diminished sexual desires. Women's uncurtailed continuous hypersexuality would drastically interfere with maternal responsibilities; and (b) with the rise of settled agriculture economies, man's territorialism became expressed in property rights and kinship laws. Large families of known parentage were mandatory and could not evolve until the inordinate sexual demands of women were curbed.

Since women are capable of "insatiable" orgasmic experience and much more so through clitoral eroticism, with the potential for ultimate destruction of human society, therefore, clitoris must be regarded as the arch enemy of human civilization. In other words, Sherfey, while first appearing to be a defender of clitoral sexuality, turns out, in the long run, to be a protege of gynophobes and misogynists.

It is rather amusing to see that Western academicians and sex volunteers (a legitimized title for those who consent for coition in the name of High Priest of Objective Science) continue to wrestle with the question of anatomical basis of female sexuality, without achieving much by way of resolution. For example, during a recent study of twenty-seven coitally experienced volunteers, vaginal eroticism could be elicited in 89% of the subjects by means of systematic digital stimulation of both vaginal walls. This study supported previous findings; however, it did not support the existence of the discrete anatomical structure called the Grafenberg Spot (G. Spot, for the common). The author concludes that this study supports the contention that there are two distinct types of orgasms—vaginally-evoked and clitorally-evoked. Moreover, it also supported the finding that some women expel, during orgasm, a fluid through the urethra. In this study, the fluid was chemically indistinguishable from urine.

In Islam :

> Canonically and theologically, circumcision has no privileged status. It is not one of the five pillars of Islam... It is merely a *sunna.* The ritual surrounding it is loose, imprecise, and more spontaneous than organic. It is accompained by no prayer. The age at which the operation is performed is not fixed in any strict way and may take place any time between one and twelve years. The fiqh is hardly concerned with it and the Quran not at all. Furthermore there is a systematic concern on the part of Muslims to distinguish themselves from the Jews on this matter.

Indeed, the Qur'an does not make mention of circumcision for either sex. Quite a few *ahadith* are, however, cited on this subject. For example, the oft-quoted *hadith*— "If the two circumcised parts have been in touch with one another, *ghusl* is necessary,"— is interpreted to be an approval by the Blessed Prophet for both female and male circumcision. Certain *fuqaha'* were of the opinion that in light of this *hadith,* female circumcision was not forbidden by the Prophet but he just disapproved total clitoridectomy. In the judgement of al-Mawardi: "the excision limits itself to removal of the kernel-shaped skin of the upper tip of the organ. One should cut, therefore, merely the protruding epidermis without removing the organ as such."

According to another *hadith,* the Prophet is said to have addressed a woman, *Umm 'Atiyah,* who was reportedly operating on a girl : *idha khafadti fa-ashimmi wa-la tankhaki fa innahu adwa li'l-wajh wa-ahza 'ind al-zawj*—i.e., just touch the surface lightly and do not cut deep; her face will grow beautiful and her husband will rejoice.

Moreover, *ahadith* alluding to *khifad* (female circumcision) and *khitan* (male circumcision) are quoted as : "Circumcision is my way for men, but is merely ennobling for women," and addressing a newly converted woman to Islam on the subject of circumcision, the Prophet said, "Do not inflict trouble on yourself, because that is painful to a wife, but pleasing to a husband."

The historical evidence is that the female circumcision was prevalent in pre-Islamic Arabia. Common expressions like *Ibn al-Bazra* and *Ibn al-Lakhma* indicate the perceived social meanings of circumcision relative to its absence. For instance, Khalid ibn. 'Abd-Allah al-Kasri, whose mother was a Christian from Greece, had her circumcised to absolve himself of the satirical title of *Ibn al-Bazra.'*

The Muslim juridical opinion of *khitan* differs from total prohibition to the practice being considered *makrumah,* an act of piety, or *wajib,* an obligation. Imam Nu'man bin Thabit bin Zuta

Abu Hanifah (81-150/701-68) does not accept female circumcision. However, it is also believed that both Imam Abu Hanifah and Imam Abu 'Abd-Allah Malik bin Anas (d. 179/795) did not consider either female or male circumcision as obligatory acts. They deemed them praiseworthy. According to Imam Ahmad ibn Hanbal (164-241/780-855), circumcision is imperative for the males but a commendable act for the females. In the opinion of Imam Muhammad bin Idris al-Shafi'i (150-204/767-820.) both *Khifad* and *Khitan* represent a duty. Imam Muhy al-Din Yahya al Nawawi (631-76/1233-78), in his commentary on *Sahih Muslim,* presents the following opinion about the Shafi'i verdict on female circumcision :

> Circumcision is obligatory *(wadjib)* according to al-Shafi'i and many of the doctors, *sunna* according to Malik and the majority of them. It is further, according to al Shafi'i, equally obligatory for males and females... As regards females, it is obligatory to cut off a small part of the skin in the highest parts of the genitals.

In essence, in the absence of the Qur'anic injunction on circumcision, *ahadith* became the sole source to enact the permissibility of this practice. In its social context, the circumcision came to be recognized as the emblem of inclusion in Muslim society, at least for the males. Compared to the festivities attached to the male circumcision that are observed in almost every Muslim country, female circumcision, wherever it is prevalent in the Muslim world, is devoid of such fiesta.

The Western critics of clitoridectomy, as it is practised in certain Muslim countries, fail to differentiate between the act proper and *khifad.* Granted that female circumcision is permitted according to *ahadith,* there is overwhelming evidence that it is not an obligatory act. In its social context, it is neither synonymous nor analogous to *khitan*- male circumcision. Moreover, the authorization of *khifad,* as derived from certain *ahadith,* in no way, tantamounts to total clitoridectomy. As a matter of fact, the *hadith* makes a specific prohibition for the same. Thus, the Western diatribe over clitoridectomy that characterizes it as an indigenous Islamic dictum is false.

The historical evidence on female circumcision and its variants does not attribute its genesis to Islamic teachings. On the contrary, it was the mythical beliefs and later Judaic practices, combined with the Christian compromises, that helped spread this loathsome practice through many cultures. It is the spectrum of the covenant of Judaism stretching to the perpetual virginity of Christianity that forge the social context for these crimes against women. Furthermore, it is the misogynic Western culture that deceptively reinforces these practices at many other societal levels. If the *Sunnah* of the Blessed Prophet accorded a recognition to circumcision (more so to the male one), it was in the pervasive Qura'nic spirit of emulating the Abrahamic tradition, that is not necessarily synchronous with the Judaic facade as we know it today.

The reported incidences of clitoridectomy and infibulation in Muslim countries (such as Egypt, the Sudan, South Yemen, Nigeria, Malaysia and Indonesia) are definitely in defiance of the Islamic verdict. Yet, there are a number of Muslim countries—Afghanistan, Pakistan, Algeria, Morocco, Libya, Tunisia—where such genital mutilations are unknown. Nevertheless, a statistical differential does not exonerate those who indulge in these un-Islamic pursuits. In so doing, they are no different from the gynophobes of Western culture. Ironically, by calling clitoridectomy the *Sunnah* circumcision, they are making a mockery of the teachings of the Blessed Prophet. Apart from biopsychological maladies (including orgasmic insensitivity or extremely delayed threshold) that women have to suffer through these mutilations, men are condemned to seek endless virility. Little wonder that addition to *hashish* and other "aphrodisiacs" has been a corollary of clitorophobia, at least in Egypt.

Islam, unlike any other religion, bestows upon woman an ralienable right to sexual gratification. Whatever may be intricacies of the purported clitoral and vaginal orgasms, the clitoris remains the biological basis for sexual pleasure in women. To deprive a woman of her fundamental right to sexual bliss—through total clitoridectomy. Pharaenic circumcision or infibulation is to ostracize Islamic dictates in this context. Bullough has made a succinct observation :or extremely delayed threshold) that women have to suffer through these mutilations, men are condemned to seek endless virility. Little wonder that addition to *hashish* and other "aphrodisiacs" has been a corollary of clitorophobia, at least in Egypt.

Islam, unlike any other religion, bestows upon woman an ralienable right to sexual gratification. Whatever may be intricacies of the purported clitoral and vaginal orgasms, the clitoris remains the biological basis for sexual pleasure in women. To deprive a woman of her fundamental right to sexual bliss—through total clitoridectomy, Pharaenic circumcision or infibulation is to ostracize Islamic dictates in this context. Bullough has made a succinct observation :In Muslim countries one of the contradictions inherent in female circumcision... is that is the Muslims believe and teach that the clitoris is the source and wellspring of all female passion. This implies that clitoral excision is more or less deliberate attempt to make women less sensuous and, is contrary to the Koran.

Bouhdiba voices a similar opinion, except that he unwittingly falls into the Freudian trap of the "castration complex"But for the young Arab girl in the Middle East excision is hardly less traumatic. Excision, which, despite the canonical regulations, is very often quite simply a clitoridectomy, is merely the first step in 'a veritable plot intended to frustratethe women of her share of fulfillment'... This 'blinding' felt by men. In both cases one can speak of a castration complex inherent in all Muslim child rearing.

Definitely, in his search for the social context of circumcision, he is at loss to declare both male and female circumcision a generic Muslim cultural trait. This is not true even of the Arab culture *per se,* what to relate to the extremely diverse Muslim societies.

It would be a folly to assume that Islamic moral order is contingent upon a pair of scissors that excises the clitoris of a young girl. The pre-Islamic pagan rituals of clitoridectomy and infibulations must come to a halt in Muslim countries. The dignity, honour and right to sexual fulfillment that Islam guarantees to all women must be restored by a total ban on all non-medical surgical manipulations of female genitalia.

REFERENCES

1. Robin Morgan and Gloria Steinem, "The international crime of genital mutilation." M.S. 7 (March 1980), 66.
2. Abdelwahab Bouhdiba, Sexuality in Islam, London, 1985.
3. Otto Meinardus, "Mythological, historical and sociological aspects of the practice of female circumcision among the Egyptians," Acta Ethnographica Acad Scient. Hungari., 16 (3-4) (1967), 388.
4. Fazlur Rahman, Health and medicine in the Islamic tradition: Change and identity, New York, 1987.
5. J A Verzin, "Sequelae of female circumcision," Tropical Doctor 5 (October 1975), 163.
6. Mahmoud Karim and Roshdi Ammar, Female circumcision and sexual desire, Cairo, 1965.

(Revised and edited; originally published in Islamic Culture, July 1989).

14

Institution of Waqf

MOHD. ZAIN B. HAJI OTHMAN

(Abstract: Waqf or religious endowement, or family trust, is an institution which in Muslim usage is a purely religious matter...Charity is at the root of the development and extension of waqf. Waqf is no part of the Quran. But the doctrine has been given due recognition from the earliest times in Sharia, and so law relating to endowements is the most important branch of Islamic law).

The institution of waqf has always been, in the conscience of the Muslims, more closely connected with religion than other legal matters, and therefore generally ruled by Islamic law. As an important part of the law of real estates it has been popular in most, if not all, Muslim countries. The silence of the holy Qur'an on the subject of waqf is one of the most remarkable facts in relation to the development of Islamic law. Waqf is also the most important part of the law, for it remains interwoven with the entire religious life and social economy of Muslims.

According to Islamic law, the very concept of property involves the idea of its being owned by someone possessed of full powers of disposition over it, though such powers of some may be in suspense for a temporary cause. As an exception to this general rule the law recognises the validity of a waqf which is a form of alienation by which a property passes from ownership. The institution of waqf and its literature is rather vast, and it is the most difficult branch. There are conflicting decisions; the texts differ among themselves widely, which is not at all surprising. The social, economic and cultural life of the people in countries such as North and West Africa, Egypt, Turkey, Arabia, Palestine, Persia, Central Asia, Malaysia, Pakistan, India, etc., differs so widely that such divergences are only to be expected. Furthermore, in all Muslim countries vast funds, properties and agricultural lands are donated as waqf; hence it is necessary to give a brief general account of the law dealing with the waqf.

Waqf (plural *awqaf*), in Islamic law, covers religious endowments, family trust, etc., while in North Africa, in particular, the term *hubs* (*ahbas*) or *habis* (*hubus*) is more commonly used. The word *tasbil* is also used in the same sense, i.e. devoted to the way of God (*sabil Allah*). The only point concerning waqfs on which all Muslim lawyers seem agreed is that their basic purpose is a "good work" (*gurbah*), or "an approach to God" (*taqarrub*).

Waqf or *hubs* is in fact an Arabic *masdar* (noun of infinitive, in Arabic), and literally means " to prevent, to restrain." In Muslim legal terminology it means primarily :" to protect something, to prevent it from becoming the property of a third person." In Malaya and Java, the form 'wakap' has slight phonetic modifications. Among the Muslims of the East Indian Archipelago, the institution is well-known; estates made 'wakap' are however of isolated occurrence only: they always serve religious purpose, while in Malaysia, in particular, the term waqf, spelt "wakaf," is more commonly used.

However the definition of waqf may have been formulated, it is interesting to see the following differences of opinion between Muslim jurists with regard to waqf in the language of law.

According to Abu Hanifa (d.A.H.150)

(a) It signifies the appropriation of any particular thing in such a way that the founder's right in it shall continue, and the advantage of it go to some charitable object.
(b) It is the detention of a specific thing in the ownership of founder (*waqif*), and the devoting or dedicating of its profits or usufruct in charity to the poor, or other good

> objects in the manner of *'ariyah* or commodate loan. This does not mean that the profits are merely to be lent, but the objects of waqf are to havé the same benefit from it as if the subject of it were lent to them in the manner of an 'ariyah, when they would have the use of it, or, in other words, its profit or usufruct for their on benefit so iong as it remained in their possession. It is not at all to be binding on the founder; and he may revoke the waqf or sell the subject of it. However, there are two ways in which it may be made obligatory; one is by the sanction of the Qadi making it so, and the other by the use of words of bequest in its constitution, as by saying "I have bequeathed the product of my mansion," in which case also the waqf becomes obligatory. It is also binding when made in favour of a mosque or burial ground.

Thus waqf, according to Abu Hanifa, was analogous to *'ariyah,* and had all the essential characteristics.of *ariyah.*

(1) The corpus remained with the founder and, as future usufruct could not be taken possession of, the contract was revocable at will.

(2) The waqf ended on the death of the grantor, but this could be modified, either by obtaining a decree from Qadi making the waqf irrevocable, or by making it in the form of a bequest—when as there was no one who could revoke it, it was valid and binding in the same way as a usufructuary bequest to the extent of bequestable third. Abu Hanifa held that upon the failure of the object, the property returned to the founder and his heirs, the founder's right could not end without its being transferred to some other person, as the law does not admit the idea of anything during its existence leaving the possession of all proprietors. The only exception recognised by him was a waqf for a mosque and a testamentary waqf upon the death of the testator.

According to the two disciples of Abu Hanifa- Abu Yusuf (d.A.H.182) and Imam Muhammad (d.A.H.189):

(a) Waqf signifies the appropriation of a particular article in such a manner as subjects it to the theoretical rules of divine property where the founder's rights in it are extinguished, and it becomes a property of God by the advantage of it resulting to His creature;

(b) Waqf is the detention of a thing in the implied ownership of Almighty God in such a manner that its profits may revert to or be applied for the benefit of mankind, and the appropriation, when once made, is absolute, so that the thing appropriated can neither be sold, nor given away as a gift, nor inherited.

According to Abu Yusuf, the waqf becomes absolute by the mere declaration of the founder that he has constituted or constitutes any particular property as waqf; while Muhammad held that the right of the founder does not cease until the appointment of a curator (*mutawalli* and the delivery of the property into his hands. Abu Yusuf was well aware of the benefit of the institution of waqf in the community and so based his theory on the assumption that a waqf was analogous to "*ijarah* and sale, and it was void if made temporarily. Although he is reputed to have allowed a waqf for a limited period in favour of the poor, provided it was made for a period of at least a month, he did so merely in the sense that it took effect as a perpetual waqf, as by saying, " A man makes waqf of his house for a day or a month or any limited period, the waqf being valid and perpetual, but if he should say `I make this waqf for a month and after that it is void,' the waqf then is void immediately."

Shafi'i's view was more or less the same as of Abu Yusuf, as the corpus was transferred to God, and if the beneficiaries failed the usufruct only reverted to the founder's heirs.

According to the Maliki school, however, a waqf may be limited as to time or as to a life or several lives, and after the expiration of the time or extinction of the life or lives specified, it reverts in full ownership to the founder or his heirs. This view was closer to Abu Hanifa's view, for it has been said that "the bare ownership remains with the founder, in reality during his life, and fictitiously after his death. Among the distinguished Hanafi Jurists, Muhammad ibn al- Hasan al Shaybani insisted that even a family waqf could not be validly created without an explicit mention of the poor, or some other charity of a permanent character as its ultimate beneficiary. His insistence on this was emphatically not in order to import a charitable element which would not otherwise exist, but rather to ensure an element of perpetuity which might otherwise be lacking. Abu Yusuf, indeed, on the other hand, made no such stipulation but maintained that the very use of the word "waqf" must be regarded as sufficient implication of such perpetuity, in the absence of any provision inconsistent with this presumption, and as an adequate indication that the waqf income should be devoted to the poor, when all other beneficiaries become extinct. Only in the Hanafi law the income of waqf is paid to the poor during any year in which the named beneficiaries are for some reason temporarily lacking. The dominant Shafi view also made no such stipulation and expressly laid down how the income of the waqf should in fact be expended after the named beneficiaries had died out. Ibn Hajar al Haythami, who is considered throughout Malaysia as the decisive authority in the Shafi'i school, says in his *Tuhfa* :

> Should he say, "I have made a waqf in favour of my children" or "in favour of Zaid and his descendants" or some similar object which lacks perpetuity and should he say no more than this, then the authentic view is that the waqf is valid. This is because its purpose is an approach to God and perpetuity. So, if its first beneficiaries are indicated, it can be easily perpetuated in favour of some good purpose. If therefore, the named beneficiaries pass away, the more authentic view is that it should continue as a waqf wince perpetuity is of the nature of waqf. The more authentic view, then, is that the income should be paid to the nearest relative of the founder. Regard should be had to the poor, not the rich among them. Should none of his relatives be available or should they all be

> rich, then the ruler should expend the income in the interest of the Muslim community. Others again say it should be devoted to the poor or to the poor of the town where the property is situated.

Also Zayn al-Din Al-Malibari in his *Fath al Mu'in* says :

> If he say, "I have made this waqf in favour of my children" and mentions no one to follow them or "in favour of Zayd and then his descendants" or some similar object which lacks perpetuity, the income should be paid to the poor persons nearest related to the founder.
>
> This is because charity to relatives has priority over the general charity, and the best charity of all is to the nearest of kin and the greatest in need. Failing such relatives, the ruler should spend the income in the interests of the Muslim community. Many, on the other hand, say it should be paid to the poor and indigent of the town where the property is situated. But the waqf will not in any case be vitiated, but will be maintained.

This, too, is the dominant view in the Hanbali school. It would appear rather significant, however, that the reason explicitly given for the other and less authentic opinion in the Shafi'i' schools, i.e., that a waqf which does not include any ultimate dedication to the poor is invalid, is that a "waqf must be in perpetuity,, so when it has no beneficiaries left it becomes a waqf for an unknown object; this is not valid, in just the same way as though the first beneficiary had been unknown. Somewhat similar differences concern the type of property which may be donated as waqf, the person and the powers of the administrator, and the concept of where the ownership of the property concerned must be held to lie. Nevertheless, the fact is that the classical texts make no distinction whatsoever between what are now termed "charitable waqfs" on the one hard and "family waqfs" on the other. Both alike were regarded as perfectly valid according to the doctrine of all four Sunni schools of law.

The General view prevalent in the present conditions accepts the view of Abu Yusuf, which is the general Hanafi rule that a waqf must be perpetual for validity, and it cannot be revoked even by reserving such a power.

Charity is at the root of the development and extension of waqfs. The institution of waqf itself is no part of the original, unchangeable Qur'anic revelation. But the doctrine has been given due recognition and proper place from the earliest times in the Muslim system of law, and so the law relating to endowments is by far the most important branch of Islamic law. Historically, its origin is attributed to the direct prescriptions of the Prophet (p.b.u.h.). The Qur'an contains no specific reference to Waqf, though it abounds in charitable injunctions :

> They ask thee what they should spend (in charity). Say : Whatever ye spend that is good, is for parents, and kindred, and orphans and those in want, and for wayfarers. And whatever ye do that is good. God knoweth it well.
>
> By no means shall ye attain righteousness unless ye give (freely) of that which ye love; and whatever ye give of a truth God knoweth it well.

There are three questions which may arise in charity:

1) What shall ye give ?
2) To whom shall ye give? and
3) How shall we give

The answer to that is this :

Give anything that is good, something that you value greatly, is useful or helpful. It may be property or money; it may be a This helping hand; it may be advice; it may be a kind word; :whatever ye do that is good" is charity. On the other hand, if you throw away what is useless, there is no charity in it. Or if you give something with a harmful intent, e.g. a sword to a madman, or a drug or sweets or even money and the like to someone whom you want to entrap or corrupt, it is no charity but a gift of damnation. To whom should you give ? It may be tempting to earn the world's praise by a gift that will be talked about, but are you meeting the needs of those who have the first claim on you ? If you are not, you are like a person who defrauds his creditor: it is not charity. Every charity is judged by its unselfish character and there is no set of unselfishness, however small or intangible, but is well within the knowledge of God. How many it be given ? As in the sight of God; shuts out all pretence, show and insincerity.

REFERENCES

1. Ameer Ali, Muhammadan Law, Tagore Law Lectures, 1884, vol. i, Calcutta, 1912.
2. J Schacht, "Islamic law in contemporary states" Amer. J. Compar. Law, 8 (1959), 139.
3. J N D Anderson, "The religious element in waqf endowments", JRCAS, July 1951, p. 292.
4. Abd al-Jalil Abd al-Rahman Ashub, Kitab al-waqf, Cairo, 1915.
5. M Z al-Abyani, Mabahith al-waqf, Cairo, 1911.
6. Hilal al-Ray, Ahkam al-waqf, Hyderabad, 1355/1936.

(Revised and edited; originally published in *Islamic Culture,* Jan. 1984).

15

Studies on Islamic Education: An Interpretive Essay

MUNAWAR AHMAD ANEES & ALIA N. ATHAR

(Abstract: 'Islamic education' as a term is interpreted in a braod sense; it is all-encompassing term denoting the literature of traditional Islamic education and also Muslim discourses in sciences, logic, philosophy, etc.)

Almost a quarter of a century ago, Bayard Doge while concluding his article on 'The Subjects and Titles of Books Written During the First Four Centuries of Islam,' made an important observation:

> 'Well may modern Muslims be proud of the vast and varied literary activity of their forefathers. If we realize the difficulty of writing books without comfortable desks, electric lights, cheap paper, convenient libraries, or even fountain pens, we can appreciate the genius and devotion of the early scholars. In our modern age of mechanical conveniences, it is for us to emulate their work and to keep alight the lamp of learning, which shone so brightly during the first-four centuries of Islam.'

Indeed, the first revelation of the Glorious Quran wa the divine proclamation on knowledge (*ilm*). This proclamation (and what followed it) transformed the *Jahiliyya* into the intellectual leaders of the world. Seyyed Hossein Nasr has eloquently described this phenomenon of the *Umma al-Kitab:*

'Taken as a whole the Qur'an is like existence itself like the

> Universe and the beings who move through it. It contains all the elements of universal existence and for this reason is in itself a universe in which a Muslim places his life from beginning to end. Being composed of words the "composition" of the Qur'an naturally leads to the symbolism of Pen and the Tablet that is so well-known in Islam . . . According to many Hadiths, God also wrote the inner reality of all things on the Guarded Tablet (*al-lawh al-mahfuz*) before the creation of the world a symbolism which has played an important role in Islamic cosmology. The Pen symbolizes the Word, the Logos, the Intellect, and the Tablet Universal substance so that it can also be asserted from this point of view that "It is by the Word that al things are made." In a metaphysical sense, then the Qur'an contains the prototype of all creation. It is the pattern upon which things were made. That is why in Islam one distinguishes between a Qur'an that is "written" and composed (*tadwini*) and a Qur'an which is "ontological" and pertains to cosmic existence (*takwini*). This is not to say that there are two Qur'an but that, metaphysically, the Qur'an has an aspect of knowledge connected with its text as a book and an aspect of being connected with its inner nature as the archetypical blueprint of the Universe.'

The *Ummi* of Arabia, the Holy Prophet Muhammad (peace be upon him) emerged as the foremost educator. The pursuit of knowledge became obligatory for all Muslim men and women. The Prophet's Mosuqe was turned into men's academy; his house into a centre of learning for women. *Al-Kitab* and the *Sunnah* of the Holy Prophet together formed the mainspring of knowledge and wisdom. The quest for knowledge on the part of Muslims was thus a manifestation of their submission to the will of Allah.

Resenthal has observed that:

'Neither practical utilitarianism however which made an acquaintance with medicine, alchemy and the exact sciences appear sesirable to Muslims, nor theoretical utilitarianism which prompted them to occupy themselves with philosophical theological problems might have sufficed to support an extensive translation activity, had not the religion of Muhammad stressed from the very beginning the role of knowledge (*ilm*) as the divine force in religion and, thereby in all human life.

Arabia the seat of the monotheistic Abrahamic tradition, also became the birth-place of the greatest intellectual revolution in human history. Devotion and love for knowledge is summed by al-Attabi: "Books smile as pens shed tears.' A relentless exploration began. It was Medieval Islam that gave birth to experimental science as opposed to the abstractions of the Byzantine Greeks. It was in the cradle of Islam that life was breathed into today's modern civilization. It was the period of freeflowering of the intellect in which scientific pursuit was invigorated by religious zeal. Bibliophilics were all around.

Unfortunately, socio-economic causes and gradually permeating traditionalism in the Muslim Empire set in motion an intellectual decline. Stagnation took its toll and by the fifteenth century (C.E.) the Islamic intellectual heritage entered into a tripartite oblivion, caused by religious. Political and linguistic assaults.

Now Italy was at the receiving end. The age of Islamic transmission of knowledge began. Latin translations of Arabic works mushroomed. The West, enlightened by the 'Wisdom of the East', liberated itself. The revolt ignited by the Islamic spirit of intellectual freedom became the precursor to the oft-boasted 'Revolution', The revolution took place thousands of miles away from Arabia. This time the second revolution of Islam was showering its blessings upon the unbelievers and testifying to the inherent truth of its Wisdom.

For some time the East remained indifferent to the 'materialistic' growth of the West. For instance, as early as the eighteenth century, an Indian Muslim traveller to Europe, Mirza Abu Taleb Khan seemed to have paid no attention to the religious and cultural foundations of the Western world, albeit noting the indifference of fellow-Muslims towards learning about the West. As for the West?

Perhaps the jet-set age has kept them ignorant. Iseman noted recently: 'For most Americans, the place is evocative perhaps of childhood geography.' Nevertheless, the post-colonial period has witnessed the growth of literature aimed at 'mutual' understanding between the West and the Muslim countries.

Dodge's comments have prompted the authors to survey the current literature to see how well we have been able to 'kept alight the lamp of learning. What follows, therefore, is a recapitulation of recent works on the Islamic education.

For the purposes of the current study, `Islamic Education' has been interpreted in broad terms. It has been interpreted in broad terms. It has been taken as an all-encompassing term that denotes the literature of traditional Islamic eduction as well as Muslim discourses in the fields of science and technology, logic, philosophy and allied areas. The compilation of this bibliography has been carried out with the aim of fulfilling a gap in writings on the history and philosophy of Islamic education. It is hoped that it will serve a very useful purpose for those engaged in research on Islamic education.

The bibliography is not an attempt to record the original works of Medieval Islamic scholars. Instead, it is concerned with the literature documenting the origin, evolution, impact and adaptation of those original works. It excludes the literature published on individual Muslim scholars because good bibliographies are already available at least for certain authors, such as al-Kindi, al-Farabi. It is limited to English language literature, mostly periodical, that has appeared since the drawn of twentieth century.

The classification scheme of the following bibliographic compilation is arbitrary. It has been done for the sake of convenience in evolving a better classification scheme. Obviously, many titles can be cross-referenced. Unfortunately the system followed by the Quarterly *Index Islamicus* (which also suffers from an inadequate coverage of the pertinent literature, aggravated by frequent typographic mistakes) is not conducive to a conceptual scheme of keyword indexing of the literature on the subject. It is, therefore, in the fitness of things that we should suggest to the professional information scientists that they give thought to developing an efficient classification for the vast literature on Islamics. It would be helpful in the speedy retrieval and storage of these works.

Islamic Education-- A Bibliographic Survey

This selection delas with the studies on the Quranic concepts of knowledge and their relationship with modern knowledge; or the studies interpreting modern knowledge in terms of Quranic verses:

Abdul Quddus, Muhammad (1971) The Quranic idea of evolution: A work which elucidates the meaning of existence and life on the basis of a new theory of volitional motions, Karachi, The author.

Anees, Munawar Ahmad (1968) `Cell reveals God', Islamic Education, 1:4, 7-15.

el-Bakry, Ehsan (1917) `How the Quean gave a new impetus to education and scientific learning', Islamic Review, 5:416.

Bucaille, Maurice, The Bible, the Quran and Science: The Holy Scriptures examines in the light of modern knowledge, Indianapolis, American Trust Pub.

el-Fandy, Muhammad Jamaluddin (1967) On cosmic verses in the Quran, Studies in Islam series, no.5, Cairo, The Supreme Council for Islamic Affairs.

al-Ghisr, Shaikh Nadim, (1968) `The Quan on Islamic education', Islamic Culture, 42:1, 1-24.

Gordon, B L. (1955) `Medicine in the Koran', J. Medical Soc.,New Jersey, 52: 513-18.

Khan, Majid Ali (1977) `Science and Islam on the origin of life,' Islam and the Modern Age 8:1, 63-85.

Quarterly Index Islamicus is still a useful source to identify the materials on Islamics. An up-to-date bibliography on Quran is listed in the Muslim World Book Review (London), and a full bibliography of Quranic studies is `World Bibliography of Quran' (Istanbul); Islamic Education Quarterly (London) is a useful source of information: Editor.

(Revised and edited; originaly published in *Islamic Quarterly*)

16

The Social and Political Functions of the Mosque in the Muslim Community

ASGHAR FATHI

(Abstract: The Iranian, Moroccan and Pakistani cases are discussed to point out that there is a revival of the political and social functions of the mosque).

Throughout the history of Islam the mosque has played a dominant role in the development of socio-political issues, and has been involved in many social movements. The significant place of the mosque in modern times, during which the impact of Western powers, ideas, and ways of life has created unrest and uprisings in the Muslim lands, is specially noticeable. The objective of this article is to arrive at a better understanding of some of the recent developments in Muslim societies by discussing the evolution of the mosque and its cultural background.

Historical and Cultural Bases of Mosque

In Arabic the word for mosque is *masjid,* a place where one prostrates oneself, or a place of worship. However, the Prophet Muhammad had instructed the Muslims that each of the five daily prayers should be performed wherever they happened to be. Therefore, in the early years of Islam the mosque as a place of worship did not exist. The original Muslim community in Mecca had no special place for the people to congregate and listen to their leader. It was not until the Prophet migrated to Medina in A.D. 622, where as head of the community, he governed, collected taxes, dispensed justice, and made peace and war, that he felt the need to build the first mosque next to his house. (Goitein : 1968 ; "Masdjid," 1953 : 330-331).

Reports about the first mosque indicate that it had nothing of the character of a sacred place. There was no specially dedicated ritual object. Believers and unbelievers went freely about in the mosque, tents were erected, disputes and affairs were settled. It was also a place where the Prophet addressed his followers and discussed issues and problems with them. From there he controlled the political and religious community of Islam. After Muhammad, during the time of his first four successors, the Orthodox Caliphs (A.D. 632-661), mosques in many places consisted of military camps built by the Muslim commanders on their expeditions ("Masdjid," 1953 : 330-331, 347).

It would be misleading to consider the mosque as the Islamic equivalent of the Christian church. The mosque was the centre of the Muslim community, like the Roman forum and the Greek agora (Grabar, 1973 : 107, 109 and 124; "Masdjid" 1953 : 336). Governors representing the caliph built the mosque, government offices, and military barracks side by side in the towns they founded after their conquests. ("Masjid," 1953 : 331, 336 and 347)

The importance of the mosque as a Muslim community centre, having more political than religious significance, is well illustrated by a discussion of the Friday prayer of the assembly. Friday in Islam is not a sabbath, or a day of rest. Before the Prophet migrated of Medina there was no Friday service in Mecca. Public worship was held in Medina at the initiative of the new Muslims. As the Muslim community grew, it became necessary to designate a time when all the members could congregate in the mosque so that the Prophet could meet them regularly in order to guide them and discuss the events which affected them. (Goitein : 1968; "Masdjid," 1953 : 347-348)

Thus prayer on Friday at noon was made obligatory for every free adult male Muslim. Attendance was regarded as an act of allegiance. The Prophet, and eventually his successors, the caliphs and provincial governors, became *imams,* or leaders of the collective worship. Some sort of address rather than religious sermon would be made at the gathering which was identified as a political community. Therefore, from the beginning, Friday worship had the character of a political meeting (Goitein, 1968). It was the time not merely for a pietistic performance but also the announcement of news pertaining to the whole group and even for the making of certain collective decisions. As Grabar notes, "The time for Friday prayer served thus as the time when, as social scientists might put it, communications took place between the collectivity and its leaders." (Grabar, 1973 : 105-106)

In addition to the fact that the caliph or his governors originally addressed the congregation personally and conducted the prayer of the assembly on Friday (Goitein, 1968; "Masdjid," 1953 : 336 and 347), the political nature of these meetings is further revealed by other requirements of these weekly gatherings. To begin with, soon after the death of the Prophet, a distinction was made between *masjid* and *masjid al-jami*, the mosque of collectivity, sometimes called the catherdal mosque of Friday mosque. It was long held that the Friday service should be only in provincial capitals where the representative of the Islamic government had his seat, and that it should be performed in the main mosque, i.e., the Friday mosque. ("Masdjid," 1953 : 336-337; Grabar, 1973: 112)

Secondly, it was the *jami*, or Friday mosque, which was directly supervised and paid for by the central Muslim authority, even after A.D. 900, when local governors had achieved considerable political autonomy. For the *Masjid al-jami* was the place where allegiance was sworn to the successor of the Prophet, and not merely to the local governor. (Grabar, 1973: 112)

Finally, there was the ban on female participation. From a spiritual viewpoint in Islam woman is equal to man. However, from a political point of view, she did not belong to the body politic of which only free men bearing arms were members. (Goitein, 1968)

Associated with the prayer of the assembly in the mosque on Friday noon is the *khutba* or oration which is delivered either before or after the prayer. The *khutba* is delivered from the *minbar*, which is an elevated seat. The Prophet frequently spoke from an elevated place while addressing the Muslim congregation. ("Masdjid," 1953: 343-345)

The *minbar* gradually became a kind of throne used on official occasions by state officials. In his inauguration ceremony the caliph would sit on the *minbar*, take the oath of office, and deliver a *khutba*. In the provinces the governors stood in the same relation to the mosques as the caliph in the capital: they made their formal entry into office by ascending the *minbar*, which, as already noted, existed only in the Friday mosques of the provincial capitals. ("Masdjid," 1953: 343-345, 347)

The *minbar* was also used for defending certain policies, stirring public emotion, or for propaganda. For example, when 'Uthman, the third caliph, was killed by those unhappy with his administration (A.D. 655), his governor in Syria, Mu awiya, the founder of the Umayyad dynasty, became the rival of 'Ali, the forth caliph. Throughout his caliphate 'Ali was plagued by Mu'awiya, who plotted and waged wars against him. During his civil war the mosque assemblies played a significant role in the struggle between the two.

There also developed the custom for the enemies of the ruler and his party to be cursed from the *minbar*. Along with this tradition there emerged the practice of bestowing a blessing upon the ruler in whose name the Friday *khutba* was delivered. Later, this custom became the usual form of expressing loyalty to the caliph, after whose name that of the local ruler was usually mentioned. ("Masdjid," 1953: 347-348 and "Khutba," 1953 : 259)

According to the *Shorter Encyclopaedia of Islam*,

> In general, the mosque... was the place where official proclamations were made... as early as the time of the Prophet...

> Al-Walid [the Umayyad caliph] announced from the minbar the deaths of two distinguished governors...; the results of battles were announced in khutbas... In the Fatimid and 'Abbasid periods also proclamations, orders, edicts about taxation etc., by the ruler were announced in the principle mosque...; document appointing the more important officers were also read upon the minbar...; frequently people trooped into the mosque to hear an official announcement... ("Masjid," 1953 : 351).

After the Umayyads the Abbasid dynasty (A.D. 750-1258) came to power through profession of religious zeal and emphasis on patronage of religious activities. But the Abbasid caliphs' love the ceremonial and the traditions of the Persian monarchy, and the expansion of the Islamic domain, prevented them from delivering the *khatba* personally. ("Khalifa," 1953 : 237). THerefore, during the Abbasid period a man leanred in religious matters was appointed to the position of *khatib,* or orator ("Masdjid," 1953 : 351).

However, there was a more profound factor responsible for this change. After Muhammad, the caliphs inherited the Prophet's sovereign position as head of the Muslim community, but unlike the Prophet, they were not considered sources of religious law, nor did they have authority over Muslim religious conceptions and practices. From the beginning, people without priestly status or institutional support, had on their own given themselves over to the study of religion. Gradually the scholars in each locality grouped themselves into exclusive bodies, each adhering to a common method and a common body of law under the name of a great teacher. The scholars in these schools studied, commented on religious matters, and became involved in the administration of the law and community affairs as judges, administrators and teachers. They gained social and religious leadership of the masses, who turned to them rather than to the caliphs for religious instruction and moral guidance. (Lapidus, 1975)

In course of time a split developed in the ranks of the religious leaders. After the time of the Orthodox Caliphs, there arose two distinct versions of the religion. According to the first, religion was primarily the regulation of life by laws and rituals systematized by the religious institutions that were represented by the scholars. The second version emphasized the emotional aspect of religion. Popular preachers through edifying tales brought to the illiterate masses a more humanized and comprehensible version of religion : they served to bridge the gap between the spiritually distant "ecclesiastical" establishment and the popular need for guidance. (Pedersen, 1953; Kass, 1976: 734 ; Bosworth, 1976 : 27)

Along with this differentiation, there developed a distinct separation between the religious scholars and the popular preachers due to the latter's informal interpretations of the Qur'an and the Islamic tradition, which differed from the systematic discussions offered by the learned scholars (Pedersen, 1953). Some well-known common preachers were very influential, and their popularity was so great that their followers and audiences were prepared to defend them against any authority. ("Hanabila," 1971 : 158-162)

In this way, with the expansion of Islam, the appearance of imperial caliphal administration and the development of independent religious authorities, the mosque became less an instrument of polity and more a place for religious practice. The *khutba*, which in earlier days was pronounced by the sovereign himself or his governors and generals, and dealt with political, military and other state affairs, became less important. It gradually became more of a divine service, or sermon, and the ruler was no longer the *Khatib*.

With the dwindling of the political function of the mosque, its purely religious aspect increased. The *mihrab*, the niche indicating the direction of Mecca for prayer, grew in size and decoration, and acquired an mystical character (Grabar, 1973 ; 124, 126). One could not any more enter the mosque at random. The followers of other faiths were no longer permitted to enter. While in the earlier days the building of the mosque was the obligation of the ruler as the representative of the community, gradually ordinary people began to build mosques, and influential persons erected magnificent monuments as a religious duty. ("Masdjid," 1953 : 335)

Even so, the political character of the mosque, though diminished, never disappeared. Utterance of prayers for the ruler during the *khutba* was one of the recognized tokens of sovereignty in Islam: its omission was a signal of revolt. The political character of the mosque has also been retained in another sense. In the case of a major crisis or when the community members were dissatisfied, they flocked to the mosque to discuss the problem and seek remedy and redress. Thus, throughout the history of Islam the mosque has been the centre and the scene of numerous uprisings, revolts, and social movements, often led by popular preachers from the pulpit. Many princes as well as rebels have tried to influence public opinion by attempting to control the mosque. The role of the mosque during periods of unrest in the Islamic societies of the nineteenth and twentieth centuries is specially noticeable.

The Mosque in Modern Times

Muslim leaders were shocked by the increasing political, commercial, and technological influence of the Christian West that accompanied the colonization of Islamic lands during the last two centuries. In response to the agonizing problems that the increasing incursions of the West brought, the intellectuals were roughly divided into three groups. The pure traditionalists believed that the situation was of a transitory nature and that traditional Islam would eventually triumph. The reformists thought that seeking certain pragmatic values and the freer use of human reason in reinterpreting traditional Islamic ideas would increase the political and military power of the Islamic states. The modernists sought salvation by uncritical imitation of the Christian West. Except for the last group, the assemblies in the mosque have been used by all parties to fight the West and one another, and so persuade the masses to follow them.

Again, with the exception of the orthodox preachers and teachers, other users of the mosque in the nineteenth and twentieth centuries, frequently tried to introduce borrowed ideas and institutions to the Muslim societies via a reinterpretation of traditional Islamic teachings. although the reformist preachers and the intellectuals involved in day-to-day politics have been reluctant to admit this novel function of the mosque as an instrument of social change, some devout Muslim social scientists of today openly recommend such use of the mosque. An examination of this phenomenon with examples from Iran, Morocco and Pakistan follows:

> Our first example for demonstration the role of religious assemblies in the mosque, in the context of anti-colonialist movements, comes from Iran. To understand the Iranian situation we need to become familiar with Twelver Shi'ism, the Muslim sect which has been the main religious belief in Iran since A.D. 1502. According to Twelver Shi'ism, legitimate authority belongs to the Hidden Imam, a descendant of Muhammad who is in an occult state. In a belief similar to the second coming of Christ, the followers expect the Hidden Imam to reappear and fill the world with justice and righteousness. On the basis of this belief the state has not been regarded as possessing legitimate authority. The Shi's religious leaders do not represent the authority of the Hidden Imam either; their authority lies rather in their supplying a living source of leadership for the day-to-day activities of the Shi'a community. (Tabataba'i, 1975)

In this long-standing conflict between the religious leaders and the state in Iran, the former have often been the refuge of the oppressed, the malcontent, and the opposition parties. In 1890, for instance, when Nasir al-Din Shah Qachar granted a concession to a British subject for the control and sale of tobacco in Iran, Iranian tobacco growers and merchants sought assistance from the religious leaders, who were also displeased with the influence of Christian Europeans in the country. The religious leaders in two major cities and the capital assumed the leadership, and the mosque was effectively used for mobilizing the people against the tobacco concession. Since the Shah refused to backdown, a *fatwa* (a ruling on a point of holy law) was proclaimed from the pulpit banning the use of tobacco, and was accepted by all throughout the country, including the members of the Shah's household. To prevent an open rebellion the Shah cancelled the concession in 1891. (Lambton, 1970)

Fourteen years later the conflict between the religious leaders and the state was an important factor in the development of the constitutional movement in Iran. A handful of intellectual reformists were ineffective without the support of the masses, who were illiterate and ignorant about misgovernment, foreign influence, and possible reform. It was in this context that the alliance between the reformists and the religious leaders helped develop a truly national movement in which the mosque played a significant role. (Lambton, 1970)

A full account of the 1905-1911 Constitutional movement in Iran is not intended but it is necessary to point out that two of the most influential pro-constitutional preachers, who played a vital role in arousing the public, did not believe in Islam in spite of their religious garb. Undoubtedly there were also less prominent preachers in the same position whose aim was to use the religious assemblies in the mosque to disseminate modern ideas among the masses. (Fathi, 1980)

The question of fighting colonialism and legitimizing new ideas and practices via the mosque has gained more prominence in recent years, as reflected in the following report concerning Morocco and contemporary occurrences. Whereas in Shi'a Iran the split between the state and religious leaders turned the latter into a natural opposition party, the tradition of the fusion of state and religion has been revived in Sunni Morocco to the former's advantage.

In 1912 Morocco became a protectorate of France (Spencer, 1980: 6). As a result, an Islamic intellectual movement (Salafiya), which had apparently originated in Egypt in response to Western domination, was progressively transformed into an anti-colonial nationalist movement in Morocco (Spencer, 1980 : 97). Although most of the religious leaders believed in resistance to France and defence of Islam, those who were younger and exposed to Western style education advocated the adoption of new practices, such as the appointment of young, reform minded preachers, and changes in the archaic format of the Friday sermon in the mosque for effective communication of political ideas (Al-Fasi, 1970 : 186, 202-203,172). The fact that the Arabic press was under the control of French authorities made this reform more urgent. (Al-Fasi, 1970: 112,127,253).

The fusion of state and religion in early Islam and the role of the ruler as both temporal and spiritual leader was also revived. For instance, in the case of Muhammad V (1927-1961) the fact that he claimed descent from the Prophet was one reason why his official proclamation as king was performed in the grand mosque by prominent religious leaders (Al-Fasi, 1970: 86). King Muhammad, while convinced of the necessity of social changes in Morocco, insisted that his personal image should remain traditional (Crawford, 1965). He couched his public speeches in religious terms, and as spiritual leader of the people led the prayer of the assembly on Fridays and gave sermons in the mosque. (Crawford, 1965; Al-Fasi: 1970 : 276-277).

In his desire for modernization, the King, as commander of the faithful, ordered that loud-speakers be installed in the mosque, and in his Friday sermons urged the adoption of modern practices. He also clashed with the French authorities; for example, in 1947 he deleted from his Friday sermon a statement by the French Resident General advocating cooperation with France. (Al-Fasi, 1970 : 226, 276-278).

The French authorities, who were aware of the anti-French character of the mosque assemblies, did not like the Moroccan ruler to lead the Friday prayers and deliver sermons, and sought ways to prevent him from entering the mosque. They often restricted public access to the mosques in times of unrest; sometimes the army occupied the mosques or even closed them. If these measures failed the French authorities interfered with the mosque meetings or ordered the army to drive out the assembly forcibly. (Al-Fasi, 1970 : 121-125, 134, 186, 192, 228).

While King Muhammad of Morocco used the mosque to promote his modernist policies in the garb of "true Islamic traditions" and to amalgamate social change and nationalism with the tenets of Islam, in another Muslim country the mosque is openly recommended as an instrument for achieving social change and for transforming traditional life styles.

Thus our third example of the revival of the social functions of the mosque concerns a plan according to which the rural mosque in Pakistan could be profitably used as the action centre of an organized mass movement for the development of rural life. What is interesting in this proposal is the admitted novelty of this practice.

The author, who is a social scientist, believes that rural people in Pakistan could be reached extensively and effectively through the Friday *khutba,* which should be made more simple in language and relevant to the daily problems of the rural population. The problems of apathy, ignorance, ill-health and low productivity can be effectively solved with the help of communication via the pulpit, backed by such measures as a well-planned training programme for the mosque leaders and promoting the attendance of women and children at the Friday prayers. The utilization of the rural mosque as a community centre as well as a place for literacy classes is indicated.

What differentiates this plan from the Moroccan Government's use of the mosque is that in the Pakistani case the religious against assembly in the mosque is not confined to political communication alone. By implication it is claimed that with creative planning and imaginative use, the Friday sermon could compete with the cinema, radio, television, and novels, which promote alien, harmful cultural values and deviant behaviour standards, especially among youth. (Rauf, 1963; 1964; 1973).

Conclusion

The Iranian, Moroccan and the Pakistani cases discussed all seem to point to the revival of the political and social functions of the mosque. In the case of Shi'a Iran, because of long-standing split between the state and the religious leaders, since the turn of the century the mosque has increasingly become a rallying point the government. In this light the 1979 revolution against the Shah should not appear as a unique event.

In the case of Sunni Morocco, because of the revival of the fusion of state and religion, the government has consistently used the mosque to its own advantage. A similar situation exists in Egypt, where in recent years the mosque has become an arm of the government, and not infrequently has been used as an instrument for the legitimization of government programmes. For instance, since Naser, a bone of contention between the fundamentalist Muslim Brotherhood and the Egyptian Government has been the latter's strict control of the mosque. (Berger, 1970).

The Muslim intellectuals' attention to indigenous institutions, such as the mosques as a means of establishing rural community development programmes, and the pulpit as a medium of public communication for preventing the harmful effects of modern mass media and their alien content, as exemplified by the Pakistani case, is no less pertinent.

REFERENCES

1. Shorter Ency. of Islam, New York, 1953, for articles on "Kass", "Hanabila", "Khalifa", "Khutba", "Masjid" and "Madrasa".
2. A. Rauf, "Dynamic role of the mosque in national reconstruction", Pakistan Rev., 11, 1953, 15-19.
3. A. Rauf, "The cultural role of the mosque", The Punjab Educational J., July & Aug., 1964, 3-20.
4. A. Rauf, "A mosque-centered rural development plan", Islamic Education, Jan-Feb. 1973, 26-36.

(Revised and edited; originally published in *Islamic Culture,* July 1984)

17

New Moon's Visibility and Monthly Lunar Date Lines: Calculations for Important Dates in 1979

M. ILYAS

(Abstract: Seeing the new moon, for fixing dates of significant events, is important in Islamic life and hence this has always interested Muslim scientists.)

Introduction

There has been an ever growing need for a close examination of the available astronomical systems for possible assistance in fixing the lunar-sighting based on important events lime Idds. The possibility of holding such celebrations together on a single date globally has also received considerable attention. Although widely accepted practice has been to use sighting (or at least highly probable sighting) for such events, suggestions for using the astronomically new moon (conjunction) have also been made. In a few instances, such suggestions have been made with a misunderstanding that the new moon's presence above the horizon after sunset (however small the angular separation from the setting sun) means its visibility if the sky is clear. (I am sure that generally people dealing with lunar observations are aware that for a very young moon, its visibility depends not merely on its above horizon presence but on its angular separation from the setting sun, even though not all may be aware of a more precise astronomical criterion). Much of these suggestions are based upon the simple argument that the moon is anyway present above the horizon. However, this argument does not appear to be sound since the moon comes above the horizon every day of the year as rightly pointed out by the late Mufti Mohammad Shafi.

Therefore, our attempts for possible solutions to the above-mentioned problems must be based on the visibility rather than its mere presence since, to my knowledge that is a Quranic requirement. With this in mind, I have been exploring the astronomical predictability and its use for possible global celebrations, and a primarily qualitative discussion was presented recently " Therein the existing criterion for lunar visibility was explained which is of empirical nature (having been derived from a set of actual new moon's observations primarily at mid-latitudes) and allows us to speak in terms of the probability of visibility rather than a simple yes or no.

Lunar Date Lines (Monthly)

More recently, I have successfully developed a self-contained algorithm suitable for calculations of lunar and solar positional parameters needed for subsequent visibility test according to the existing criterion involving lunar separation from the setting sun along the horizon (azimuthal) and upwards (zenithal). For each latitude, the longitude where minimum visibility requirements are satisfied is identified, the visibility condition to the west of this point (along the latitude circle) improves increasing with longitudinal separation since the angular separation at local sunset increases due to the longitudinal time lag in the sunset of 1 hr/15^0 due to the earth's rotation. A line is then drawn joining the minimum visibility longitudes for different latitudes towards the high latitudes, the minimum angular separations meeting visibility- criterion for a given longitude is seen to be met one or more days later (especially in abnormal zones). The lines so drawn thus from a boundary of first possible sighting and for a given latitude, the probability of sighting increases with longitude to the west of the line. The lines may be conveniently referred to as monthly Lunar Date Lines (LDL) for use in (probable) visibility based Lunar calendars. Both the geographical location and the shape of LDLs varies from month to month due to the Lunar (synodic) month's length of 29.53 (average) solar days. The lunar month is begun on the evening at a Date Line (LDL) and proceeds to the west (as the solar date) along the latitude circles completing 24 hours back to the initial point from the eastern direction. However, as one crosses the LDL (International Date Line) at 180^0 (remembering that the two ends of the globe are jointed together at 180^0 lines), there is a conventional solar date change; thus at any one latitude circle, the lunar date will extend over two solar dates but in time will be only 24 hours long (evening to evening)

Use of LDL

(i) Calendars : As the calculated monthly LDLs provide the closest approximation to the actual visibility based LDLs, sighting based calendars, (like Islamic) may be globally prepared using the calculated LDLSs This would standardize the lunar calendars globally, i.e., lunar dates between any two countries will be related in a universally known manner and the calendars thus mode will have a geographical continuity. (Observance of the events like Mi'raj, Miladun Nabi, etc., on the basis of such a calendar will provide global continuity — as historical events of fixed times (dates) should— and will maintain a fixed length of the repetitive cycle, i.e. lunar year globally). If the LDL passes through a country (as will be the case in practice) it may be treated as if passing along the eastern boundary.

(ii) Religious Events : The visibility-based events if they commence at the locations on the LDL and proceed to the west will occur on the same lunar date with a global continuity (finishing round the globe in 24 hrs., as with the solar based activities like Magbrih or Christmas). It is my understanding that as for the dates like first of Ramadan and Idds, actual visibility is essential which is effectively (supposed to be) done by individual Muslim communities on national or sub-national (regional) basis. In an extremely important comment, Mufti Mohammad Shafi has said that celebrations like Idds on a national level are permissible on the basis of a single sighting anywhere in a country— no matter how big geographically—

provided a system consisting of a National Committee along with local Qadi's Office is established and one or more sighting reports—duly verified in the local Qadi's office (are transmitted to the national body which alone should have access to the mass media (radio, T.V., News papers, etc._) for making the announcement nationally. (This kind of system is already in operation in many countries with India as an important exception). Effectively this means that an actual visibility boundary is established by observations at national levels which should be close to the calculated boundary (weather permitting). Here is an important question for the ulama; If an actual visibility boundary is established (as the calculated one) involving an internationally coordinated effort (an international committee consisting of national/ regional committees as representatives), could places to the west of the observational LDL assume the moon sighted. If permitted, this will be an extension of the above- mentioned national situation (in which a sighting anywhere in a country is taken as sufficient nationally) into a global one. A global system so based will automatically take care that the lunar month is between 29 and 30 days. (Places to the east of LDL upto the preceding LDL will have the month of 29 days elsewhere 30 days).

Future Work

The existing empirical visibility criterion is based upon observations primarily at mid-latitudes and may have to be significantly modified for tropical latitudes and needs sufficient testing (and adjustment if necessary) for ascertaining the degree of reliability. Once a reliable criterion is established, it may then be considered for possible actual usage. Accordingly, arrangements should be made for the charts of global LDL for each of the twelve months to be prepared annually using the existing criterion. These should be widely distributed for the preparation of calendars nationally and for attempts of visibility globally. The feedback on actual visibility (for clear weather) at all locations on an extended period would then enable us to test and modify (if necessary) the existing criterion. There may be an International Committee to deal with this aspect under the Masajid's Council which may also explore assistance from astronomical observatories and the Astronomical Almanac Office. In due course, LDLs should become a permanent feature of the annual astronomical Almanac (s) since other communities also will find the information useful.

(Revised and edited; originally published in *Islamic Culture,* April 1979).

18

The Muslim Community and the Place of Mosque in its Life

MUSHIRUL HAQ

(Abstract: The important role of the mosque in the community life of the Muslims was that it served as a check on the entire community....The collective cosciousness had become the real driving force in the life of the community...This institution has disappeared, so the community has lost its direction).

The call of the *Qur'an* to obey only one God and surrender before the authority of the Prophet Muhammad was a complete break away from the past in which the Arabs lived. It did not only shatter their religious belief and practices but also gave a new direction and new meaning to the word 'community'. The Arabs had certainly had a sense of living in a community, but it was very exclusive and non-universal. Their history which we know mostly through their literature tells us that despite the fact that even though they were united on the point of not worshipping one universal God, still that vital 'link' was missing from them which could bring people from outside into their fold. In their case the unifying link was chiefly the tribal affinity : religion was certainly not the link. The right and wrong were determined not on the basis of any religious ideal but on the basis of the membership of a particular tribe. A person was always right in the eyes of his fellowmen if he had not broken the accepted tribal norms which prohibited him from doing any wrong to the members of his own tribe. So long as the others remained on receiving end the individual had the protection of his tribesmen. Each tribe was thus a community in spite of the fact that in their mode of worship they did not appear different from each other.

Islam indeed brought a remarkable change in their social set up.

Tribal affinity did no longer remain the link in Islamic community. It was now God who assumed the central place in the life of the new community. All those who believed in Him and acted according to His dictates became the full members of the new community. The criteria for judging right and wrong were now the *Qur'an* and the Prophet. Certain tribal concepts were retained, however, but with new meanings. For example, in the tribal society of Arabia everyone had to stand by his brother whether he was right or wrong. In Islamic community this togetherness was retained but for a higher ideal. The Prophet once told his followers that they should help their brother whether he was an oppressor or an oppressed one : *Unsur Akhaka, Zaliman Au Mazluman*. It was so strange an advice that people could not believe that they had heard him correctly. They asked : "O Prophet of God, we understand the meaning of helping our oppressed brothers, but how could we help those who are oppressors ? "Stop them from committing wrong, and that will be your help to him," replied the Prophet. That was exactly in line with the teachings of the *Qur'an*. It asked them: "O believers, Be ye staunch in justice, witness for God even though it be against yourselves or (your) parents or (your) kindered." A new social order was thus launched of which the membership was open to all provided they believed in the oneness of God, submitted to the authority of the Prophet and accepted the *Qur'an* as their code of conduct. The community therefore had to live and work within the limits prescribed by God, *Hudud Allah*. No one was allowed to cross the limits, and those who did were dealt with.

The term and conditions in which the first batch of Medina Muslims were asked to give their allegiance to the Prophet at Aqaba left no doubt in what the community was going to be. They all had to repeat:

> We take allegiance to the Prophet that we should associate nothing with God, not steal, not commit fornication, not kill our offsprings, not slander our neighbours, not disobey him in what was right ; if we fulfill this paradise will be ours, and

> if we committed any of these sins, we should be punished in this world and this would serve as expiation; if the sin was concealed until the day of resurrection, then it would be for God to decide whether to punish us or to forgive us.

It is significant to note that even at the time of the first ʿAqaba allegiance when no one could possibly think of the emergence of a well organized community the pioneers from Medina had willingly agreed to surrender themselves before an authority who could punish them for their wrongdoings. This authority was none but the Prophet whom the people had to obey as much as they were to obey God. The membership of the community was bound to be terminated if one challenged the authority of the Prophet. The membership of the community also entitled a man to receive rich rewards both here and hereafter from God provided he remained within the limits. According to the *Qur'an* the members of the Muslim community are those who are steadfast in their prayers and behave justly towards their fellowmen. They are sympathetic to one another but very ruthless to unbelievers in matters of God's limits. They are to renounce the old habits particularly those which create disrespect and insolence of each other. At one place the creed and the ethics of the Muslim community are set forth by the *Qur'an* in the following way :

> Serve God and associate none with Him. Show kindness to your parents and your kindred, to the orphans and the needy, to your near and distant neighbours, to your fellow travellers, to the wayfarers, and to the slaves whom you own.

Thus the Muslim community which emerged in the time of the Prophet was based on the identity of faith transcending the barriers of race, colour, language and nation. The only condition was that it must accept the *Qur'an* as its code, and the Prophet as its leader.

But how was the community going to survive after the death of the Prophet. It was only the Prophet who was in direct communication with God, and none but he could receive divine guidance at critical moment. People certainly knew that one day he would die but they had so much become dependent on him that when it actually happened they refused to believe it. Umar the great was so shocked that he was going to kill those who dared say that Muhammad was dead. It was only Abu Bakri who came forward and announced that those who had been worshipping Muhammad must know that Muhammad was dead. But those who worship God must know that God is all living; death can never reach Him. The situation was changed and Abu Bakr was then elected to lead the community. But unlike the Prophet he did not have access to God--nobody could have for that matter. He was only their commander—*Amir al-Mu minin.*

Time and again the Prophet had advised the people to obey their commander but his obedience was not unconditional. On the question of obedience the sentiments of the people were well expressed by a bed bedouin who stood to answer the question of Umar when he asked the audience whether or not would they obey him. The bedouin told him that he would be obeyed as long as he remained within the limits, but would certainly be beheaded if he transgressed them. The answer was appropriate, but it certainly posed a big question : who was to decide the transgression? The Prophet had time and again told that the community affairs were to be decided by consultation. It was thus the collective consciousness of the community which became responsible for its own affairs. And as the Prophet had assured that the community as a whole never go wrong the consensus of the community become pivot on which its life depended. On this point the institution of mosque in the life of the Muslim community becomes too important to be overlooked.

Mosque here must not be confused with the brick and lime structure. The building is only the symbol of the collectivity and the consensus. Since mosque as a symbol of unity provides a sense of belonging and togetherness the buildings, therefore, have acquired an important place in the life of the Muslim community. Mosque cannot privately be owned, cannot be rented out or sold. To desecrate a mosque is as good or as bad as to defile the commujnity. Mosque and community are thus co-existent, one cannot live without the other. The first thing which the Prophet did after his arrival in Medina was that he built a Mosque which became the never centre of the community. People had to come there for offering their thankfulness to God, to have their cases decided by the Prophet, to discuss their problems, and to receive foreign emissaries. The mosque was their house of worship, their parliament, their secretariat, their government house, their meeting place, their centre of learning. In short it was all in one. Because of this the Muslims were advised to build a mosque in all their settlements. The architectural studies of Muslim towns of medieval times reveals the fact that the cities were usually built around a mosque. The people living in various directions from the mosque thus had to cover almost equal distance to come to mosque. Houses of the people in authority were generally built close to mosque. This was an indication to their responsibility towards its maintenance. All the famous schools of the early period were located in mosque : in them were also made important political decisions. These were the functional aspects of the mosque, so far as the buildings were concerned. But the institution of mosque, as such was not confided within the four walls of the buildings.

The important role of the mosque in the community life of the Muslims was that it served as a check on the entire community. The mosque helped sustain people who made the following *Qur'anic* injunction the motto of their life. .

And hold fast, all together, into the bond with God, and do not draw apart from one another. And remember the blessings which God has bestowed upon you; how, when you were enemies [npto one another], He brought your hearts together, so that through His blessing you became brethren; and [how, when] you were on the brink of a fiery abyss. He saved you from it. In this way God makes clear His messages unto you, so that you may find guidance, and there may grow out of you a community who invite unto all that is good, and enjoin the doing of what is right and forbid the doing of what is wrong : and it is they, they who shall be graced with good everlasting.

The act of inviting people to good and forbidding them from committing wrong is not confined only to the members of the community of the believers. Being a Muslim every member of the community is bound to participate in the world's affairs and to consider the whole world as his own. If a Muslim fails in this he will do harm not only to himself but also to his community, and the world at large. He cannot shirk his responsibility on the excuse that it is the others who are wrong doers. The Prophet has stressed to his people to get themselves involved in the improvement of the world. Once he told his companions that those who abstained from taking active part in world's affairs were like travellers on a double-deck ship in which water was stored on the upper-deck and the people travelling in the lower deck were to climb up everytime they needed water. This annoys the upper-deck people and they close the connecting door. Consequently, some people on the lower-deck decide to drill a hole in the bottom of the ship in order to draw water directly from the river. This is a grave and alarming situation. If the people travelling on the upper-deck do nothing and the travellers in the lower-deck do not stop those who are drilling the hole, all will indeed be drowned, even though many of them had nothing directly to do with the drilling of the hole.

This advice is certainly not meant to apply only in such cases where both the parties are Muslims, for if this is so, we would be allowing others to drill a hole in the ship in which we too are travelling.

The community which the *Qur'an* calls the best of the community, can exist only when every Muslim considers himself responsible before God for the improvement of the world. "Everyone of you is a shepherd," says the Prophet, "And very shepherd will one day be asked about the faithful which appears to be exclusive becomes really inclusive because of its involvement and participation in world's affairs.

We have seen that in Islam there was no authority after the Prophet, absolute and infallible. The collective consciousness had become the real driving force in the life of the community. This force was symbolized in the form of mosque. The long and hazardous journey which the Muslim community had to undertake in its history was possible only because there was mosque before them as a light house. The development of law, theology, philosophy and other sciences was due to the fact that the collective consciousness, concretized in the form of mosque, provided necessary encouragements. But a time, however, came when the community lost its vitality, and gone with it was the real mosque. Now we have all over the world beautifully built, well decorated, fully ornamented mosque but without any real link. The institutions has disappeared, so the community has lost its direction.

(Revised and edited; originally published in *Studies in Islam,* October 1978).